THE Margaritaville® COOKBOOK

"...I'm livin' on things that excite me,
Be they pastry or lobster or love..."

— FROM "The Wino and I Know"
on LIVING AND DYING IN ¾ TIME

THE Margaritaville® COOKBOOK

Olaf Nordstrom

Margaritaville

Key West, Florida · New Orleans, Louisiana
Orlando, Florida & Charleston, South Carolina

This edition of
The Margaritaville Cookbook
is published exclusively for
The Margaritaville Stores
Key West, Florida · New Orleans, Louisiana
Orlando, Florida & Charleston, South Carolina
by
The Peninsula Press · Cape Cod 02670 USA
Donald W. Davidson
Publisher
w w w . m a r g a r e a d e r . c o m

Additional copies of this book may be ordered directly through
The Coconut Telegraph at 1–800–COCO–TEL
or
w w w . m a r g a r i t a v i l l e . c o m

Library of Congress Catalog Card Number:
Nordstrom, Olaf.
  The Margaritaville Cookbook
  The Peninsula Press, ©2000.
  ISBN 1-883684-22-6

Second edition
Manufactured in the United States of America
6 7 8 9 0/ 09 08 07 06 05

CONTENTS

JIMMY BUFFETT'S MARGARITAVILLE® BOOKS

THE ESSENTIAL BOOK OF BOAT DRINKS
& ASSORTED FROZEN CONCOCTIONS

THE MARGARITAVILLE COOKBOOK

THINGS YOU KNOW BY HEART:
1001 Questions from the Songs of Jimmy Buffett

JIMMY BUFFETT'S SHIPWRECK EDITIONS®

Available exclusively at The Margaritaville® Stores:
1 - 8 0 0 - C O C O - T E L
or
w w w . m a r g a r i t a v i l l e . c o m

OLAF NORDSTROM is a bartender/writer/fisherman/carpenter/philosopher/sailor/substitute teacher/ survivor/raconteur of little repute who hails originally from the shores of Cape Cod. After forsaking nearly everything which was his (including his own name), he set up life aboard his sailboat, *Honky's Dory*, then took a bearing south by southwest to gunkhole among the Elizabeth Islands. Much of what little time he spent ashore was usually around the docks and bars of Woods Hole on the Cape, as well as those on Nantucket and the Vineyard. Not one to drop his anchor for long, though, Nordstrom eventually set his course even further south to Crab Key, where he now cooks, eats, drinks, fishes, sails, reads, writes, plays his saxophone, and spends as little time working as the rest of the world will allow. Needless to say, Nordstrom loves the now.

In his spare time, he has also compiled *The Essential Book of Boat Drinks & Assorted Frozen Concoctions*, as well as *Things You Know by Heart: 1001 Questions from the Songs of Jimmy Buffett*.

Swallowing the Equator

"There ain't anything
that is so interesting to look at
as a place that a book
has talked about."

MARK TWAIN
—in TOM SAWYER ABROAD

JIMMY BUFFETT didn't write this book, but he most certainly set out most of the menu in his writings and his lyrics. Accepting the advice of Mark Twain to "write what you know about," Jimmy has spent more than a quarter of a century telling us quite a bit of what he knows: the places he's been, the stuff he's imbibed, and, yes, even the food that he's eaten. And believe me, it's more than just kosher pickles and sponge cake.

From peanut butter and popcorn to paté foie de gras, Jimmy has set out quite a buffet for those fans who tend to eat up his every word. And as a literary remora of sorts, feeding off the crumbs of Jimmy's writings, I decided to tinker with some of Twain's other thoughts and came up with this corollary: There ain't anything that is so interesting to eat as a meal that Bubba has written about. So, I've gone over all the songs and the books to make a catalogue of all that food. When I was done, I read back through my list and tossed out some of the extremes in his taste. For example, the can of sardines in "The Peanut Butter Conspiracy" from the early years, as well as the cucumber and tomato sandwiches from his most recent best-selling book, *A Pirate Looks at Fifty*. Then, I avoided most impulses to come up with (m)any Buffettesque names for stuff, so you won't find any Riddles in the Sandwich or Tiramisu So Badly or Caribbean Sole. For the most part, then, the final menu consists of things you'd be likely to find from a vagabond whose work has kept him comfortably in the tropics. To be sure, there is the occasional foray to New Orleans, Nantucket, and even to France, but much of this diet tends to linger among those little latitudes. So, it's sort of like swallowing the equator, and I think you'll be pleasantly surprised at what our friend has recounted for us over the years.

Now and then, Jimmy says that he's going to write a cookbook of his own someday, but I really don't see that anywhere on the horizon. Not that he wouldn't be able to do it, but when would he ever find the time? So, 'til that day, this collection will just have to do.

Of course, it always goes without saying that I could not have completed this project on my own. Aside from the fact that work of any sort never seems to make it on to my list of "Things to Do," there's also only so much space to be filled in any sailor's galley before one's forced to seek some help ashore. And you can bet your bottom sand dollar that I've sought my share of that. To all my friends on shore, then, I must admit to an enormous debt of gratitude.

To a long-time friend, Francophile, and true gourmand, Jan Brosius, many thanks for pardoning my French; to another long-time friend and islander, Karen Meeks on Buzzards Bay, thanks for advising me in this and other matters; to Tom Bednark, thanks for the use of your Swiss Army® knife for the cover photo; to Sheila Stagman, thanks for the loan of your gecko for the cover, too; to Andy Scherding, Roxy Hambleton, and Jeanne Goodwin, thanks for assisting with the editorial and design; and to the good folks at the Margaritaville Cafes, including Bret Brown and Chef Joe Tusa, thanks for sharing some culinary secrets.

Thanks to all of those places whose food Jimmy has found worth mentioning over the years, including: Le Select on St. Barthelemy, French West Indies; Ruby's on Harbour Island, the Bahamas; La Bodeguita del Medio in Havana; the Dew Drop Inn in Mobile; Rotier's in Nashville; Tujaque's, the Cafe du Monde, Galatoire's, the Camelia Grill, and the Central Grocery in New Orleans; the Flora-Bama® Lounge and Package in Perdido Key; Herbert's Market in Palm Beach; La Taza de Oro in Miami; Alabama Jack's and the Caribbean Club on Key Largo; the Big Pine Inn on Big Pine Key; Bobalu's Southern Cafe on Big Coppitt Key; and Louie's Backyard, Pepe's, BO's Fish Wagon, Blue Heaven, and Fausto's in Key West.

I think it's safe to say that none of this project would have progressed very far were it not for the support of the very patient people at the Margaritaville home office, especially Sunshine Smith and Nina Avramides, who've manage to put up with my foolish messages, but still come back with smiling answers to my questions. Thanks, of course, to Jimmy not only for having been willing to swallow a lot of things that many of us otherwise might have pushed away, but also for having the good sense to shun some others that certainly would have given us the shudders, if not the dry heaves. I have found no mention of rocky mountain oysters, frogs legs, and sweet breads, and I pray that I *never* do!

OLAF NORDSTROM
Adrift on a new moon tide
7 November 1999

MARGARITAS & MORE

Margarita ❦ Genuine Boat Drink
Bloody Mary ❦ Daiquiri ❦ Mojito
Cajun Martini ❦ Oyster Shooter
Striped Bass ❦ Mimosa ❦ Petit Punch
Lemonade ❦ Iced Tea ❦ Root Beer Float
Milkshakes in Motion ❦ Aztec Hot
Chocolate ❦ Café Noir ❦ Café Au Lait
Lait Chaud ❦ Café Con Leche
Coco Frio

Margarita

— FROM "Margaritaville"
on HAVANA DAYDREAMIN'

Yields 1 serving

Basically, this is the concoction that created the Americanos' taste for tequila in the 1960s. Before this, tequila (which is technically a brandy) was best known in Central America and Mexico. Tax records in the Mexican town of Tequila note that 3 barrels of "mezcal wine" had been shipped to Texas in 1873, and American troops in pursuit of Pancho Villa had brought some back in 1916. Still, folks north of the border had not quite taken to the taste of tequila. Even when there was a shortage of gin during World War II, the gringo interest in tequila proved to be nothing more than a flirtation.

Then California college students discovered the MARGARITA, and the rest (as they say) is history.

As for the creation of the drink itself, several bars and bartenders have staked a claim. The Caliente Racetrack in Tijuana boasts of its origin around 1930, as does Bertita's Bar in Tasca, Mexico. Later claims have been insisted upon not only by the Garci Crespo Hotel in Puebla, Mexico, around 1936 (where the bartender says he named the drink for his girlfriend), but also by a couple from San Antonio, Texas, who spent many an hour wasting away during the 1950s at the bar of the Flamingo Hotel in Acapulco, where they owned a home. (Her name, of course, was Margarita.) And not to be denied a piece of the legend is an LA restaurant called The Tale of the Cock, where they claim to have created this recipe first during the Eisenhower Administration.

But the most documented story comes from Danny Herrera, who owned Rancho La Gloria between Rosarito Beach and Tijuana. In the late 1940s, a showgirl named Marjorie King stopped there quite often, and she had a drinking "problem" of sorts: she was allergic to every form of booze except tequila, which she needed mixed.

Among the many tequila experiments that Danny Herrera tried was a concoction consisting of 3 parts white tequila, 2 parts Cointreau, and 1 part fresh lemon juice. These he shook together in a container of shaved ice, then served up in a short-stemmed glass rimmed with lemon juice and salt. This she liked, and so he gave the new drink the Spanish name for Marjorie: *Margarita*.

MARGARITA (Basic)

Yields 1 serving

INGREDIENTS:

> 1 jigger Margaritaville Tequila® Oro
> ½ jigger triple sec
> 1 jigger lime juice
> 2 t coarse salt
> 1 lime wedge, garnish

PREPARATION:

First, salt the rim of the glass by placing coarse salt on a saucer, rubbing the rim of the glass with the lime, then dipping rim into the salt for a thorough coating.

Fill your shaker with cracked ice.

Add the Margaritaville Tequila Oro, triple sec, and the lime juice, then shake.

Strain into salted glass.

Garnish with the remaining wedge of lime.

MARGARITA (Frozen)

Yields 1 serving

INGREDIENTS:

> 2 jiggers Margaritaville Tequila® Blanco
> ½ jigger triple sec
> 1 jigger lime juice
> 2 t coarse salt
> 1 lime wedge, garnish

PREPARATION:

First, salt the rim of the glass by placing coarse salt on a saucer, rubbing the rim of the glass with the lime, then dipping rim into the salt for a thorough coating.

Fill your blender ¼ with cracked ice.

Add the Margaritaville Tequila Blanco, triple sec, and lime juice, then blend medium until smooth.

Pour into salted glass.

Garnish with the remaining wedge of lime.

NOT A MARGARITA

Yields 1 serving

INGREDIENTS:

> ½ c limeade concentrate
> ½ c orange juice
> ¼ c grapefruit juice, unsweetened
> 10 to 15 ice cubes
> Lime wedge, for garnish
> Coarse sugar or salt

PREPARATION:

First, sugar or salt the rim of the glass by placing coarse sugar or salt on a saucer, rubbing the rim of the glass with lime, then dipping rim into the sugar or salt for a thorough coating.

Add the limeade concentrate, orange juice, and grapefruit juice to blender, then cover and blend low until smooth. As the blender hums away, drop 1 ice cube at a time through the hole in the cover until this becomes a slushy concoction.

Pour into glass.

Garnish with lime wedge.

Genuine Boat Drink

Yields 1 serving

— FROM "Boat Drinks"
on A1A

Jimmy says that one February night in Boston during the '70s they were trying to ward off the frigid weather by passing time in Derek Sanderson's bar, Daisy Buchanan's. That episode inspired the song; this drink, the anti-freeze.

While this recipe calls for a dark rum, if it's made with white rum, it's the drink of preference among expatriates in Amerigo (formerly called *Kinja*) as noted in Herman Wouk's *Don't Stop the Carnival*.

INGREDIENTS:

1 jigger Barbados rum
8 oz tonic
Juice of ½ lime
Lime slice, for garnish

PREPARATION:

Fill a tall glass with ice.

Pour in the rum, add the tonic, then stir.

Garnish with the lime slice.

Bloody Mary

Yields 1 serving

— FROM "Tryin' to Reason
with Hurricane Season"
on A1A

When Papa Hemingway introduced this cocktail to Hong Kong back in 1941, he wrote that he "did more than any other single factor except the Japanese Army to precipitate the Fall of that Crown Colony." Still, he hadn't been the inventor of this concoction.

That distinction falls upon a bartender in Paris named Ferdinand "Pete" Petiot years earlier at a place called Harry's New York Bar. Having had his own first encounter with vodka in 1920, Petiot the next year combined it with tomato juice and some seasonings. One wag thought it ought to be named after a Chicago nightclub called the "Bucket of Blood." They did that, but no one in Paris was impressed.

By 1933, Petiot was invited back to New York to tend the King Cole Bar at the St. Regis. Made with gin, they called the drink a RED SNAPPER, billed as a cure for hangover; however, others called the vodka recipe by its current name, after the bloody reign of Mary Tudor (Mary I of England and Ireland) against the Protestants.

Though this has also been made with gin or rum and kept its name, mixing the basic recipe with tequila makes this a BLOODY MARIA; with Japanese *sake*, a BLOODY MARY QUITE CONTRARY; and without any alcohol at all, a BLOODY SHAME!

Having begun this little history lesson with a Hemingway drinking story, I feel I should close it with his own recipe from a note to Bernard Peyton.

"To a large pitcher (anything smaller is worthless)," wrote Papa, "add:

> 1 chunk ice (the biggest that will fit)
> 1 pint vodka
> 1 pint chilled tomato juice
> 1 tablespoon 'Worcester' sauce [sic]
> 1 jigger fresh lime juice
> Pinch celery salt
> Pinch cayenne pepper
> Pinch black pepper
> Several drops Tabasco® sauce

"Keep on stirring and taste it to see how it is doing. If you get it too powerful, weaken with more tomato juice. If it lacks authority, add more vodka."

Of course, if that recipe makes too much BLOODY MARY for you, then I suppose that it's up to you whether To Halve or Halve Not. *Let's drink!*

BLOODY MARY (BASIC)

Yields 1 serving

INGREDIENTS:

> *1 jigger vodka*
> *1 jigger thick tomato juice*
> *Dash lemon juice*
> *Dash fresh black pepper, cracked*
> *2 dashes salt*
> *2 dashes cayenne*
> *3 dashes Worcestershire*
> *Lime slice, for garnish*

PREPARATION:

Fill your shaker with crushed ice.

Add to your shaker the vodka, tomato juice, lemon juice, cracked black pepper, salt, cayenne, and Worcestershire.

Shake and strain into glass.

Garnish with the lime slice.

BLOODY SHAME

Yields 1 serving

INGREDIENTS:

> *½ cup tomato juice*
> *1 jigger Heinz 57®*
> *Juice of ½ lemon*
> *¼ T garlic salt*
> *2 dashes Worcestershire*
> *1 dash Crystal® sauce*
> *Fresh black pepper, cracked*
> *1 large shrimp, peeled & deveined (tail on)*
> *Lemon wedge, for garnish*

PREPARATION:

Fill your shaker with cracked ice.

Add to your shaker the tomato juice, Heinz 57®, lemon juice, garlic salt, Worcestershire, Crystal®, and cracked black pepper.

Shake altogether well and strain into rocks glass.

Garnish with the shrimp and the lemon wedge.

Daiquiri

— FROM "The Weather is Here,
I Wish You Were Beautiful"
on COCONUT TELEGRAPH

Yields 1 serving

Sometimes spelled with a capital letter, this fruity concoction is named after a Cuban town not far from Santiago, where Americans ventured to work the mines after the Spanish-American War (1898). Spending long days working underground, the Yanks would relax weekends at the Venus Hotel and slug these rum drinks down. The DAIQUIRI was given its name by Jennings S. Cox, chief engineer of the mining project, and many credit him with its creation.

A generation would pass, though, before the first printed reference to the daiquiri would appear in Fitzgerald's *This Side of Paradise.*

As with the BASIC DAIQUIRI, the frozen concoction also has some literary connections, for it was first blended at the La Florida Bar in Havana, a place known affectionately as "Floridita" when Hemingway still occupied a seat there. A.E. Hotchner (Paul Newman's partner in the *Newman's Own*® line of food products that benefits children's causes, as well as author of *Papa Hemingway: A Personal Memoir*) recounts the role of the FROZEN DAIQUIRI in their very first meeting:

"Hotchner," he said, shaking hands, "welcome to the Cub Room." His hands were thick and square, the fingers rather short, the nails squared off. The bartender placed two frozen daiquiris in front of us; they were in conical glasses twice the size of my previous drink. "Here we have the ultimate achievement of the daiquiri-maker's art," Hemingway said. "Made a run of sixteen here one night." "This size?"

"House record," the barman, who was listening, said.

Hemingway sampled his drink by taking a large mouthful, holding it a long moment, then swallowing it in several installments. He nodded approval.

Oh, what I would have given to have been in Hotchner's seat . . . or at least one stool over.

The daiquiris kept coming as we discussed Robert Flaherty's documentary films, which Hemingway greatly admired, Ted Williams, the Book-of-the-Month-Club, Lena Horne, Proust, television, swordfish recipes, aphrodisiacs, and Indians, until eight o'clock, not threatening the Hemingway daiquiri-record but setting an all-time Hotchner high of seven. Hemingway took a drink with him for the road, sitting in the front of the station wagon next to his chauffeur, Juan; and I somehow managed to retain in the rum-mist of my head that he was going to pick me up the following morning to go out on his boat.

How many Parrotheads have hung around Jimmy's old haunts and hoped for such a similar encounter?

DAIQUIRI (Basic)

Yields 1 serving

INGREDIENTS:

1 jigger light rum
½ jigger lime juice
1 t superfine sugar
Lime slice, for garnish

PREPARATION:

Fill your shaker with ice.

Add the light rum, the lime juice, and the superfine sugar, then shake.

Strain into a chilled glass.

Garnish with the lime slice.

DAIQUIRI (Frozen)

Yields 1 serving

INGREDIENTS:

1 jigger light rum
½ jigger lime juice
1 t superfine sugar
Lime slice, for garnish

PREPARATION:

Fill your blender ¼ with ice.

Add the light rum, the lime juice, and the superfine sugar, then blend on low until smooth.

Pour into a chilled glass.

Garnish with the lime slice.

FROZEN FRUIT DAIQUIRI

Yields 1 serving

INGREDIENTS:

1 jigger light rum
½ jigger lime juice
½ jigger fruit liqueur*
1 jigger cream
Fruit*, for garnish

PREPARATION:

Fill your blender ¼ with ice.

Add the light rum, lime juice, fruit liqueur, and the cream, then blend on low until smooth.

Pour into chilled glass.

Garnish with the piece of matching fruit.

* Fruit should match your liqueur. If fruit is not sweet, add ½ jigger of honey.

Mojito

— FROM "Hooked in the Heart"
in TALES FROM MARGARITAVILLE / P.192

Yields 1 serving

The ingredients of the MOJITO (moe-HEE-toe) are very similar to a BASIC DAIQUIRI. And knowing what you now know of Hemingway's role in drinking history, I think you'll have some inkling to the significance of his supposedly frequent saying: "My daiquiri at Floridita; my mojito at the Bodeguita." (If you haven't a clue, that just means that he enjoyed these drinks at the bars of Havana's La Florida and La Bodeguita del Medio hotels.) And though the word *mojito* is Cuban, it has no particular meaning other than this particular drink.

Now, as the sun pulls away from the shore and the ship sinks in the west, we must wave goodbye to the last of my Hemingway stories.

The Mojito's ingredients aside, the thing that seems to set this apart from the rest of the mix is the colorful stirring utensil used by the Habañeros. Relying on neither a shaker, nor a blender, the traditional preparation of this drink requires a wooden swizzle stick from the base of which radiates (what has best been described as) "a bird's foot." After the bartender adds the first 4 ingredients, this utensil is inserted to the bottom of the glass and the upright "leg" is rolled between the palms of both hands, thus blending the drink and ensuring that the sugar at the bottom is dissolved.

INGREDIENTS:

> 1 jigger light rum
> ½ jigger lime juice
> 1 t superfine sugar
> Fresh mint, crushed
> Club soda

Lime slice, for garnish

PREPARATION:

In the bottom of a rocks glass, muddle the fresh mint with the lime juice and sugar.

Pour in the rum, then swizzle!

Add ice cubes and club soda to your liking.

Garnish with the lime slice.

Cajun Martini

— FROM "We Are the People Our Parents Warned Us About" on ONE PARTICULAR HARBOUR

When the MARTINI itself first came to print in an 1862 drink mixing guide called *The Bon-Vivant's Companion,* written by a bartender at the Occidental Hotel in San Francisco, the name was "Martinez." There was less gin and more vermouth than in the cocktail we know today, but the drink gradually moved on to equal proportions, and then 2 parts gin to 1 part dry vermouth just before Prohibition kicked in. By the time the Volstead Act was repealed and WW II had ended, there was very little vermouth in the recipe at all. Arguments then turned to the rightful place of a lemon twist or an olive.

Meanwhile, Ian Fleming arrived on the scene in 1960 with James Bond, a British spy who cared not at all for the gin, but preferred vodka instead. While you might want to pause here and debate the merits of *Shaken v. Stirred,* it is more relevant that you thank 007 for having given us the VODKA MARTINI, forerunner to this particular cocktail.

The CAJUN MARTINI remains a favorite in New Orleans, especially at K-Paul's Louisiana Kitchen, where it is said to have been created by Chef Paul

Prudhomme and his wife, Kay. This can be made with commercially-prepared pepper vodka, or you can prepare your own spicy vodka or gin. To do so, carefully wash 3 fresh cayenne peppers, 2 fresh jalapeño peppers, and 1 habeñero pepper. Gently puncture the peppers so that the alcohol will be able to flow through and become infused with their flavors. Add the peppers to a bottle of quality vodka or gin, then refrigerate for at least 3 days. After a week, any remaining alcohol must be strained.

INGREDIENTS:

   1 jigger pepper vodka

½ jigger dry vermouth
1 small jalapeño pepper, for garnish

PREPARATION:

Fill your shaker with ice.

Add the pepper vodka and the dry vermouth.

Shake altogether well, then strain into a chilled cocktail glass.

Garnish with a jalapeño pepper.

Oyster Shooter

Yields 1 serving

— FROM *"Beyond the Low Water Mark"*
in WHERE IS JOE MERCHANT? / P. 108

Slide your butt over, Elmo. As long as we've got that bottle of pepper vodka out for the CAJUN MARTINIS, we might as well do a couple of shooters. If you think you don't like oysters, this might just be the cure-all for *that* neurosis. When your head sweats, your ears ring, and your nose runs, you won't worry about some oyster sliding around in your gullet.

INGREDIENTS:

   1 oyster, raw on the half-shell
   1 T Crystal® sauce
   ½ t horseradish
   1 jigger pepper vodka

PREPARATION:

Slip the raw oyster from the shell into a shot glass.

Add the Crystal® sauce and horseradish.

Pour in the pepper vodka.

Slug it all down in one fell swoop!

Striped Bass

Yields 1 serving

Yes, it is true that this one came to me in a dream. That is, if you accept the notion that the semi-conscious stages of a drunken stupor are very, very much like a dream state. The concept obviously is from the traditional beer blending known as a BLACK & TAN, wherein one mixes equal parts of light, Pilsner beer and an Ale.

INGREDIENTS:

> *6 oz Red Stripe Jamaican Beer®*
> *6 oz Bass Ale®*

PREPARATION:

Ummm, pour some of your Red Stripe® into a chilled mug.

Let's see. Then pour some of your Bass Ale® into the same mug.

Yell out: "Hey, this should be called a *Striped Bass!*"

Drink up before anybody realizes who's making such a ruckus.

Mimosa

— FROM "I Wish Lunch Could Last Forever"
in TALES FROM MARGARITAVILLE / P. 151

Yields 1 serving

Let us now toast both Isabella Rivière and Slade Patterson, who not only share a passion for life, but also great taste in food. As with the BLOODY MARY, MIMOSAS are most often associated with brunch. And the proportions of the ingredients are really a matter of taste.

INGREDIENTS:

> *3 oz fresh orange juice*
> *3 oz Cristal champagne*
> *Splash of Grand Marnier, Cointreau, or*
> *Triple Sec*
> *Orange slice, for garnish*

PREPARATION:

Pour the fresh orange juice into a large, chilled wine glass.

Add the champagne to taste, along with your splash of preference, then stir gently.

Garnish with the orange slice.

Petit Punch

Yields 1 serving

— FROM "I Wish Lunch Could Last Forever"
in TALES FROM MARGARITAVILLE / P. 144

Time was when people old enough to drink were also old enough to know the meaning of a record player. If you happen to fall into that category, then now's the time to dig out some old records and mix up this favorite from Isabella's island of Martinique.

INGREDIENTS:

> *1 oz white rum*
> *½ ounce of Cointreau*
> *½ ounce of sweet vermouth*
> *Juice of ½ orange*
> *Orange slice, for garnish*

PREPARATION:

Fill your shaker with ice.

Add the white rum, Cointreau, sweet vermouth and orange juice, then shake.

Pour into a chilled cocktail glass.

Garnish with the orange slice.

Lemonade

— FROM "One Small Bass" in A PIRATE LOOKS AT FIFTY / P.43

Yields 4 servings

No one seems to remember just how to make LEMONADE the way they used to make it. Somewhere between then and now, we've come to believe that lemonade begins its life either as a powder, or as some frozen clump of something or other.

Though this recipe does take a little work, it begins with the making of a SIMPLE SYRUP (½ water/½ sugar), which can be stored and used at a later time. When I know that I'm going to make more lemonade during the course of a week, I'll freeze part of my first batch in ice cube trays. That way, the ice cubes don't dilute the flavor of the lemonade.

INGREDIENTS:
For the simple syrup:
> *2½ c cold water*
> *2½ c sugar*
> *Zest of 3 lemons*

For the lemonade:
> *Juice of 3 lemons*
> *3 to 4 c water*
> *Lemon slice for garnish*

PREPARATION:

For the simple syrup:

Put the 2½ c of cold water into a saucepan, then stir in the 2½ c of sugar and lemon zest.

Over low heat, bring the mixture to the slow boil and simmer for 2 minutes.

Remove the saucepan from the heat and allow the syrup to cool.

When cooled, the syrup can be strained to remove the zest; however, allowing it to remain will not detract from the taste of the lemonade.

For the lemonade:

In a pitcher, combine the lemon juice with 3 c of cold water.

Add 1 c of the SIMPLE SYRUP. Stir well and taste. If necessary, add more water.

Add ice to a tall glass, then fill with lemonade.

Garnish each glass with a lemon slice.

Iced Tea

— FROM "Take Another Road"
in TALES FROM MARGARITAVILLE / P. 37

Yields 1 gallon

There is ICED TEA, and there is SWEET TEA. Their ingredients are all but indistinguishable, and yet their preparation and taste are a world apart.

In the South, SWEET TEA is a common beverage that is simply not understood in places north of some mysterious line. Ask for SWEET TEA in some eatery above that cultural divide, and someone is likely to just slide a glass of ICED TEA in front of you and point to the sugar or the sweetener. But ask for SWEET TEA in the land from whence it comes and you'll get what you asked for. The recipe is so deceptively simple that you'll have no excuse not to try it. And once you do, you'll never again want to drink any of that stuff they sell as iced tea in a fancy schmancy bottle or a can.

INGREDIENTS:

2 qts water, boiled
4 quart-size tea bags
2 qts water, cold
2 c sugar

PREPARATION:

In a large pot, bring 2 qts of water to the boil.

Add the tea bags, then remove the pot from the heat and allow the tea to steep for 8 minutes.

Meanwhile, place the 2 qts of cold water in a gallon container.

Add the 2 c sugar to the cold water and stir to dissolve. Do not cheat on this step. The sugar must be dissolved in cold water, not in cold tea.

Add the 2 qts of steeped tea to the gallon container with the dissolved sugar and water.

Allow the batch of sweet tea to cool to room temperature, then cool and store in the refrigerator.

You might want to freeze some of each batch in ice cube trays so that plain water ice doesn't dilute the flavor of your sweet tea. Otherwise, serve in a chilled glass.

Root Beer Float

Yields 1 serving

— FROM "The Wind is in from Africa" in WHERE IS JOE MERCHANT? / P. 117

By now, I'll bet that you've read the last couple of recipes, then flipped to the cover just to make certain that you weren't reading some book called *Margaritas for Morons* or something similar. After all, most people who need a recipe for ICED TEA are probably going to have trouble operating a spoon, right? Well, here's a twist on a ROOT BEER FLOAT that will at least make it worth buying yourself some of those flexible straws. This is not exactly a traditional ROOT BEER FLOAT (or BROWN COW, if you're a Steely Dan fan). It's almost a Root Beer Parfait with a shot of Root Beer tossed in. And while it still has the great flavor of sassafras and vanilla, you might try grating in a bit of cinnamon or ginger.

INGREDIENTS:

> *2 12-oz bottles of premium root beer*
> *1 qt of premium* VANILLA ICE CREAM
> *Fresh cinnamon or ginger, grated for garnish*

PREPARATION:

Pour 1 12-oz bottle of root beer into an ice cube tray and allow to freeze into cubes.

Once you have frozen root beer cubes, assemble all of your ingredients, utensils, and soda glasses so that you can work quickly.

Empty your tray of root beer cubes into a food processor. Gently and briefly pulse the cubes until they become the consistency of dry slush. Don't overpulse and melt the ice into a liquid.

Spoon enough root beer slush to cover the bottom of each soda glass.

Add enough ice cream to cover the slush.

Top the ice cream with more slush and repeat until you run out of room in the glass or out of ingredients

Gently pour enough root beer from the second bottle to create the consistency of a FLOAT.

Garnish with fresh cinnamon or ginger.

Milkshakes in Motion

Yields 2 servings

— FROM "The Wino and I Know"
on LIVING & DYING IN ¾ TIME

How difficult can it be to put a milkshake in motion? Well, it first depends upon your definition of a MILKSHAKE. In some places, a MILKSHAKE is nothing more than milk and flavoring that is "shaken." In others, however, the MILKSHAKE also has ice cream. And, even then, the ice cream can range in proportion from a single scoop to an overwhelming amount that freezes the entire shake. In fact, those so-called "shakes" served by fast food franchises don't contain any milk whatsoever. They're a frozen, flavored, frenzied vegetable oil base. (*Yuck!*)

So, what shall we do?

Well, I don't want to insult you by telling you how to add 2 T of some syrup to 12 oz of milk. (I tried that insult with the ROOT BEER FLOAT.) Or even to toss in a scoop or two of ice cream. (Ditto. Plus, that sounds similar to the recipe for the BANANA SPLIT.)

So, I thought we might consider some basic recipes that not only vary the ingredients from the more traditional ones, but which also do something about that shaking motion. After all, the *true* milkshake mixer is *definitely not* a blender in the household sense. The true mixer has that single vertical shaft that stirs, rather than blends. And the household blender has those little blades that chop and whip, creating a lot of air bubbles and whipping the bejeezus out of any ice cream you might want to add. (What's up with *that*?)

So, the short answers to the problem are these: First, try using some Margaritaville flavors, such as the ICE CREAMS, SORBETS, FROZEN YOGURTS, and GRANITAS found in a later chapter. Second, keep the milk in milkshake by using different varieties, such as coconut milk or condensed milk (thick and sweet) with a fruit juice. Third, use a cocktail shaker to put that milkshake in motion. This is especially fine for those who do want to include ice cream in their recipes, because shaking keeps much of the scoop intact, yet it enables the ice cream to lower the temperature of the milk. Besides, any lack of creativity in the recipe is compensated for with your shaking panache.

CARIBBEAN SHAKE

Yields 1 serving

INGREDIENTS:

> 2 small bananas, peeled & cut in chunks
> 4 T coconut milk
> 4 T lime juice
> 4 oz orange juice
> 4 oz pineapple juice
> 1 t fresh ginger, peeled & grated
> 6 ice cubes
> Orange slice, for garnish

PREPARATION:

Place all the ingredients into your blender, then blend on low until smooth.

Pour into a tall, chilled glass.

Garnish with the orange slice.

JAMAICA SHAKE

Yields 1 serving

This recipe is not from the island, it simply contains all the Jamaican flavors.

INGREDIENTS:

> ½ cup freshly brewed strong coffee, cooled
> ½ t fresh ginger root, grated (or to taste)
> 2 t brown sugar
> ¼ t nutmeg
> ¼ t cardamom
> ¼ t cinnamon
> 3 scoops of CHOCOLATE ICE CREAM

PREPARATION:

Place the coffee, ginger, brown sugar, nutmeg, cardamom, and cinnamon in your shaker, then shake until you feel that they are mixed well.

Add the CHOCOLATE ICE CREAM, then shake another 30 seconds.

Pour into tall, chilled glass.

Dust with cinnamon.

LAST MANGO FRAPPE

Yields 1 serving

INGREDIENTS:

> 1½ c ripe mango, chopped
> 1 c milk
> 2 T sugar
> ¼ t vanilla extract
> 3 scoops of MANGO SHERBET
> Small slice of mango, for garnish

PREPARATION:

Chop a fresh, ripe mango into ½-inch pieces, then place the chopped pieces in your freezer for 30 minutes.

To your blender add the mango, milk, sugar, and vanilla, then blend until smooth.

Pour the blended mix into your shaker, then add the MANGO SHERBET.

Shake 30 seconds.

Serve in a tall, chilled glass.

Garnish with the mango slice.

GEORGIA PEACHES & CREAM

Yields 1 serving

INGREDIENTS:

> 1½ c fresh peaches, cut in ½-inch pieces
> ¼ c heavy cream
> 1 T sugar
> 3 scoops of PEACH ICE CREAM

PREPARATION:

Place the peaches, cream, and sugar into your blender, then process until smooth.

Pour the blended mix into your shaker, then add the ICE CREAM.

Shake well for 30 seconds.

Pour into a tall, chilled glass.

LOUISIANA MILKSHAKE

Yields 1 serving

INGREDIENTS:

> ½ c milk
> 1 t vanilla extract
> ¼ c of powdered milk
> 3 scoops of VANILLA ICE CREAM
> ½ cup Dr. Pepper®

PREPARATION:

Add the milk, vanilla, and milk powder to your shaker, then shake well for nearly 1 minute.

Add the ICE CREAM to the shaker, then shake well another 30 seconds.

Pour the Dr. Pepper® into a tall, chilled glass.

Pour the ingredients from your shaker into the glass with Dr. Pepper®.

CHOCOLATE PUDDING SHAKE

Yields 1 serving

INGREDIENTS:

> 1 c very cold milk
> 2 T instant chocolate pudding, any flavor
> 2 scoops of CHOCOLATE ICE CREAM

PREPARATION:

Add the milk, pudding mix, and ICE CREAM to your shaker, then shake vigorously for 1 minute.

Pour into tall, chilled glass.

Aztec Hot Chocolate

Yields 1 serving

— FROM "Waiting for the Sails to Fill"
in WHERE IS JOE MERCHANT? / P. 374

Tequila is not the only great drink from South of the Border. Though you might not think of Mexico and chocolate as being synonymous, Mexicans do take their chocolate very seriously. Often, in fact, unsweetened chocolate is put in non-dessert foods, such as chili. (Try it! You'll like it!)

And though Alaskan hot chocolate might be what Frank and Trevor drank to keep them warm, perhaps the best hot chocolate in the world is made with Mexican chocolate, which is made from roasted cocoa beans ground together with sugar and cinnamon. Quite often, almonds are also included. Shaped in thick round blocks, this is available in Mexican markets, gourmet shops, and mail-order catalogues.

INGREDIENTS:

3 oz Mexican chocolate, grated
3 c milk

PREPARATION:

In a small saucepan, bring the 3 c of milk to the boil over medium heat.

Meanwhile, grate the 3 oz of Mexican chocolate into your kitchen blender.

BEFORE YOU ADD THE BOILING MILK TO YOUR BLENDER, TAKE SOME SAFETY PRECAUTIONS.

First, be certain that the base of the blender's glassware is tightly secured to the blender. Second, make certain that you remove the vent from the cover of your blender. Finally, have a clean towel handy to wrap around the top of the glassware and the top to prevent any boiling milk from splattering up and out.

When you've taken all of the above precautions, pour the milk over the chocolate in the blender.

Place the vented cover on the glassware of the blender, then wrap the vented top with your towel.

Blend the milk and chocolate at medium speed until they have combined and the drink is frothy.

Pour the hot chocolate into heated cups.

The Coffee is Hot

— FROM "The Wino and I Know"
on LIVING & DYING IN ¾ TIME

— FROM "I Wish Lunch Could Last Forever"
on OFF TO SEE THE LIZARD

— FROM "Boomerang Love"
in TALES FROM MARGARITAVILLE / P. 102

— FROM "I Wish Lunch Could Last Forever"
in TALES FROM MARGARITAVILLE / P. 140

— FROM "Livin' on Island Time"
in WHERE IS JOE MERCHANT / P. 173

— FROM "Rolling with the Punches"
in WHERE IS JOE MERCHANT / P. 239

— FROM "Beach Music, Beach Music"
in WHERE IS JOE MERCHANT / P. 258

We know damn well that the Café du Monde serves hot coffee, because that's what the song says. What Jimmy doesn't tell you, though, is that the black coffee (CAFE NOIR) is not only hot, but also very, very, *very* strong. So, if you go to the French Quarter of New Orleans, make certain you order CAFE AU LAIT with your BEIGNETS. Otherwise, you might be in your seat for hours just trying to finish your coffee, hot or not.

While the French might hold some culinary advantages, no coffee in the world can match *Cafe a la Creole* perfected in Creole households. From early morning to late into the wee hours of the next day, there is a coffee drink for every aspect of Louisiana lifes. The secret lies not only in the process, but also in the ingredients. Creole coffee requires the very best of the Java and Mocha beans, as well as roasted chicory. (Not the kind you put in your salad.)

But the hot coffee in "The Wino and I Know" is not the only coffee brew that Jimmy savors thoughout his writings. His tastes run the full gamut of roasts with various proportions of milk, cream, or neither.

CAFE NOIR

Yields 4 cups

Traditionally, your morning dose of CAFE NOIR would be made in the basic sort of drip coffee pot that utilizes a straining basket. If you sold yours long ago in a tag sale for a quarter, you can buy a new one for under 10 dollars. The main thing to keep in mind is that you're not going to put the coffee pot on to boil. As the water percolates through this recipe, the coffee in the pot does not sit on any heat.

The next best piece of kitchenware to use would be a coffee press; however, it's just not the same. And don't even think of using that Joltin' Joe coffeemaker. It just won't do.

INGREDIENTS:

> *1 c Creole blend coffee*
> *4½ c cold water*
> *Sugar cubes, to taste*

PREPARATION:

Bring the 4½ c of water to the boil.

In a coffee mill, grind 1 c of roasted coffee beans from Mocha and Java, along with the roasted chicory. (*This blend is available from gourmet shops and through mail-order.*)

Place your coffee pot on top of the stove, but *not* on a burner. You are *not* going to boil your coffee.

Place the ground coffee in the strainer of your coffee pot and moisten with 2 T of the boiling water. Allow the water to settle throughout the grounds for about 5 minutes in order to prepare the oils from the beans.

Add just enough more of the boiling water to the strainer to make the grounds froth and bubble. Cover the strainer and the spout to prevent any steam from escaping from your pot. Allow the water to seep through the grounds into the pot.

DO NOT ADD ANY MORE WATER UNTIL THE GROUNDS HAVE SETTLED AND STOPPED BUBBLING.

Add just enough more of the boiling water to repeat this process.

Continue until you have depleted your water and filled your coffee pot.

Serve in heated cups. Sweeten, to taste, with sugar cubes. Do not add any milk or cream. *C'est noir!*

CAFE AU LAIT

Yields 4 cups

If you really wish that lunch could last forever, then this is the way Jimmy's song says you should begin: a little COCONUT TART and a CAFE AU LAIT.

As one who firmly believes that nothing is worth any wait in line — especially coffee and except Buffett tickets — I was a long time learning the difference between "coffee light," CAFE AU LAIT, LAIT CHAUD, CAFE LATTE, and CAFE CON LECHE. (Being a Cape Cod boy, I always think of Starbuck as a fine, old Nantucket whaling family.)

Traditionally, CAFE AU LAIT is made from equal portions of freshly brewed coffee and steamed milk; LAIT CHAUD, from equal portions of coffee and milk (*not* steamed).

Okay, so now you can bust out that gizmo that steams and foams your milk while it's making an eyecup's worth of ESPRESSO. I know you tried it a couple of times before it became a dust-collecting trophy on your kitchen counter and was last seen in a box under the cellar stairs. All you need that thing for here, though, is to steam that milk.

INGREDIENTS:

> *½ c Creole blend coffee*
> *2¼ c cold water*
> *2 c milk, steamed*
> *Sugar cubes, to taste*

PREPARATION:

Brew your *Cafe a la Creole* just as you would for CAFE NOIR.

Follow the directions on your cappuccinno/espresso maker for steaming milk.

Pour the hot, brewed coffee into heated cups.

Add equal portions of the *steamed* milk to each, then sweeten, taste.

LAIT CHAUD

Yields 4 cups

One rainy Paris day at Chéz Bar-B-Q-Hill, Isabella had put on the stereo a Slade Patterson record and enjoyed this "taste of her youth" from Martinique.

For those of you who don't remember a damn thing I told you, or who simply skipped the previous section of CAFE AU LAIT, I'll restate this explanation. LAIT CHAUD is simply the same as CAFE AU LAIT, except that the milk is not steamed. Though the milk is generally room temperature, it might be chilled.

INGREDIENTS:

> ½ c Creole blend coffee
> 2¼ c cold water
> 2 c milk
> Sugar cubes, to taste

PREPARATION:

Brew your *Cafe a la Creole* as for CAFE NOIR.

Pour the hot, brewed coffee into heated cups.

Add equal portions of the milk to each, then sweeten, taste.

CAFE CON LECHE

Yields 1 cup

At last, the time has come to make full use of that espresso machine, or else get thee to a Cuban bodega.

The Cuban Coffee Queen has now disappeared from the corner of Green and Ann Streets in Key West, only to be replaced by a SUSHI bar! Still, you can find yourself a great CAFE CON LECHE at Five Brothers on the corner of Eaton and Grinnell, or even the Dennis Pharmacy at the corner of United and Simonton.

This Cuban brew requires that elaborate contraption, as well as those dark and bitter roasted beans used for ESPRESSO. That Italian word has nothing to do with a "fast cup" of coffee, but means "pressed out." Just as *Cafe a la Creole* is one process, so is *espresso* another. The pressure of the water and steam extract the essential oils and flavors of the freshly ground beans so that the half-cup serving is highly concentrated.

The true difference between CAFE CON LECHE and CAFE LATTE is the amount of milk allowed by the proper-sized cup. CAFE CON LECHE should be served in an 8-oz cup; CAFE LATTE, in a 6-oz cup.

INGREDIENTS:

> 1½ oz brewed espresso
> 5 oz milk, steamed

PREPARATION:

Brew your *espresso* according to the directions with your machine.

Steam 5 oz milk according to the directions with your machine.

Serve in an 8-oz cup.

Coco Frio

Serves 1

— FROM "The Wind is in from Africa"
in WHERE IS JOE MERCHANT? / P. 119

This is my old "good news/bad news recipe." The good news is that you can't find a simpler drink to make than this one. (Unless, of course, you can't find a green coconut.) Face it, a monkey could serve this drink!

The bad news is that the liquid inside the coconut is *not* coconut cream or even coconut milk. (They're found in tin cans.) The stuff inside a coconut is coconut *water*: COCO FRIO.

End of story, end of recipe.

INGREDIENTS:

1 green coconut, chilled on ice

PREPARATION:
Being careful that you don't spill the coconut water inside, whack off the top of the coconut with your macheté.

Count the fingers on your coconut-holding hand. If you still have 5 entire fingers attached, insert a straw in the coconut and enjoy!

On the other hand (no pun intended), if you do not have a macheté, then you can drill 2 holes about 3 inches apart in the top of the coconut. One hole is for the COCO FRIO to come out; the other, for air to enter.

Insert a straw into one hole and enjoy! (Remember, you must sip on the outside end of the straw in order to enjoy.)

GALLEY NOTES:

BREAKFAST STUFF

Granola ❧ Banana Pancakes
Pecan Waffles ❧ French Toast
Pain Perdu ❧ French Toast with Mango
Huevos Rancheros ❧ Huevos Habañeros
Crab Omelette ❧ Cheddar Cheese Omelet
Beignets ❧ Cosmic Muffins ❧ Croissants
Breakfast Grits

Granola

— FROM "Blame It on Lord Baden-Powell"
in A PIRATE LOOKS AT FIFTY / P. 89

Yields 8 servings

Rock & roll lore has it that for the Beatles' classic "Yesterday," Paul McCartney had given the tune the working title of "Scrambled Eggs" until they could come up with a lyric. Well, let me assure you that there is absolutely no truth to the legend that Jimmy had used "Granola" as the working title for "Creola" on the *Floridays* LP. (That said, though, I am still tracking down rumors that the working title for "Boat Drinks" was actually "Goat Cheese!" I'll let you know what I find out.)

Meanwhile, here's a throwback to Jimmy's days of incense and patchouli oil.

INGREDIENTS:

> 6 c oatmeal
> 1 c wheat germ
> 1 c All-Bran® cereal
> 1 c toasted almonds, chopped rough
> 1 c coconut
> ½ c brown sugar
> 1 t fresh cinnamon, grated
> 1 t fresh nutmeg, grated

1 c honey
½ c canola oil

PREPARATION:

Preheat your over to 300° F.

In a large bowl, mix together the oatmeal, wheat germ, All-Bran® cereal, chopped almonds, and coconut.

Add in the brown sugar and cinnamon, then toss well.

In a small, heatproof bowl, combine the honey and oil, then microwave them about 45 seconds. Stir together the heated honey and oil, then pour over the dry ingredients in the larger bowl.

Mix everything together well, then spread upon a baking sheet.

Place the baking sheet on the center rack of your oven and bake for 25 minutes, stirring the mix every 10 minutes.

With an oven mitt, remove the baking sheet from the oven and allow your GRANOLA to cool.

Store in an airtight container.

Banana Pancakes

Yields 4 servings of 4 pancakes

— FROM "Christmas Morning
with Cecil B. DeBuffett"
in A PIRATE LOOKS AT FIFTY / P. 107

People who like to pride themselves in light, fluffy pancakes will love this recipe, not only because it uses eggs whites to keep the air inside, but also because the banana is part of the batter.

If you'd rather not make them yourself, then order up a stack at the Blue Heaven in Key West.

INGREDIENTS:

1 c all-purpose flour
½ c oat bran
1 T sugar
2 t baking powder
1 t salt
½ t fresh cinnamon, ground
¼ t fresh ginger, grated
1½ c water
½ c plain yogurt
½ c ripe banana, mashed
2 T vegetable oil
1½ t vanilla extract
4 egg whites, beaten to soft peaks

PREPARATION:

In a large mixing bowl, combine the flour, bran, sugar, baking powder, salt, cinnamon, and ginger.

In another mixing bowl, mix together the water, yogurt, mashed banana, vanilla, and 1 T of the oil.

To the mixing bowl of dry ingredients, stir in the bowl of wet ingredients. Mix just enough to incorporate them.

Use a mixer to beat the egg whites until they form into soft peaks.

Add ½ of the whites to the batter, then stir well.

Gently fold the remaining ½ of the egg whites into the batter.

Over medium heat, bring your pan to a temperature where a drop of water will bounce off its surface. Coat the surface of the heated pan with the remaining 1 T of oil.

For each pancake, ladle ½ c of batter into the hot pan.

When the wet surface of the pancake has become perforated by broken air bubbles that have risen through from the bottom and the edges of the pancake are dry, then it can be flipped.

Pecan Waffles

Yields 8 waffles

— FROM "I Wish Lunch Could Last Forever"
in TALES FROM MARGARITAVILLE / P. 144

Waffles made the proper way are not something you make on impulse. The toughest part, though, is not the making of a yeast batter the night before, but the trying to fall asleep while thinking of the next morning's breakfast.

INGREDIENTS:

> 1¾ c milk
> 1 t salt
> 1 T butter
> 2¼ t active dry yeast
> ¼ c warm water
> 2 c flour
> 1 c pecans, shelled & chopped
> 2 eggs, separated

PREPARATION:

In a small saucepan, combine the milk, salt, and butter over medium heat.

Bring to the boil, then remove from the heat.

In a small mixing bowl, proof the yeast in warm water until small bubbles foam on the surface.

When the yeast has proofed and the scalded milk cools to lukewarm, stir the yeast into the milk.

In a large mixing bowl, combine the flour with ¾ c of the pecans (reserve ¼ c for garnish), then stir in the warm liquid ingredients. After they have been incorporated, beat them together well.

Cover the bowl loosely with plastic wrap and allow the batter to rise overnight.

In the morning, separate the eggs. Place the yolks in a small mixing bowl; the whites in a larger one.

Preheat your waffle iron.

Beat the yolks well. Set aside.

Beat the whites until they form stiff peaks.

Stir the beaten egg yolks into the batter, then gently fold the beaten whites into the batter.

Spread enough batter on your iron to form a waffle, then cook until it is golden brown on both sides.

Top each waffle with soft butter and a garnish of chopped pecans, as well as cane or maple syrup.

French Toast

Yields 4 servings

— FROM "Twenty-six Miles Across the Sea"
in A Pirate Looks at Fifty / p. 148

French Toast in France is known as *ameritte*, but in New Orleans it's called PAIN PERDU ("lost bread," not "hurting chicken"). While Americans and Europeans generally make the recipe with WHITE BREAD, the Creoles and Cajuns alike insist that PAIN PERDU be made with FRENCH BREAD, though the crust is optional.

INGREDIENTS:
> 12 slices of white bread
> 2 eggs, beaten
> ½ c cream
> ½ t fresh cinnamon, grated
> 2 T butter

PREPARATION:
Heat your griddle or frying pan to a high temperature over medium heat.

In a wide-rimmed plate, whisk together the eggs and cream.

Grate in the fresh cinnamon and stir well.

Melt ½ T of the butter in the pan, but do not let it brown.

One at a time, dip into the beaten eggs-and-cream only as many slices of bread as you can cook at one time, then shake the excess egg wash off each.

Place the slices of bread into the pan and sauté until each is lightly golden on the bottom.

Flip each slice over and sauté on the second side until golden.

Remove the toasted bread from the pan and place on a warmed platter in a warm oven.

Repeat the process until all your slices have been cooked.

Serve with butter, syrup, and/or powdered sugar.

PAIN PERDU

Yields 4 servings

INGREDIENTS:

   1 loaf FRENCH BREAD, *(crust optional)*
   1 egg, beaten
   1 t brandy
   1 t orange water
   1 t sugar
   ½ t lemon zest
   2 T butter
   Powdered sugar, for garnish
   Fresh nutmeg, grated for garnish

PREPARATION:

In a wide bowl, beat together the egg, brandy, orange flower water, sugar, and orange zest.

If you wish, you can trim the crust from the bread; otherwise, slice the loaf into thick pieces.

Allow slices to soak in the egg mix for 30 minutes.

Melt the butter in a medium hot skillet, but do not allow it to brown.

Sauté each slice of soaked bread until golden brown on each side.

Remove the sautéed bread from your skillet, then sprinkle with powdered sugar and nutmeg.

Serve hot.

FRENCH TOAST WITH MANGO

Yields 4 servings

INGREDIENTS:

   2 eggs, separated
   1 t vanilla extract
   1½ cups soft bread crumbs
   1 loaf FRENCH BREAD, *cut into 8 slices*
   6 T butter
   2 fresh mangos, peeled & chopped
   1 c sour cream
   ¼ c brown sugar
   ¼ t fresh cinnamon, grated
   1 c cream

PREPARATION:

In a medium mixing bowl, combine the sour cream and the fresh cream.

Add the mangos, brown sugar, and grated cinnamon, then stir together well. Set aside.

In a wide-rimmed dish, beat together the egg yolks, vanilla, and cream.

In a medium mixing bowl, beat the egg whites until frothy.

Spread the bread crumbs in a flat dish.

Melt the butter in a medium-hot skillet, but do not allow it to brown.

Soak each slice of French bread in the yolk mixture for 10 seconds per side.

Dip the soaked bread slice into the egg white, then dredge in the bread crumbs.

Sauté each bread slice in your skillet until golden brown on each side.

Remove the sautéed slices from the skillet and keep them warm until they all have been sautéed.

Arrange 2-slice servings on each serving dish and top with the mango mixture.

Huevos Rancheros

Yields 4 servings

— FROM "Take Another Road" in TALES FROM MARGARITAVILLE / P. 55

At first glance, this recipe looks to be one of those that involves too much time; however, if you want to start off with the same necessities that Tully Mars did when he landed on Key West, then you've got to crack some eggs.

INGREDIENTS:

For the sauce:

3 T vegetable oil
¾ c onion, chopped fine
½ t garlic, chopped fine
2½ c tomato sauce
3 serrano chili peppers, diced
1 t chili powder
1 t salt
2 T cilantro, chopped

For the eggs:

6 T butter, melted
Salt, to taste
Fresh black pepper, cracked to taste
10 eggs

PREPARATION:

Of the sauce:

In a large saucepan, heat the 3 T of vegetable oil.

Add the chopped onion and garlic, then cook until they're soft. Stir occasionally.

Stir into the saucepan the tomato sauce, serrano peppers, chili powder, and salt. Bring to the boil, then reduce the heat and simmer uncovered for 15 minutes.

Remove the saucepan from the heat, stir in the cilantro, and replace the cover.

Of the eggs:

Over medium heat, melt the butter in a heavy skillet.

In a large mixing bowl, beat together the eggs, salt, and cracked pepper.

Pour the eggs into the heated skillet and scramble them to your liking.

Add the tomato sauce from the saucepan to the skillet.

Serve hot.

Huevos Habañeros

Yields 4 servings

As long as you're willing to try the Key West taste that Tully Mars experienced in the previous recipe, you might as well head another 90 miles due south and try this one with Frank Bama and Rudy Breno.

Before you go too much further, though, you're going to need some small ramekins. But that's okay, because you'll also want to use them when you make your CRÈME BRÛLÉE.

INGREDIENTS:

For the sauce:

¼ c pure Spanish olive oil
1 onion, chopped fine
1 green bell pepper, chopped fine
2 garlic cloves, chopped fine
2 tomatoes, chopped
½ c pimiento, drained & chopped fine
2 T dry sherry
Salt, to taste
Fresh black pepper, cracked to taste

For the eggs:

    8 large eggs
    4 T butter, melted
    Salt, to taste
    Fresh black pepper, cracked to taste
    1 T parsley, chopped fine for garnish

PREPARATION:

Of the sauce:

In a medium skillet, heat the olive oil over low heat until it is fragrant.

Add the onion, bell pepper, and garlic, then stir occasionally until they are cooked tender, about 8 minutes.

Stir in the tomatoes, pimientos, and sherry, then cook until thickened, about 15 minutes.

Stir, taste, and adjust the seasonings with salt & fresh cracked pepper.

Of the eggs:

Preheat your oven to 350° F.

Lightly oil 4 ramekins and place them on a baking sheet.

Divide the tomato sauce equally among them.

Break 2 eggs into a saucer, then slide them atop the sauce in one of the ramekins.

Repeat this procedure with the other 3 ramekins.

Drizzle melted butter on top of the eggs, then carefully place the baking sheet of ramekins on the center rack of your oven.

Bake until the whites of the eggs have set, but the yolks are still soft, about 10 minutes.

Season with salt & pepper.

Garnish with chopped parsley.

Place each ramekin on a heat-proof dish and serve immediately with toasted, buttered CUBAN BREAD.

Crabmeat Omelette

Yields 4 2-egg omelettes

— FROM "I Wish Lunch Could Last Forever"
in TALES FROM MARGARITAVILLE / P. 151

Chéz Bar-B-Q Hill was not just Isabella's dream come true, but a place whose menu is what Jimmy calls a lifeline of her travels. But look who's talking. Considering those fictional and factual sources, let me suggest that you not save this dish just for breakfast. After all, Isabella's specialty was "déjeuner toute la journée."

INGREDIENTS:

1 lb fresh crab meat, picked & cleaned
2 T butter
2 c fresh mushrooms, sliced
8 scallions, chopped
½ c sour cream
8 eggs
2 c Swiss cheese, grated
2 T butter
Fresh parsley sprigs, for garnish

PREPARATION:

In a small skillet, melt the butter, then sauté the mushrooms until soft.

Add the crab meat to the skillet, along with the sour cream, then stir and reduce the heat to its lowest temperature to keep this mixture just warm.

In a small mixing bowl, whip together 2 eggs.

In your 8-inch omelette pan over medium-high heat, melt ½ T of the butter. Pour the eggs into the pan and allow them to set for 30 seconds.

Use a spatula to lift the setting edges of the eggs and allow the uncooked egg to flow underneath.

Sprinkle ½ c of the cheese in the center of the omelette, then place a cover on the pan and cook for 1 minute.

Remove the cover and spoon ¼ of the crab-mushroom mixture over half of the omelette's top. Replace the cover and cook until the eggs are set, about 1 more minute.

Remove the cover and slide the omelette onto a warm serving plate so that the omelette folds over onto the crab half of itself.

Garnish with a sprig of parsley and serve hot.

Cheddar Omelet

Yields 2 servings

— FROM *"Changing Channels"* in WHERE IS JOE MERCHANT? / P. 281

My spelling's just fine, thank you, but I can't help it if this egg dish is spelled more than one way. But that's the way Jimmy likes it. Isabella serves OMELETTES, while Desdemona makes OMELETS. Though spelling means nothing, that's not to say there isn't more than one way to make these things. The *French* version is pretty much the quick recipe on the previous page, but the other version is this one, sometimes called a *puffy* omelet. The difference is that the eggs are separated in this version to create a dish which is finished in your oven and must be served before it all falls down.

All of which means that this is probably *not* the recipe Desdemona would have whipped-up for Trevor in the galley of the *Cosmic Muffin*.

INGREDIENTS:

> 4 eggs, separated
> ½ c mayonnaise
> 3 t water
> 2 T butter
> 1 c cheddar cheese, shredded fine

PREPARATION:

Preheat your oven to 350° F.

In a small mixing bowl, combine the egg yolks, mayonnaise, and water. Set aside.

In a medium mixing bowl, beat the egg whites until they form soft peaks, then fold the yolk mixture into the bowl of egg whites.

In a large, ovenproof skillet, melt the butter.

Turn the eggs into your skillet, then reduce the heat to low. Cook 'til the bottom is light brown and puffy, but the top is moist, 10 minutes.

Place the omelet in the oven to bake 5 minutes.

With an oven mitt, gently remove the hot skillet from the oven and sprinkle the cheese on top.

Place the skillet back in the oven and bake until the cheese melts, about 1 to 2 minutes more.

With an oven mitt, remove the skillet again, then use a spatula to loosen the omelet from the edges of the pan.

Use a sharp knife to make a shallow cut down the center of the omelet and fold the omelet in half along the cut. Serve immediately.

Beignets

— FROM "The Wino and I Know"
on LIVING AND DYING IN ¾ TIME

— FROM "I Will Play for Gumbo"
on BEACH HOUSE ON THE MOON

Yields 2 dozen

When Jimmy sings of the hot doughnuts at the Café du Monde, he means the classic French BEIGNET, not the classic Kripsy Kreme® doughnut you get at the drive-through window.

And as if that word distinction weren't enough, let me point out that the BEIGNETS he sings of are these confections, not the deep-fried, savory FRITTERS that also carry this French name. So, when you hear Jimmy sing "doughnut," think BEIGNET. And when he sings "beignet," don't think FRITTER. There's enough confusion there to clog your brain cells as well as your arteries.

Once mixed, this dough must be refrigerated at least overnight, but it will keep well in the refrigerator for about a week and can also be frozen. In any case, you ought to allow your cut dough to rise (as much as double) before the frying. Though some recipes simply have you fry the cold dough and do not mention this proofing stage, that direction makes no use of the yeast which you take the time to proof and add to the ingredients. And whether you cut your BEIGNET in the shape of a rectangle or a triangle is more a mater of personal dexterity. An even rectangle is a tougher cut for me than a free-form triangle. The New Orleans standard has four sides. Finally, let me note that a serving at the Café du Monde consists of 3 hot BEIGNETS dusted (buried!) very generously with confectioner's sugar.

INGREDIENTS:

1½ t active dry yeast
¾ c water (100° to 115° F)
¼ c sugar
½ teaspoon salt
1 large egg
½ c evaporated milk
3½ c all-purpose flour
2 T solid shortening
Vegetable oil for deep frying
Confectioner's sugar for dusting (or burying, depending on taste)

PREPARATION:

Proof the yeast by combining the warm water and sugar in a large mixing bowl. Stir the yeast into the water until it has dissolved. Allow this to stand until bubbles appear in the surface foam.

After the yeast has proofed, stir in the rest of the sugar with the salt, egg, and evaporated milk.

Gradually stir in 2 c of the flour, then beat until smooth with a wooden spoon.

Beat in the shortening with a spoon until blended well.

Gradually add the remaining flour, again beating it in with a spoon until the dough is too stiff to stir. Use your hands to work in any remaining flour.

Grease lightly a large mixing bowl, then transfer the dough.

Seal the bowl tightly with plastic wrap and refrigerate overnight.

Before frying, lightly dust a pastry cloth, then roll the dough to a ¼-inch thickness.

Use a sharp knife or pastry cutter to cut the dough into 2½- by 3½-inch rectangles.

Cover your cut dough with a damp cloth and set in a warm place to proof.

Heat the oil to 360° F.

When your beignets have about doubled in size, carefully place 3 or 4 in the hot oil. Fry this batch until they are golden brown on each side. Their puffing will cause them to rise to the surface of the oil, so use a pair of tongs to turn each just once. Altogether, each batch should take about 3 minutes.

Use your tongs to remove each beignet and place on a platter lined with layers of paper towel. They can be kept warm in a 200° F oven.

To serve, generously bury each hot beignet with confectioner's sugar.

Cosmic Muffins

— FROM "Desdemona's Building
A Rocket Ship"
in WHERE IS JOE MERCHANT? / P. 67

Years and years ago, when Jimmy used to perform at the Club Passim in Cambridge, Massachusetts during the 70s, there was also an astrologist named Daryl Martinie who appeared as "The Cosmic Muffin" each morning with Charles Laquidara on WBCN-FM. 'BCN has long remained one of the pioneers in progressive radio, but the last I heard of "The Cosmic Muffin," he was somewhere in Florida. Coincidence? I think not.

Meanwhile, there is no specific muffin mentioned anywhere in all of Jimmy's words about Desdemona's baking. Still, I couldn't pass up the opportunity to share some possible breakfast goodies for rested Margaritians. I hope that these make Desdemona proud and that she finds them worthy of their cosmicity. (I think I just made up a word.)

ORANGE~GINGER

Yields 12 muffins

INGREDIENTS:

1¾ c all-purpose flour

1½ t baking soda
1½ t baking powder
½ t salt
1 orange, peeled, seeded & chopped fine
2 t orange zest
½ c butter, softened
¾ c sugar
1 egg
½ c orange juice
¼ c crystallized ginger, chopped fine

PREPARATION:
Preheat your oven to 375° F.

In a medium mixing bowl, combine the flour, baking soda, baking powder, and salt. Set this aside.

Before you peel and seed the orange, grate 2 t of zest from the peel, making certain that you don't get any of that white pith just beneath the orange coloring. Set this aside.

Peel and seed the orange, then chop it fine. Set this aside, too.

In a large mixing bowl, beat together the butter and sugar until they are light and fluffy.

Add the egg to the butter and sugar, then beat this in.

Stir the orange zest and chopped orange into this mixture.

Alternate adding and mixing the dry ingredients and the orange juice into the larger mixing bowl of beaten butter, sugar, and egg. Do not overmix this batter.

Stir in the crystallized ginger.

Lightly grease your muffin pan, then fill each

almost to the top with an equal portion of the batter.

Place the muffin pan on the center rack of your preheated oven. Bake until the muffins are golden brown and a toothpick inserted in the center comes out clean, about 18 minutes.

With an oven mitt, remove the muffin pan from the oven and allow to cool before serving.

MANGO

Yields 12 muffins

INGREDIENTS:

¼ c cream cheese
½ c sugar
2 eggs
1 c peach yogurt
½ c heavy cream
1 t lemon juice
Zest of 1 lemon
1 mango, peeled & chopped
2½ c self-rising flour
¼ c slivered almonds, toasted
¼ c raw sugar

PREPARATION:
Preheat your oven to 350° F.

In a large mixing bowl, cream together the sugar and cream cheese.

Beat into this mixture the eggs, cream, lemon juice, and yogurt.

Add the mango and lemon zest, then mix together.

Gradually fold in the flour. If the batter does not seem stiff enough, add up to an additional ½ c of flour.

Lightly grease your muffin pan.

Divide the batter equally, then top with toasted almonds and raw sugar.

Place on the center rack for 25 minutes.

With an oven mitt, remove the muffin pan from your oven and allow the muffins to cool.

KEY LIME

Yields 12 muffins

INGREDIENTS:

> 1 c all-purpose flour
> 1 t baking powder
> ½ c sugar
> 1 t salt
> 4 T butter, melted
> Juice of 3 key limes
> 2 eggs
> Zest of 1 key lime

For the topping:

> 4 T butter, melted
> 1 T lime juice
> ½ c sugar

PREPARATION:

Preheat your oven to 375° F.

In a large mixing bowl, combine the all-purpose flour, baking powder, ½ c of sugar, and salt, then mix well.

In a small saucepan, melt the butter. Remove the saucepan from the heat, then stir in the lime juice and the zest.

Add the butter mix to the mixing bowl, along with the eggs.

Stir together until just mixed.

Lightly grease your muffin pan.

Divide the batter equally, then place on the medium rack of your oven.

Bake until browned, about 15 to 20 minutes.

With an oven mitt, remove the muffins from the oven and allow to cool for 5 minutes.

Meanwhile, melt the remaining butter, remove from the heat, and stir in the remaining juice.

Place the remaining sugar in a small dish.

With an oven mitt, turn the muffins out of their pan onto a cooling rack.

While they are still warm, dip the top of each muffin into the melted butter and lime juice, then into the sugar.

Serve warm or cooled.

COCONUT CREAM

Yields 12 muffins

INGREDIENTS:

> 3 T butter, melted
> 1 c coconut cream
> 1 c coconut, shredded coarse
> ¾ c pineapple, chopped
> 2 eggs
> 1 T rum
> 2 t baking powder
> ½ c sugar
> 1¾ c all-purpose flour

PREPARATION:

Preheat your oven to 400° F.

In a small saucepan, melt the butter. Remove the saucepan from the heat, then stir in the coconut cream, pineapple, and shredded coconut.

In a large mixing bowl, combine the butter mix with the eggs and rum.

In a smaller bowl, combine the baking powder, sugar, and all-purpose flour.

Add the dry ingredients from the smaller bowl to the wet ingredients in the larger one, then stir until just mixed.

Lightly grease your muffin pan.

Divide the batter equally, then sprinkle some shredded coconut on top.

Place the muffin pan on the medium rack of your oven.

Bake until browned, about 15 to 20 minutes.

With an oven mitt, remove the muffins from the oven and allow to cool for 5 minutes.

Serve warm or cooled.

BANANA

Yields 12 muffins

INGREDIENTS

2½ c all-purpose flour
¾ c sugar
1 T double-acting baking powder
½ t salt
6 T butter
3 ripe bananas, cut up
2 eggs
½ c milk
1 t vanilla extract

PREPARATION:

Preheat your oven to 400° F.

In a large mixing bowl, combine the flour, sugar, baking powder, and salt with a fork.

Use your fingertips to cut in the butter until the mixture is coarse and resembles cornmeal.

To your blender add the cut bananas, eggs, milk, and vanilla, then blend briefly until the bananas are just chopped.

Add the wet ingredients from the blender to the dry ingredients in the larger bowl, then stir until just mixed.

Lightly grease your muffin pan.

Divide the batter equally among the muffin cups, then place the pan on the medium rack of your oven.

Bake until browned, about 20 to 25 minutes.

With an oven mitt, remove the muffins from the oven and allow to cool for 5 minutes.

Serve warm or cooled.

BLACKBERRY*

Yields 12 muffins

INGREDIENTS

3¼ c all-purpose flour
1½ c sugar
1 t salt
4 t baking powder
1 t baking soda
Zest of 1 whole lemon, grated
2 eggs
2 c buttermilk
½ c vegetable oil
2 c fresh blackberries
½ c pecans, chopped
Sugar, for topping

PREPARATION:

Preheat your oven to 375° F.

In a large mixing bowl, sift together the flour, sugar, salt, baking powder and baking soda.

Stir in the zest of the lemon and the pecans.

In another large mixing bowl, whisk together the eggs, buttermilk, and oil.

Add the dry ingredients that have been sifted and stir until everything is just mixed.

Gently fold the blackberries into the batter so that they are distributed throughout.

Lightly grease your muffin pan.

Divide the batter equally, then sprinkle the top of each muffin with sugar.

Place the muffin pan on the medium rack of your oven.

Bake until browned, about 20 to 25 minutes.

With an oven mitt, remove the muffins from the oven and allow to cool for 10 minutes.

Serve warm or cool them completely on a wire rack.

Sure, you could use Blueberries or Huckleberries.

PLANTATION STYLE

Yields 12 muffins

INGREDIENTS:

1 20-oz can crushed pineapple, drained
1 c pecans, chopped
2 c all-purpose flour
1 t salt
1 t baking soda
3 oz cream cheese, softened
1 c sugar
2 t vanilla
1 egg, beaten
½ c sour cream

PREPARATION:

Preheat your oven to 400° F.

In a large mixing bowl, sift together flour, baking soda, and salt.

In another large mixing bowl, beat cream cheese, sugar, and vanilla, then add the egg.

Alternate adding to the cream cheese mixture the sifted dry ingredients and then the yogurt. Mix after adding each.

Gently fold the drained pineapple.

Heavily grease your muffin pan.

Divide the pecans among the muffin cups, then divide the batter equally.

Place the muffin pan on the medium rack of your oven.

Bake until browned, about 20 to 25 minutes.

With an oven mitt, remove the muffins from the oven and allow to cool for 10 minutes.

Serve warm or cool them completely on a wire rack.

GINGER

Yields 12 muffins

INGREDIENTS

2 oz fresh ginger, unpeeled & grated
¾ c plus 3 T sugar
2 T lime zest, grated
½ c butter, softened
1 c buttermilk
2 eggs
2 c all-purpose flour
½ t salt
¾ t baking soda

PREPARATION:

Preheat your oven to 375° F.

In a small saucepan, combine the ginger and sugar, then cook over medium heat until the sugar melts and becomes hot. Do not leave this pan unattended, because this happens much quicker than you might think.

Remove the saucepan from the stove and allow the ginger mix to cool.

In a food processor, combine the lime zest and the 3 T of sugar.

Stir this into the ginger mixture and set aside.

In a large mixing bowl, beat together the butter and ¾ c of sugar.

Beat in the eggs, then blend in the buttermilk.

Stir in the flour, baking soda, and salt.

Add the ginger-lime mixture, then stir well.

Lightly grease your muffin pan, then divide the batter equally among the muffin cups.

Place the pan on the medium rack of your oven and bake until browned, about 15 to 20 minutes.

With an oven mitt, remove the muffins from the oven and allow to cool for 10 minutes.

Serve warm.

GEORGIA PEACH

Yields 12 muffins

INGREDIENTS:

> ¾ c all-purpose flour
> ¼ c whole wheat pastry flour
> ½ c raw sugar
> 1 T baking powder
> 2 fresh peaches, diced into ¼-inch pieces

> 1 T butter, melted
> 2 eggs
> 1 c milk
> 1 t almond extract
> 2 T fresh cinnamon, grated for topping
> 2 T raw sugar, grated for topping

PREPARATION:

Preheat your oven to 400° F.

In a large mixing bowl, combine the all-purpose flour, the whole wheat pastry flour, the raw sugar, and the baking powder.

Fold in the chopped peaches.

In a smaller mixing bowl, combine the melted butter, eggs, milk, and almond extract, then mix together well.

Add the smaller bowl of wet ingredients to the larger bowl of dry ingredients, then stir until just mixed.

Lightly grease your muffin pan.

Divide the batter equally among the muffin cups, then top with a mix of cinnamon and raw sugar.

Place the pan on the medium rack of your oven and bake until browned, about 15 minutes.

With an oven mitt, remove the muffins from the oven and allow to cool for 10 minutes.

Serve warm.

HAWAIIAN MUFFINS

Yields 12 muffins

INGREDIENTS:

> 2 c all-purpose flour
> ½ c sugar
> 2 t baking powder

½ t salt

1 c salted roasted macadamia nuts, chopped

¾ c coconut, flaked

½ c dried pineapple, chopped

¾ c milk

½ c butter, melted & cooled

1 egg, lightly beaten

1 t vanilla extract

PREPARATION:

Preheat your oven to 400° F.

In a large mixing bowl, combine the all-purpose flour, sugar, baking powder, and the salt.

Add the macadamia nuts, coconut, and pine-apple, then stir until coated.

In a smaller mixing bowl, combine the butter, egg, milk, and vanilla extract, then mix together well.

Add the smaller bowl of wet ingredients to the larger bowl of dry, then stir until just mixed.

Lightly grease your muffin pan.

Divide the batter equally among the muffin cups, then top with a mix of cinnamon and raw sugar.

Place the muffin pan on the medium rack of your oven and bake until the muffins are browned, about 15 to 20 minutes.

With an oven mitt, remove the muffins from the oven and allow to cool for 10 minutes.

Serve warm or cooled.

FRUITCAKE MUFFINS

Yields 12 muffins

INGREDIENTS:

2 c all-purpose flour

1 c sugar

2 t baking soda

2½ t fresh cinnamon, grated

1 t salt

1 carrot, peeled & grated

1 c zucchini, grated

½ c raisins

½ c pecans, chopped

1 c coconut, grated

1 Granny Smith apple, cored & grated

3 large eggs

¼ c vegetable oil

¼ c apple sauce

½ c buttermilk

1 T vanilla extract

PREPARATION:

Preheat your oven to 350° F.

In a large mixing bowl, sift together flour, sugar, baking soda, cinnamon, and salt.

Add carrots, zucchini, raisins, pecans, coconut, and apples, then stir until coated.

In a smaller mixing bowl, combine the eggs, vegetable oil, apple sauce, buttermilk, and vanilla extract, then mix together well.

Add the smaller bowl of wet ingredients to the larger bowl of dry, then stir until just mixed.

Lightly grease your muffin pan, then divide the batter equally among the muffin cups.

Place the muffin pan on the medium rack of your oven and bake until browned, about 25 to 30 minutes.

With an oven mitt, remove the muffins from the oven and allow to cool for 5 minutes.

Cool on a wire rack.

Croissants

Yields 1 dozen

— FROM *"Beach Music, Beach Music"*
in Where is Joe Merchant? / P. 258

— FROM *"Fly-Boy in the Ointment"*
in Where is Joe Merchant / P. 297

Perhaps the phrase "labor of love" was created especially for those who have the stamina to bake these delicate delights. One saving grace, however, is that the dough can be made and frozen.

INGREDIENTS:

1½ t active dry yeast
1 T sugar
¼ c warm water
1 t salt
2½ c unbleached flour
1 T butter
1 c milk, warm
1 c cold butter

PREPARATION:

Proof the yeast by combining the ¼ c of warm water and sugar in a large mixing bowl. Stir the yeast into the water until it has dissolved. Allow this to stand until bubbles appear in the surface foam.

In a large mixing bowl, combine the flour, salt, and the 1 T of butter.

Add the 1 c warm milk to the large mixing bowl, along with the proofed yeast, then stir well until the dough is smooth.

Lightly butter a large mixing bowl.

Transfer the dough to the buttered bowl, then cover and allow the dough to rise until double in bulk, about 1½ hours.

After the dough has doubled, place the dough in the refrigerator for 30 minutes.

Prepare the butter by spreading a piece of plastic wrap on your work surface, then sprinkling 2 T of flour on the plastic wrap.

Place the butter onto the floured plastic wrap, then sprinkle the butter with flour.

Cover the butter with plastic wrap.

Use a rolling pin to gently pound the butter flat so that it will be workable without being either brittle cold or greasy warm. Keep it refrigerated until you are ready to work it into the dough.

After 30 minutes, remove the dough from the refrigerator and turn it out on a floured surface.

Roll the dough into a rectangle that is ¼ inch thick. Place the rectangle so that one narrow side (end) is close to you, then use a table knife to mark it in 3 equal sections.

Remove the butter from the refrigerator and spread it over the 2 equal sections closest to you. Of the 3 equal sections of the rectangle, then, the furthest section will remain unbuttered.

Fold the unbuttered far section toward you until it covers the buttered center section.

Fold the buttered section near you over the other 2 doubled sections. The dough should now be more a square than a rectangle.

Turn this square of dough 1 turn clockwise.

Roll the dough once again into a rectangle that is ¼ inch thick.

Without adding any more butter, repeat the same folding procedure as above.

Wrap the dough and refrigerate for 2 hours.

Remove the dough from the refrigerator, then once again roll and fold the dough. Turn the dough, then roll and fold once more. Altogether, you will have rolled and folded 4 times to create layers and layers of dough with butter between them. When baked, this will create a flaky crescent.

For the last time (*fer cryin' out loud!*), roll the dough into a rectangle that is ¼ inch thick.

With a sharp knife, cut dough in 3-inch squares.

Cut each of these squares diagonally to form 2 triangles from each square.

Beginning with the widest side of each triangle, roll up the dough and shape into a crescent (or, as they say in France, *croissant*).

Place the croissants on a baking sheet and chill in the refrigerator for 30 minutes.

Preheat your oven to 400° F.

Place the baking sheet in the upper third of your oven and bake the croissants for 10 minutes. Reduce heat to 350° F, then bake them for another 15 minutes.

With an oven mitt, remove the baking sheet from your oven. Use a thin metal spatula to remove the croissants immediately from the hot baking sheet to a wire rack. Otherwise, the bottoms of the croissants are likely to burn.

Au Pain Chocolat

Yields 1 dozen

If you have survived the process of baking CROIS-SANTS, then you are set to create this variation. Essentially, you are using the exact same recipe and procedure; however, before you roll the croissants you must add 1 oz of quality semisweet chocolate as a filling.

Ingredients:

1½ t active dry yeast
1 T sugar
¼ c warm water
1 t salt
2½ c unbleached flour
1 T butter
1 c milk, warm
1 c cold butter
12 oz of fine semisweet chocolate

Preparation:

Follow the same directions as for the croissants, except that you add the chocolate (as you did the butter) after rolling the second rectangle.

Breakfast Grits

— from *"Take Another Road"* in Tales from Margaritaville / p. 34

Get this straight: there are LOOSE GRITS and there are BAKED GRITS. And they're *much* better than their critics would ever have you believe. There are also shrimp grits and sausage grits and whatever grits. But we'll stick with the breakfast basics, not unlike those that Tully Mars had for his very first time at the Chat 'n Chew Cafe near Blytheville, Arkansas.

Basic Grits

Yields 4 servings

Ingredients:

4 c water
1 c quick (not instant!) grits
1 t salt
4 T butter

Preparation:

In a medium saucepan, bring the water to the boil. Add the salt to the boiling water, then steadily stir the grits into the saucepan.

Allow the grits to boil until they stop foaming.

Reduce the heat, cover, and simmer until the grits have become thick, about 5 to 7 minutes.

Remove the grits from the heat and add the butter.

Serve hot.

BAKED CHEESE GRITS

Yields 4 servings

INGREDIENTS:

> 2 t salt
> 1 c regular grits
> 4 c milk, divided
> 2 eggs, beaten
> 1 c extra sharp cheddar cheese, shredded & divided
> ½ c butter
> 1 t Worcestershire sauce
> Fresh black pepper, cracked to taste

PREPARATION:

In medium saucepan, bring 3½ c of milk to the boil over medium heat.

Steadily add and stir the grits into the saucepan.

Stirring constantly, allow the grits to boil until they stop foaming.

Reduce the heat, simmer, and beat the grits often until they begin to thicken. Stir in the remaining ¼ c of the milk, as well as the butter, then cover and remove the pan from the heat.

Preheat your oven to 350° F.

Butter a 2-quart baking dish.

Add to the saucepan the eggs, ¾ c of the cheese, the Worcestershire sauce, the baking powder, the pepper, and the salt. Stir together well to blend, then transfer the grits to the baking dish.

Place the uncovered baking dish on the center rack of your oven and bake for 30 minutes.

With an oven mitt, remove the baking dish from the oven and sprinkle the top with the remaining ¼ c of cheddar.

Place the uncovered baking dish on the center rack of your oven and bake for 15 more minutes.

With an oven mitt, remove the baking dish from the oven.

Serve either hot, or re-heated.

APPETIZERS & SNACKS

Pommes de Terre Soufflées
Conch Fritters ❧ Eighth Deadly Sin
Deviled Eggs ❧ Caviar ❧ Fried Okra
Desdemona's Tortillas ❧ Guacamole
Thy Neighbor's Wife's Popcorn
Fried Crab Claws ❧ Peanut Butter

Pommes de Terre Soufflées

Yields 4 servings

— FROM "I Wish Lunch Could Last Forever"
in TALES FROM MARGARITAVILLE / P. 151

When Slade and Isabella had ordered POMMES DE TERRE SOUFFLÉES as part of their celebratory feast at Galatoire's, my fractured knowledge of French told me that this might be some sort of potato soufflé. Though I might have been wrong, I was joined in this error by all sorts of well-meaning gourmands who helped me locate a recipe. In the end, our search to the motherland of POMMES DE TERRE found a recipe which fulfilled our misunderstanding. When I finally thought of checking the veritable *Larousse Gastronomique* (a big reference book whose name in French means something about something) therein was the *truth* about "puffed potatoes" attributed to an unnamed chef at a restaurant outside Paris.

A popular favorite at Antoine's restaurant in New Orleans, this recipe was brought to America in the late 19th century by Antoine Alciatore himself, who had been an apprentice to a Chef Collinet of the Hôtel de Noailles in Marseilles. As the story goes, Collinet was the chef who had awaited the arrival by train of King Louis Philippe at Saint-Germain-en-Laye near Paris.

At the request of the railway company, the chef prepared the king's meal, including his favorite fried potatoes. They were already frying as word came that Louis had been removed from the train for security reasons when the locomotive had trouble chugging uphill, and he was finishing his journey by carriage. So, Collinet scooped the slices from the cooker and set them aside. When the king finally made his appearance, the chef put the once-fried, now cold potato slices back into the hot oil and *voila! Up they all puffed!*

The chef was surprised, the king was delighted, and they all lived fattily ever after.

"The famous analytical chemist Chevreul," adds *Larousse*, "who was informed of this phenomenon, studied it experimentally and established the conditions under which it occurred and could be produced at will."

So, Collinet kept on puffing the potatoes, which he then taught to Antoine, who (in turn) brought them to America, where they are beloved in New Orleans, and are savored by Jimmy through Slade and Isabella.

Though they do share some of their technique of FRENCH FRIED POTATOES, POMMES DE TERRE SOUFFLÉES have nothing to do with any recipes for a mashed potato soufflé. Still, my many thanks to all who tried to help this cause. *Merci.*

INGREDIENTS:

> *2 lbs potatoes, cut lengthwise in 1¼-inch slices about 1/8-inch thick*
> *Vegetable oil*
> *Salt, to taste*

PREPARATION:

The traditional kitchen tool for making such thin slices would be a mandolin, but a less expensive slicer is certainly adequate.

Soak the slices in cold water for 30 minutes.

Drain and dry the potato slices.

In a large skillet, heat your oil to 275° F.

Carefully place a layer of potato slices in the hot oil, then use a wooden spoon to move the slices around until they puff up.

With a slotted spoon, remove the puffed potatoes to a clean layer of paper towel and allow them to cool for a few minutes.

Heat your oil to 400° F.

Again, place the once-fried slices into the hot oil until they are puffy and crisp.

With a slotted spoon, remove the puffed slices to a clean paper towel to drain.

Salt, to taste, and serve hot.

Conch Fritters

Yields 2 dozen

— FROM "Tickets to Ride"
in WHERE IS JOE MERCHANT? / P. 154

The French seem to have a word for everything. And that word apparently is BEIGNET, which can mean (as in this case) a FRITTER, or it can be a DOUGHNUT.

CONCH FRITTERS remain a popular appetizer in Key West, though no one makes them better than they do at the Margaritaville Cafe and at B.O.'s Fish Wagon. All too often in most other places, there's just not enough conch in the batter to make them pass any truth-in-advertising standards. Maybe that's why Jimmy never found any great urge to write about them until he got around to serving them as dog treats for Frank Bama's faithful pooch, Hoagy. Nonetheless, this recipe will make your guests roll over and beg for more. (Just don't let them jump up on the furniture!)

Most fish markets can order a 5-pound box of conch meat for you rather inexpensively. The conch meat is whole, but well-cleaned, then frozen. The fritters are best served with the Margaritaville Cafe's KEY WEST HOT SAUCE.

INGREDIENTS:

½ lb conch meat
2 T vegetable oil
¼ c onion, chopped
¼ c green pepper, chopped
1 celery rib, diced
1 T garlic, chopped
2 eggs, beaten
1 c buttermilk
1 t baking powder
2 T Crystal®
½ c self-rising cornmeal
¾ c all-purpose flour
Solid vegetable shortening, for deep-frying
Salt & cayenne pepper

PREPARATION:

Use a meat mallet to pound the conch into a flat ¼-inch steak, then dice the conch into small pieces with a knife. If you use a food processor to do this, the conch meat is likely to become a bit more gummy than you want and will be difficult to mix with the other ingredients.

In a large skillet, heat the 2 T of vegetable oil over medium temperature.

Add the onions, pepper, and celery, then sauté for about 3 minutes.

Season the conch with cayenne pepper, then add the conch to the skillet. Sauté for 2 minutes.

Add the garlic to the skillet, then stir.

Remove the skillet from the heat and allow this mixture to cool.

In a large mixing bowl, combine the eggs, milk, buttermilk, baking powder, 1 t of salt, and the Crystal® sauce.

In a smaller mixing bowl, combine the self-rising cornmeal and flour.

Gradually add the cornmeal and flour mixture, ¼ c at a time, to the larger bowl of wet ingredients and incorporate until the batter is smooth.

Fold the conch mixture from the skillet into the batter.

Heat the shortening to 360° F.

Use a tablespoon to drop the batter, one spoonful at a time, into the hot oil.

As the fritters rise to the surface of the hot oil, use a slotted spoon to roll them until each is evenly browned.

Remove the fritters with the slotted spoon and drain on paper towels.

Season with salt and cayenne pepper, then serve warm.

KEY WEST HOT SAUCE

Yields 2½ cups

INGREDIENTS:

2 c chili sauce
1 T Matouk Pepper Sauce (Flambeau)
2 T prepared horseradish
½ t fresh cracked black pepper
¼ t fresh lemon juice
½ t dry mustard
1 t olive oil
1 t garlic, minced

PREPARATION:

In a small skillet, heat the olive oil and sauté the garlic over medium heat. Be careful that you do not burn the garlic.

In a small mixing bowl, combine the chili sauce,

pepper sauce, prepared horseradish, black pepper, lemon juice, and mustard.

Add the sautéed garlic with the olive oil to the bowl of other ingredients, then mix all the ingredients together well.

Store any remaining hot sauce in a sealed container in your refrigerator.

Eighth Deadly Sin

Yields 4 servings as an appetizer

— FROM "Bank of Bad Habits"
on BAROMETER SOUP

If pizza is truly the Eighth Deadly Sin, then grilled pizza only makes matters worse. Once you've tried this, you'll discover that it's an entire sin unto itself. And don't be afraid of the fact that it's baked on your barbecue grill. Just follow these instructions and nothing will go wrong. (Now, repeat after me: "Nothing will go wrong . . . . Nothing will go wrong . . . .")

Let me put in a word or two here, though, about your grill. Yes, you can use a gas grill, but make certain that you've cleaned off all that crud on your grill from your last cookout.

But if you use a charcoal grill, you should *not* use charcoal briquets. Old fashioned hardwood charcoal is truly the best and most certainly worth the effort of looking around for it. Plan ahead, because this is often difficult to find in the "off season."

When using charcoal (or if your gas grill has dual burners), you might want to build your fire to one side of the grill (or use only one of the two burners). That way, you have only half of the pizza over the heat at any one time, and you can control its baking. *Nothing will go wrong.*

INGREDIENTS:

For the dough:

> 2½ t dry active yeast
> Pinch of sugar
> 1 c water, warm
> 2½ t sea salt
> ¼ c white cornmeal, ground fine
> 3 T whole wheat flour
> 1 T olive oil
> 2½ to 3½ c white flour, unbleached

For the topping:

> ¼ c olive oil
> ½ t fresh garlic, minced
> ½ c fontina cheese, shredded
> 2 T fresh Pecorino Romana, grated
> 6 T canned tomatoes, chopped & in purée
> 8 basil leaves

PREPARATION:

Of the dough:

In a large mixing bowl, combine the warm water with the yeast and sugar to dissolve.

In a small mixing bowl, combine the salt, cornmeal, and whole wheat flour.

When the yeast has begun to proof and show bubbles upon the surface of the water, stir in the olive oil, then add the combined dry ingredients from the small bowl. Mix together well.

Gradually, stir in the white flour until the dough becomes quite stiff.

Flour your work surface, then transfer the dough and begin kneading. Work the dough for several minutes and continue to add flour only if the dough becomes sticky.

Once the dough is shiny and smooth, it should be allowed to double in bulk. Most often, you can place the dough in a large mixing bowl that has been brushed with olive oil, then brush the surface of the dough as well. Cover the bowl tightly with plastic wrap.

What I like to do, however, is oil the inside of a large, resealable freezer bag, then seal the dough within. The gases from the yeast will cause the bag to inflate as the dough grows in bulk. I find this good for dough that I'm going to refrigerate and allow to rise later. And I find this especially great when I'm going to mix up several pizza doughs at a time. I place each bag in the refrigerator, then take them all out at the same time to rise in a warm place for about 2 hours.

In any case, once the dough has doubled, punch it down and knead it again. Then, let it rise for another 40 minutes.

(This is a good time to prepare your charcoal fire or to begin heating your pizza stone on the gas grill.)

Finally, punch down the dough a third time. If it seems sticky, dust it with flour and knead it just a bit more.

Of the pizza:

If you're baking *without* a stone, then oil a large baking sheet.

Place the dough on the oiled sheet, then use your hands and fingers to flatten it into a crust that's about ¼-inch thick and anywhere from 10 to 12 inches in diameter. Don't try to form a perfect circle. *Nothing will go wrong.*

Check the heat of your fire.

Once the fire is hot, move the baking sheet near to the grill so that you can work rather quickly.

Gently lift the edge of the dough closest to you with your fingers and carry it above the grill.

Nothing will go wrong.

There is probably an edge of the dough that is dangling down, away from you. Catch this dangling edge on a part of the grill that is NOT above the hot coals, then allow your fingers to drape the rest of the dough over the grill directly above the heat.

Nothing will go wrong.

In just about a minute, your pizza crust will begin to puff up. The bottom will bake to a more controllable stiffness, and the grill will burn some marks into the crust.

Nothing will go wrong.

With a pair of tongs, move the crust away from the heat and flip it over.

Brush the top (cooked side) with about half of the olive oil.

Sprinkle the garlic and cheese across the surface, then use a spoon to place dollops of the tomato atop the garlic and cheese. Don't try to spread this small amount of tomato around the entire surface. The tomato has been kept to a minimum to prevent the pizza from becoming soggy (and falling through the grill!)

Nothing will go wrong.

Drizzle the rest of the olive oil all over the pizza.

Use your tongs to position the pizza back over the heat, and every 15 seconds or so rotate the pizza to keep the crust from burning.

Nothing will go wrong.

The pizza is done when the cheese has melted and the toppings are bubbling, about 5 to 7 minutes.

With your tongs and the assist of a large spatula, remove the pizza to a clean plate and top with the basil leaves.

Nothing has gone wrong.

Serve hot.

Deviled Eggs

Yields 2 dozen

— FROM "Livingston Saturday Night"
ON RANCHO DELUXE & SON OF A SON OF A SAILOR

QUESTION: "How come we call these DEVILED EGGS when we start by boiling the hell out of 'em?" (Get it? Devil? Hell? *Ha, ha, ha!* It's only a *yolk!* Get it? *Ha, ha, ha!*)

ANSWER: Because you add some heat with pepper and mustard. It's not funny, but it's true.

INGREDIENTS:

> 12 large eggs, hard-boiled & peeled
> ½ c mayonnaise
> 2 t Creole mustard
> ½ t fresh white pepper, cracked
> 2 jalapeño peppers, seeded & diced fine
> 2 T sweet pickle relish
> Cayenne, for garnish

PREPARATION:

In a large saucepan, boil the hell out of the eggs! (*Ha, ha, ha* . . . I've *still* got it!)

Okay, in a large saucepan bring 6 c of water to the

boil. Carefully add the eggs to the pan, then allow the water to again come to the boil.

Remove the pan from the heat, cover, and allow the eggs to sit for 15 minutes.

Drain the water into the sink, then allow the eggs to come to safe handling temperature.

Shell the eggs and halve each lengthwise. There is no choice here other than *To Halve or Halve Not!* (*Ha, ha, ha* . . . I've *still* got it!)

Remove the yolks and place them in a small mixing bowl, then mash them with a fork.

Stir in the mayonnaise, Creole mustard, cracked white pepper, jalapeño peppers, and the sweet pickle relish, then mix well.

If you don't own a pastry bag, place all of the yolk mixture into a small, self-sealing sandwich bag, then snip off a small piece of one corner. Pipe the deviled yolks into the hard-boiled whites.

Garnish with a dusting of cayenne.

Cover and refrigerate the devilled eggs at least 1 hour before serving.

Beluga Caviar

— FROM "One Small Bass"
in A PIRATE LOOKS AT FIFTY / P. 43

My, my, my, just think how far Bubba has come from those days of the "Peanut Butter Conspiracy," when the best he could do was grab a lemon and a can of sardines. (Say, Bubba, can you spare a lime?) But let me be the first to point out that his reference to CAVIAR comes only in speaking of the status quo on the island. And the word, itself, is not French, but from the Turkish "havyar," which I believe was once used by the Bee Gees in their early classic "1941 Mining Disaster," ("Havyar seen my wife, Mr. Jones? Havyar heard what it's like on the outside?")

But the truth remains that you don't have to pay a lot for this stuff. For that matter, you don't even have to eat it! Still, I thought you might like to know a little more about this stuff, about how you can even make it, and then how you can even fool your friends into trying it.

For starters, let's call this by its rightful name: fish eggs! Though the Food & Drug Administration says that anything labelled as just "caviar" must be the eggs or roe of a sturgeon, caviar can also be from carp, cod, grey mullet, herring, lumpfish, salmon, tuna, or whitefish, as long as the label says so. If you make it yourself, however, you can call it whatever you want. "Polliwogs, anyone?"

Whether you buy it or make it, remember that caviar spoils very quickly above 40° F, and that you should never let it come in contact with *anything* metal. It's often served with a wedge of lemon, with black bread, on dry toast, or even on DEVILED EGGS, but I like to serve it on an ice cube. Simply heat the bowl of a spoon, then press the back of the hot spoon into an ice cube until a little ice bowl is formed. Then use a plastic spoon to fill the ice bowl with caviar! Friends are so intrigued with the ice that they forget that they're eating a whole lost generation of fish.

DO IT YOURSELF CAVIAR

In preparing your own caviar, you are basically pickling the eggs of your chosen fish. You might come across these sets of roe (basically sacks of fish eggs) in some fish that you catch, or you might just ask your local fishmonger whether or not he ever encounters roe during the course of his cleaning fish. If so, plan to have him save you some and call you when he has it. The roe must be as fresh as possible.

The only tool you'll need is some sort of non-metal screen that has a mesh that is no larger than ¼ inch. This can be found in a hardware store, and you ought to mount it on some sort of frame for stability.

The brine you'll make is nothing other than pickling salt and water, and this recipe makes more than you'll probably need. I have no idea how much roe you will be preparing, but you'll need twice as much brine in volume as you have roe.

Finally, remember that you should not be using anything metal in the preparation, storage, or serving of your caviar.

INGREDIENTS:
2¼ c pickling salt
2 qts cold water
Fresh roe

PREPARATION:
In a large mixing bowl, combine the salt and the cold water. If you're actually using a salinometer that measures the saltiness of pickling brine, then the reading should be 28.3.

Pour 2 c of this cold brine into another large mixing bowl, then place your framed piece of screening over the top.

Place some of the roe on top of the screen and gently tear the egg masses into smaller pieces. With only gentle pressure from your fingertips, work the eggs through the screen so that they fall into the bowl of brine below. I prefer to move my fingertips along the screen and brush up against the eggs with the sides of my fingers. That way, any pressure I put is upon the screen, not the fish eggs.

Once all of the eggs have been worked through the screen, add enough brine to make that approximate 2:1 volume ratio of brine to eggs.

Allow the eggs to soak in the cold brine for 20 minutes. You might want to set your bowl in a cooler of ice just to keep the brine cold.

Place a non-metal sieve or fine non-metal strainer in your sink, then drain the brine from the eggs.

Place the sieve above a large clean bowl, then place in the refrigerator. Allow the eggs to sit in the sieve and drain completely in the refrigerator for at least 1 hour.

Using non-metal utensils and containers, place

the fresh caviar into airtight containers and store at 34° F for 1 to 2 months. This will enable your caviar to cure.

After the caviar has cured, drain any residual brine and repack the containers.

Store your caviar at 0° F until you are ready to serve it.

Cowboy Caviar

Yields 4 cups

Just as there are no parts of shepherds in Shepherd's Pie, or Eskimos in Eskimo Pie®, there are no cowboys injured or maimed in the making of COWBOY CAVIAR. It's just one of those cutesy-pie names for a salsa of sorts that's very popular in the southwestern U.S. and sometimes called TEXAS CAVIAR. Having come this far, you're more likely to make this sort of caviar.

INGREDIENTS:

> 2 c black-eyed peas (fresh-cooked or canned)
> 1 T olive oil
> 1 small can of green chiles, chopped
> Dash of cayenne
> 2 T onion, minced & drained
> 2 T celery, minced & drained
> 2 T cider vinegar
> ¼ t salt
> Fresh black pepper, cracked to taste
> 1 T fresh cilantro, minced
> 2 plum tomatoes, seeded & diced

PREPARATION:

Drain the black-eyed peas, rinse with cold water, then drain once more.

In a large mixing bowl, mix together the olive oil, chiles, cayenne, onion, celery, vinegar, salt & pepper.

Add in the drained black-eyed peas and toss gently.

Cover the bowl tightly with plastic wrap, then refrigerate overnight.

Just before serving, add the tomatoes and cilantro, then toss together once again gently.

Serve with corn chips.

Mexican Caviar

Yields 1½ cups

Buzzards Bay is someplace I know you've heard sung about, and it sits between the south coast of the Massachusetts mainland and the western shore of Cape Cod. At the head of the bay is the village of Onset; just south of that, tiny Onset Island. This is where I've enjoyed Mexican Caviar the most, because it is made by my long-time friend, Karen Meeks, who sends you this recipe. She also thinks I'm nuts to think anyone will ever make CAVIAR or chop beef for CHEESEBURGERS. She may be right. I may be crazy, but that sounds more like a Billy Joel song than one of Jimmy's.

INGREDIENTS:

> 2 tomatoes, peeled & chopped
> 3 scallions, chopped
> 2 garlic cloves, minced
> 2 4½-oz cans ripe olives, chopped
> 2 4½-oz cans green chiles, chopped
> 3 T olive oil
> 2 t red wine vinegar
> 1 t fresh black pepper, cracked
> Dash of seasoned salt

PREPARATION:

In a large mixing bowl, combine the tomatoes, scallions, and garlic.

Add to the mixture the olives and chiles, as well as the olive oil, vinegar, black pepper, and seasoned salt.

Toss well, taste, and adjust the seasonings.

Cover the bowl tightly with plastic wrap and refrigerate overnight.

Serve with corn chips.

Fried Okra

— FROM "Squalls Out on the Gulf Stream"
in WHERE IS JOE MERCHANT? / P. 38

Yields 8 servings

Now that you've gotten that CAVIAR thing out of your mind, let's get back to our roots, so to speak. FRIED OKRA is the stuff of which real men are made, and I only wish Jimmy had slipped some pork rinds into his writing so that we would only have to make one trip to the cardiologist. Then, again, okra is a vegetable, so this *must* be good for you!

INGREDIENTS:

 2 lbs okra, washed & cut in ¼-inch pieces
 ½ cup self-rising cornmeal
 2 T self-rising flour
 1 t salt
 1 t pepper, cracked fresh
 1½ c oil

PREPARATION:

Carefully wash the okra of any sand and dirt, then remove any wilted leaves.

In a large mixing bowl, combine the cornmeal, flour and salt & pepper.

Add the okra pieces to the bowl and toss until coated well with the other ingredients.

Into a deep frying pan, pour the oil and heat to 400° F.

Grab a handful of okra and shake off any loose cornmeal and flour.

Carefully spread the okra across the top of the oil, then fry until golden.

Use a basket to remove the okra from the oil and drain on a paper towel.

Repeat the procedure until you have fried as much okra as you have/want.

Desdemona's Tortillas

Yields 8 10-inch tortillas

— FROM "You Can't Hide Your Mayan Eyes"
in WHERE IS JOE MERCHANT? / P. 72

— FROM "My Idea of Life Insurance"
in A PIRATE LOOKS AT FIFTY / P. 23

— FROM "I Will Play for Gumbo"
on BEACH HOUSE ON THE MOON

A refugee from the Haight, Desdemona learned to make stone-ground flour tortillas in Texas from a cook name Olinda. As for trying your own hand at these things, let me caution you that nothing seems to work quite as well as a genuine tortilla press to flatten the dough quickly into that round shape we're all accustomed to. You can buy them rather cheaply in cook shops. If you don't have access to one and really don't want to buy one for yourself, though, then you'll have to practice a bit with some other contraption found around the house. (I found that a large cement block, not a brick, works okay; however, nothing beats the press.)

Having cautioned you, let me also note that whatever lengths you go to in making your own tortillas, you'll find that nothing beats a freshly-baked tortilla. Don't expect this recipe to yield the dry, paper thin things you find in your grocery store. These are more like a pita bread, and you've really got to give them a try.

INGREDIENTS:

2 c instant corn flour (masa harina)
1½ c warm water

PREPARATION:

In a large mixing bowl, combine the corn flour and just enough of the warm water to form a soft dough. If the dough is too crumbly, add more water. If the dough sticks to your hand, it's too wet and a little more masa may be added.

Cover the bowl and allow the dough to rest for 5 minutes.

Place a seasoned, cast iron pan or griddle over medium heat and allow it to become hot. (A drop of water should dance across the surface as it evaporates.)

Take just enough dough to create a small ball about 1½ inches in diameter.

Keep the remaining dough covered with a damp cloth to prevent drying.

Place a piece of plastic wrap on the lower half of your tortilla press. Rather than placing your ball of dough in the exact center of the press, place it slightly toward the hinge of the press, because the actual pressing will move it a bit forward. Flatten the dough just a bit with your hand, then place another piece of plastic wrap on top.

Close the press firmly.

Open the press and peel away the top piece of plastic.

Dampen your hands to prevent the dough from sticking, then remove the bottom piece of plastic with the flattened dough. Flip the plastic, tortilla side down, onto one hand, then peel off the plastic with the other.

Place the tortilla on the griddle and cook about a minute.

Flip the tortilla over and cook another minute.

Remove the tortilla from the griddle and keep it warm.

If not served warm, these can be kept refrigerated up to 3 days or frozen up to 2 weeks. Always reheat the tortillas before using.

FLOUR TORTILLAS

Yields 8 10-inch tortillas

This recipe not only offers different ingredients, but also alternative method of pressing.

INGREDIENTS:

2 c all-purpose flour
½ t salt
¼ c solid vegetable shortening
½ c warm water

PREPARATION:

In a large mixing bowl, combine the flour and the salt.

Add the shortening, then work the ingredients with your fingertips until you have a fine, mealy texture.

Stir in the water to make a dough.

Turn the dough out onto a lightly-floured surface and knead for about 3 minutes.

Wrap the dough in plastic wrap and allow it to rest for 30 minutes at room temperature.

Knead the dough another minute, then divide it into 8 equal pieces.

Roll the pieces into 8 balls, then cover them with a damp cloth to prevent drying out.

Flatten a ball with your hand, turning the dough frequently, use a rolling pin to create an 8-inch circle.

Set the flattened dough aside, repeat the procedure, and stack the tortillas between sheets of wax paper.

Place a seasoned, cast iron pan or griddle over medium heat and allow it to become hot. (A drop of water should dance across the surface as it evaporates.)

Place a tortilla on the griddle and cook until the top bubbles and the bottom is flecked with brown, about 30 seconds.

Flip the tortilla over and cook for 30 seconds.

Remove the tortilla from the griddle and keep it warm.

If not served warm, these can be kept refrigerated up to 3 days or frozen up to 2 weeks. Always reheat the tortillas before using.

CRAB ENCHILADAS

Yields 6 enchiladas

INGREDIENTS:

> 6 flour tortillas (8-inch)
> 3 T corn oil
> 10 oz fresh lump crabmeat, picked & cleaned
> 1 c jalapeño jack cheese, grated
> 1 c fresh spinach leaves, shredded
> CHERRY TOMATO SALSA

PREPARATION:
Preheat your oven to 300° F.

In a sheet of aluminun foil, tightly wrap the tortillas in foil, then place them in the oven to heat through, about 10 to 15 minutes.

In a medium skillet, heat the corn oil.

Add the crabmeat to the skillet and sauté until heated through, about 2 to 3 minutes.

Remove the tortillas from the oven.

Spoon crabmeat onto the center of each warm tortilla, then sprinkle with the grated cheese and shredded spinach.

Roll each tortillas and place, seam-side down, on a heated serving plate.

Garnish with CHERRY TOMATO SALSA.

DOUBLE QUESADILLAS

Yields 6 servings

INGREDIENTS:

> 9 flour tortillas (8-inch)
> 8 oz Monterey Jack cheese, shredded
> 6 T red onion, minced
> 6 T canned mild chili peppers, drained & minced
> 8 oz cheddar, asiago, or fontina cheese, shredded
> Fresh cracked black pepper

PREPARATION:
Preheat your oven to 450° F.

Place a baking sheet on the center rack of your oven to heat.

Place 3 tortillas on your work surface and divide the Montery Jack cheese equally among them. Leave about ½ inch of exposed edge around each tortilla.

Sprinkle each tortilla with 2 T of the red onion and 2 T of the chili peppers.

Place another tortilla on top of each of the first 3 tortillas, then repeat the toppings.

Crack some fresh black pepper on top of each double stack of tortillas, then top each stack with a third tortilla.

With a baking peal or a wide spatula, carefully place the 3 quesadillas onto the heated baking sheet in the oven

Bake until the edges of each quesadilla are toasted golden brown, and they have been sealed by the melted cheeses, about 10 minutes.

With an oven mitt, remove the baking sheets from the oven, then allow the quesadillas to cool about 1 minute.

Use a spatula to transfer the quesadillas to a cutting board or serving platter, then cut each quesadilla into quarters.

Serve 2 quarters to each person.

Guacamole

Yields 3 cups

— FROM "The Lady I Can't Explain"
in WHERE IS JOE MERCHANT? / P. 56

— FROM "Que Pasa?"
in WHERE IS JOE MERCHANT? / P. 327

After you've learned some native customs, here's a word of Mexican Spanish for you to practice: *ahuacamolli*. But before you renounce your citizenship and head south, you might want to practice making some of this, because it's a helluva lot better (and less expensive) than any kind you'll buy in any store. The big difference, of course, is that the store stuff has all those preservatives to extend the shelf life, as well as to save the avocado from turning brown. *Yuck!* But that's why you add the lime juice in this recipe.

INGREDIENTS:

> *4 large ripened avocados*
> *2 T red onion, diced fine*
> *2 T serrano peppers, chopped*
> *1 large tomato, seeded & diced*
> *2 garlic cloves, minced*
> *2 T cilantro, diced*
> *½ t chili powder*
> *4 T fresh lime juice*

PREPARATION:

Cut the ripened avocados in half and remove the large seed from each.

Peel the skin from each avocado, then dice the flesh.

In a large mixing bowl, mash the diced avocados with the back of a fork.

Add to the bowl the onion, serrano pepper, tomato, garlic, cilantro, chili powder, and lime juice, then mix together well.

Cover the bowl tightly with plastic wrap and refrigerate at least 30 minutes.

Serve with tortilla chips.

CHUNKY GUACAMOLE

Yields 3 cups

When you first look at this list of ingredients, you'll probably gasp at the sight of radishes. Just remember this: it's not the *horse* in horseradish that gives some foods their heat, it's the *radish!* Not needing as much heat as horseradish could provide, though, let's leave out the horse altogether and just use the radish. (Or, as they might say, "Let's not put the horse before the radish.")

INGREDIENTS:

> 5 red radishes
> 1 small sweet onion
> 2 fresh jalapeños, seeded & chopped fine
> ½ c fresh cilantro sprigs, packed & chopped fine
> 4 ripened avocados
> 4 T fresh lime juice
> ½ t salt

PREPARATION:

Cut ¼-inch-thick slices from the outsides of the radishes, then do whatever you want with the white insides.

Dice the radish slices and the onion, then put them in a small mixing bowl with the jalapeños and cilantro.

Cut the ripened avocados in half and remove the large seed from each.

Peel the skin from each avocado, then dice the flesh.

In a large mixing bowl, mash the diced avocados with the back of a fork.

Add the ingredients from the small mixing bowl to the larger one.

Add the lime juice and mix together well.

Cover the bowl tightly with plastic wrap and refrigerate at least 30 minutes.

Serve with tortilla chips.

Thy Neighbor's Wife's Popcorn

— FROM "Bank of Bad Habits"
on BAROMETER SOUP

SAILOR JACK'S POPCORN

Yields 1¼ quarts

You'll probably enjoy the taste of this stuff, because there's no tacky prize to break your teeth.

INGREDIENTS:

½ c sugar
3 T molasses
3 T dark corn syrup
1 t butter
1 t lemon juice
¾ c peanuts
1 qt popped popcorn

PREPARATION:

Cover the surface of a cookie sheet with waxed paper, then lightly butter the waxed paper.

In a large saucepan, combine the sugar, molasses, corn syrup, butter, and lemon juice over low heat.

Continue stirring the ingredients until the sugar has completely dissolved.

Remove the saucepan from the heat.

Add the peanuts to the saucepan and stir well.

Add the popped popcorn to the saucepan and stir until it is coated with the sugar mixture.

Return the saucepan to the heat and continue stirring for 5 more minutes.

Remove the saucepan from the heat and transfer the entire sticky mixture to the buttered waxed paper.

With your spoon, spread the coated popcorn and nuts across the surface of the waxed paper.

Allow this to cool enough to handle without getting burned, then coat your fingers lightly with softened butter and shape the coated popcorn into bite-sized clusters.

Store in a covered container with sheets of waxed paper between layers.

KEY LIME BALLS

Yields 1¼ quarts

You can use any flavored gelatin powder you wish, but I thought that the green lime stuff would be appropriate here. If you use something pinkish, such as cherry or strawberry, then you'll immediately recognize these as the sort of stuff you'd see at a souvenir stand.

INGREDIENTS:

1 qt popped popcorn
8 T lime-flavored gelatin powder (undissolved)
½ c butter
16 oz marshmallows
½ c margarine, softened

PREPARATION:

Cover the surface of a cookie sheet with waxed paper, then lightly butter the waxed paper.

In a large saucepan, melt the first ½ c of butter over medium heat.

When the butter has melted, add the marshmallows and continue to stir until they are almost melted completely.

Add the powdered gelatin and stir well to mix completely.

Remove the saucepan from the heat.

Gradually add the popped popcorn to the saucepan and continue to stir.

When the coated popcorn feels cool enough to handle, lightly coat your hands with the softened margarine and form popcorn balls to whatever size you wish. (Keep re-coating your hands.)

Place the popcorn balls on the waxed paper. When they have cooled, store them in an airtight container with waxed paper between layers.

POPCORN BRITTLE

Yields 1 quart

INGREDIENTS:

1 c butter
1 c sugar
2 T water
1 T light corn syrup
1 qt popped popcorn
½ c almonds or cashews
½ c shredded coconut

PREPARATION:

Cover the surface of a cookie sheet with waxed paper, then lightly butter the waxed paper.

In a large saucepan, melt the first ½ c of butter over low heat.

When the butter has melted, remove the saucepan from the heat and stir in the sugar.

Return the saucepan to low heat and stir the sugar mixture until it comes to the full boil.

Stir in the water and the corn syrup until the mixture reaches 270° F on a candy thermometer.

Remove the saucepan from the heat.

Stir in the popcorn, nuts, and coconut.

Transfer the entire sticky mixture to the buttered waxed paper.

With your spoon, spread the coated popcorn and nuts across the surface of the waxed paper.

Allow this to cool enough to handle without getting burned, then coat your fingers lightly with softened butter and shape the coated popcorn into bite-sized clusters.

Store in a covered container with sheets of waxed paper between layers.

Fried Crab Claws

Yields 4 servings

— FROM *"Take Another Road"*
in TALES FROM MARGARITAVILLE / P. 48

Folks along the Gulf Coast bring a new appreciation to the succulent crab, which I always put on the same pedestal with lobster. So, why batter-up such a treasure? Well, as Tully Mars said of these babies at the Flora-Bama, "they taste like the ocean."

INGREDIENTS:

For the crab meat:
3 lbs of fresh claw meat, picked & cleaned
3 c all-purpose flour, for dredging

For the batter:
¾ c cornstarch
2½ c all-purpose flour
1 t salt
¼ t cracked white pepper
1¾ c water
2 egg yolks
½ c flat beer
2 t baking powder
Vegetable oil, for frying

PREPARATION:

In a large mixing bowl, combine the cornstarch, flour, salt & pepper.

In a small mixing bowl, whisk together the water, egg yolks, and beer.

Gradually whisk the wet ingredients into the bowl of dry ingredients until the batter is smooth, then whisk in the baking powder.

In a large cast iron skillet, heat the oil over medium-high temperature.

Dredge the pieces of claw meat in the flour. Shake off any excess flour, then dip the claw meat into the batter.

Carefully place each claw in the hot oil and fry until golden brown on each side, about 3 minutes.

With a slotted spoon or tongs, remove the fried crab claws from the hot oil and drain on paper towel.

Serve hot with TARTAR SAUCE.

Peanut Butter

— FROM "The Peanut Butter Conspiracy"
on A WHITE SPORT COAT AND A PINK CRUSTACEAN

— FROM "Life in the Food Chain"
in TALES FROM MARGARITAVILLE / P. 197

— FROM "Beyond the Low-Water Mark"
in WHERE IS JOE MERCHANT? / P. 114

— FROM "Kick the Tires and Light the Fires"
in A PIRATE LOOKS AT FIFTY / P. 125

Yields 1¼ cup

Cortés came upon peanuts in Mexico, and Columbus first spied them in Haiti, and it's believed that the seeds originated in Brazil; however, it wasn't until the St. Louis World's Fair in 1904 that PEANUT BUTTER first appeared as a health food concocted by a doctor. So, if your HMO doesn't cover the cost, make your own. Just keep in mind that the commercial PB has an additive that keeps the oil from separating, but this one doesn't.

INGREDIENTS:

1 c dry-roasted peanuts
¼ c peanut oil
1 T sugar
Dash of salt

PREPARATION:

In your blender, combine the peanuts, oil, sugar, and salt.

Blend the ingredients on high until you've reached the consistency you desire.

SALADS OF SORTS

West Indies Crab Salad ❀ Conch Salad
Shrimp Ceviche ❀ Crab & Mango Salad
Crawfish Salad ❀ Lone Palm Salad
Muffalata ❀ Lentil Salad ❀ Potato Salad
Salpicón ❀ Lobster Salad

West Indies Salad

Yields 4 servings

— FROM "Take Another Road"
in TALES FROM MARGARITAVILLE / P. 50

— FROM "I Wish Lunch Could Last Forever"
in TALES FROM MARGARITAVILLE / P. 155

As Tully Mars made his way from Wyoming south toward his search for "a better place," he kept a journal in a notebook he'd bought at the Indian store. On 1 April 1989, he wrote how Kirk Patterson, Slade's brother, had brought him to the Northern Lights Cafe, where Aurora and Boring Alice Porter had served him up a most incredible seafood dinner. And amongst the goodies he thought worth noting was this WEST INDIES SALAD. This must have been an item they learned from Isabella during her stay on Snake Bite Key, for she later had it on her menu at Chéz Bar-B-Q Hill.

INGREDIENTS:

1 lb fresh lump crabmeat, picked & cleaned

1 Vidalia onion, chopped

Celery seed

Capers

2 bay leaves/layer

Fresh white pepper, cracked to taste

6 oz cider vinegar

3 oz light vegetable oil
4 oz ice water

PREPARATION:

In a large mixing bowl, combine the crabmeat and chopped onion.

In a glass baking dish, spread a layer of the crab and onion mixture.

Sprinkle the layer with celery seed, capers, white pepper, and 2 or 3 bay leaves.

Repeat the layers until you have used up all of your crab and onion mix.

In a small mixing bowl, combine the vinegar, oil, and water, then pour over the layers.

Seal the glass dish tightly with plastic wrap and refrigerate overnight.

Serve chilled.

Conch Salad

Yields 4 servings

— FROM "Why I Love My Seaplane"
in THE PARROT HEAD HANDBOOK / p. 20

— FROM "Life in the Food Chain"
in TALES FROM MARGARITAVILLE / p. 197

— FROM "Where's the Party?"
in WHERE IS JOE MERCHANT? / p. 134

Maybe Charlie Fabian could hide his true identity for a while in *Where is Joe Merchant?*, but he couldn't hide his ignorance about pronouncing this dish.

"Da meal be *conch* like *honk*," the bartender corrected the mystery man, "not *conch* like *haunch*."

It's not an uncommon mistake. In fact, that's the sort of advice that even Bogie could have used in *To Have and Have Not*. But at least Bogie knew how to whistle, didn't he?

INGREDIENTS:

1½ lb conch, diced fine
1 hot red pepper, seeded & chopped fine
1 celery rib, chopped fine
1 small onion, chopped fine
1 green pepper, chopped fine
1 small cucumber, peeled & chopped fine
1 firm, ripe tomato, seeded & diced fine
¼ cup fresh lime juice
Salt, to taste

PREPARATION:

If you're using frozen conch meat which is already cleaned, then defrost the conch and soak it in a bowl of salt water for 30 minutes.

Use a sharp knife to dice the conch into fine pieces. You could use a food processor to chop the conch with the pulse switch; however, you do run the risk of making the conch gummy.

Soak the diced conch in second bowl of salted water for about 30 minutes.

Being careful not to get any of the pepper's oils into your eyes, seed the red hot pepper and dice it fine.

Seed and dice the tomato.

Dice the onion, celery, and cucumber.

In a medium glass bowl, combine all of the ingredients. Do not use any metal container when you are marinading with acidic foods.

Allow the conch salad to marinate at least 30 minutes in your refrigerator.

Serve cold on lettuce leaves.

Shrimp Ceviche

Yields 4 servings

A ceviche (or *seviche* or *escabiche*) is a recipe in which the protein in the meat is "cooked" by the acid in the marinade or vinaigrette. As with the CONCH SALAD, this SHRIMP CEVICHE always makes for a surprising appetizer, a simple beach dish, or even a hot weather meal. You can substitute another shellfish (such as scallops) or finfish (such as fresh tuna), but don't allow the fish to marinate too long or else it will become tough.

INGREDIENTS:

1 lb uncooked shrimp, shelled & deveined
1 T black peppercorns, toasted & ground
½ T coriander seeds, toasted & ground
Juice of 4 lemons
Juice of 2 key limes
Juice of 2 oranges
¼ c extra virgin olive oil
2 bay leaves, broken
Salt & pepper, to taste
4 T red onion, minced for garnish

PREPARATION:

In a small skillet, toast the peppercorns and coriander seeds over medium heat. Shake the skillet until they have toasted for 4 minutes.

Grind the toasted peppercorns and coriander seeds, then combine them in a small glass mixing bowl, along with the citrus juices, the olive oil, and the bay leaves.

Adjust the seasonings with salt & pepper.

Cut any large, uncooked pieces of your shrimp into bite-size pieces. Place them into a non-metallic bowl that allows them to be covered completely by the marinade.

Pour the marinade over the shrimp, then toss them until they are coated thoroughly. Cover tightly with plastic wrap and refrigerate at least 4 hours.

Drain and discard the marinade.

Divide the shrimp into equal portions and arrange in chilled margarita glasses.

Garnish the seviche with the chopped red onion.

Crab & Mango Salad

Yields 4 servings

Just for good measure, here's another variation of a ceviche. It's just a bit less tart than the others, but just as adaptable to other fish and shellfish.

INGREDIENTS:

> 1 lb fresh lump crab meat, picked & cleaned
> 2 ripe mangos, peeled & diced fine
> 6 pink radishes, sliced thin
> 2 mint sprigs, julienned fine
> Juice of 1 lime
> 4 oz olive oil
> Salt & pepper, to taste
> 4 bib lettuce leaves, washed & dried

PREPARATION:

In a large mixing bowl, toss together the crab meat, mango, radishes, and mint.

In a measuring cup, stir together the lime juice and olive oil.

Taste the vinaigrette and adjust the seasoning with salt & pepper.

Pour the vinaigrette into the mixing bowl, then toss together the ingredients to coat them all thoroughly.

Place a lettuce leaf on each serving dish and divide the salad among the 4 settings.

Garnish each serving with a leaf of mint.

Crawfish Salad

— FROM "I Wish Lunch Could Last Forever"
in TALES FROM MARGARITAVILLE / P. 151

Ahhhhh, mudbugs! Crawdaddies! Creekcrabs! Yabbies! While they do look a little like a lobster (or should I say they do look like a little lobster?), they still have a taste all their own . . . no matter what you choose to call 'em.

CAJUN CRAWFISH SALAD

Yields 4 servings

INGREDIENTS:

2 eggs, hard-boiled & chopped
1 lb cooked crawfish, cleaned & chopped
1 T dill pickles, chopped fine
1 t Crystal®
1 T mayonnaise
Dash of salt, if needed
½ t cayenne
½ t dijon mustard

PREPARATION:
In a large mixing bowl, combine the chopped

eggs, chopped crawfish, and chopped pickles then toss together lightly.

In a small bowl, mix together the Crystal®, mayonnaise, pepper, and mustard.

Taste, then adjust the seasoning with salt & pepper, if needed.

Add the combined seasonings to the bowl of egg, crawfish, and pickles, then mix well.

Cover the bowl tightly with plastic wrap, then refrigerate for at least 1 hour.

Serve on lettuce leaves or as a sandwich filling.

JAMAICAN SALAD

Yields 4 servings

INGREDIENTS:

2 T fresh lime juice
½ c mayonnaise
12 oz crawfish, cooked, cleaned & chopped
¼ c cucumber, diced
¼ c onion, chopped
¼ c celery, chopped
¼ c green pepper, chopped
Salt & fresh pepper, to taste
Dash Crystal®
1 lime, quartered for garnish
4 large lettuce leaves, washed & dried

PREPARATION:

In a large mixing bowl, combine the crawfish, cucumber, onion, celery, and green pepper.

In a smaller bowl, combine the lime juice with the mayonnaise, salt & pepper, and Crystal®.

Taste and adjust the seasonings, if necessary.

Add the dressing to the bowl of other ingredients, then toss lightly.

Cover tightly with plastic wrap and refrigerate at least 1 hour.

Place a lettuce leaf on each serving dish and divide the salad among the 4 settings.

Garnish with lime quarters.

Lone Palm Salad

Yields 4 servings

Mia maxima culpa! (I have absolutely no idea what that means, but I used to think that it meant, "My Nissan is a gas guzzler.") In any event, I must confess that this is one of only a few recipes in this collection with a made-up name. Basically, it's a hearts of palm salad with an equal amount of crab meat; however, you could also substitute shrimp or even fresh bay scallops.

INGREDIENTS:

1 lb hearts of palm, cleaned & blanched
2 c carrots, peeled, julienned & blanched
4 oz pecans, toasted & chopped
2 T chervil, chopped
1 c vinaigrette
2 tomatoes, in 1-inch slices
4 T Parmigiano-Reggiano cheese, grated
4 T parsley, chopped
1 lb fresh crab meat, picked & cleaned

PREPARATION:

Of the hearts of palm and carrots:
In a small saucepan, bring 2 c of water to the boil.

Meanwhile, fill a large mixing bowl with water and ice cubes.

Rinse the hearts of palm under water to remove and sand or dirt, then sort them into 4 approximate portions.

Lightly salt the boiling water, then place about one portion of the hearts of palm into the saucepan for only 1 minute.

With a slotted spoon, remove the blanched hearts of palm and immerse them in the bowl of ice water to stop any further cooking.

Repeat this process with the remaining 3 portions of the hearts of palm.

When you have blanched all of your hearts of palm, use the same boiling water to blanch your julienned carrots, placing them into the ice water, as well, to stop any further cooking.

In a colander, strain the hearts of palm and carrots, then place them on paper towels to dry.

Of the pecan meats:
In a small frying pan, toast the chopped pecans over medium heat. Continue to stir the pecans as the heat brings out their natural oils. When you begin to smell the aroma of the oils, then the pecan meats will have been toasted.

Remove the frying pan from the heat and add the pecan meats to a large mixing bowl.

Of the salad:
To the mixing bowl with the pecan meats, add the blanched hearts of palm and carrots, as well as the chervil, then toss lightly.

Add the crab meat to the mixing bowl and toss a little more.

Add about ½ c of the vinaigrette, then toss lightly once again.

Taste and adjust the seasonings with salt & pepper.

Season your tomato slices with salt & pepper, then arrange them around your serving plates.

Divide the salad equally among the serving plates, then garnish with the grated Parmesan cheese and parsley.

The remaining vinaigrette should be served on the side.

Muffalata

— FROM "Boomerang Love"
in Tales from Margaritaville / p. 94

Yields 4 servings

The first time I ever saw a MUFFALATA sandwich I was extremely disappointed, to say the least. To be sure, it was in New Orleans, where I was a mumblin' Yankee boy who had ordered a Fluffernutter®. You know, 2 pieces of gummy white sandwich bread glued together with Marshmallow Fluff® and peanut butter. I love those things, but one taste of this olive salad on its own traditional MUFFALATA BUN, and I was an instant convert. In fact, if there's one word I now enjoy saying as much as "epiphany," it's most certainly "muffalata."

INGREDIENTS:

For the muffalata:

1 c black olives, sliced
1 c green stuffed olives, sliced
2 T shallots, minced
2 t garlic, minced
2 T small celery, diced
2 T fresh parsley, chopped
1½ t fresh black pepper, cracked fine
½ c olive oil

For the sandwich:

1 10-inch MUFFALATA BUN
2 oz cotto salami, sliced thin
2 oz smoked ham, sliced thin
2 oz Genoa salami, sliced thin
2 oz mozzarella cheese, sliced thin
2 oz provolone cheese, sliced thin

PREPARATION:

Of the salad:
In a large mixing bowl, combine the black and green stuffed olives, shallots, garlic, celery, parsley, black pepper, and olive oil, then mix well. Allow this to sit for at least 1 hour.

Of the sandwich:
Split the MUFFALATA BUN in half horizontally, then remove the top half. Spoon half of the olive salad on the bottom half of the bun.

Place the cotto salami, smoked ham, Genoa salami, mozzarella, and provolone on top of the olive salad. Replace the top half of the bun, then cut the sandwich in quarters.

Lentil Salad

— FROM "Study Your Language Tapes"
in A PIRATE LOOKS AT FIFTY / P. 186

Yields 4 servings

Havana cigars were on that list. So were the daiquiris and bananas, as well as the legendary CHEESEBURGER. But is there a missing verse to that song wherein Jimmy sings about LENTIL SALAD? I don't think so. But if you read his account of learning French back in the 70s, he mentions this particular dish on St. Barth's which he even calls (in English!) "a fine meal." Perhaps it was the bottle of wine, don'tcha think? Otherwise he would have called the song "Brown Lentils in Paradise," right?

INGREDIENTS:

6 large shallots, julienned
¼ c sherry vinegar
2 T lime juice
Small pinch sugar
1 Scotch bonnet pepper, seeded & chopped
2 c brown lentils, picked & rinsed
½ t salt
¼ t black pepper, cracked fresh
½ c Spanish olive oil
½ bunch cilantro leaves, chopped fine

PREPARATION:

In a small mixing bowl, combine the shallots, sherry vinegar, lime juice, sugar, and Scotch bonnet pepper. Set aside to allow flavors to blend at room temperature.

In a large saucepan, combine the lentils with water that rises 2 inches above them. Bring the lentils to the boil, then cover, reduce the heat, and simmer until tender, about 30 minutes.

Use a colander to drain the lentils thoroughly, then add them to a large mixing bowl with the olive oil, salt & pepper.

Add the reserved bowl of the shallot mixture to the lentils, then toss them all together gently.

Allow the salad to stand for at least 30 minutes at room temperature.

Add the chopped cilantro leaves and toss once more.

Potato Salad

— FROM "Folly Chasing Death"
in A PIRATE LOOKS AT FIFTY / P. 36

Yields 4 servings

Fist fights have been known to erupt at picnics over the bragging rights to the best recipe for a POTATO SALAD, because it's always made by Mom. So, polish up those brass knuckles and line up, 'cause here's a genuine Southern-style recipe for everyone to squabble over.

INGREDIENTS:

> 2 lbs of boiled potatoes, cooled, peeled & cut in ½-inch chunks
> 3 T oil
> 1 c mayonnaise
> ¼ c sweet pickle relish
> 2 T Dijon mustard
> 4 hard-cooked eggs, peeled & diced
> ½ c red onion, diced
> Salt, to taste
> Fresh black pepper, cracked to taste

PREPARATION:

In a large mixing bowl, combine the oil, mayonnaise, relish, mustard, eggs, and onion. Stir, taste, and adjust the seasonings with salt & pepper.

Add the potato to the mixing bowl, then toss gently until all the potatoes are coated.

Cover the bowl tightly with plastic wrap and refrigerate at least 1 hour.

Salpicón

Yields 4 servings

The good people of Cuba are passionate about a number of things other than baseball, and this meat salad called salpicón is among them. Though this recipe contains roast beef and ROAST CHICKEN, you might even substitute (or include) CUBAN ROAST PORK.

INGREDIENTS:

For the dressing:

> *1 c roast beef, chopped*
>
> *1 c roast chicken, chopped*
>
> *2 c boiled potatoes, cut in cubes*
>
> *1 roasted green bell pepper, peeled, seeded & chopped*
>
> *½ c lettuce, washed & chopped*
>
> *¼ c onion, chopped fine*
>
> *1 T capers*
>
> *½ c green olives stuffed with pimiento, sliced*
>
> *2 pimientos, chopped*

For the dressing:

> *1 c olive oil*

¼ c white vinegar
Salt & cracked black pepper, to taste
Lettuce leaves, washed for garnish

PREPARATION:

In a large salad bowl, combine the chopped roast beef and chicken, along with the potatoes, bell pepper, chopped lettuce, onion, capers, sliced olives, and pimientos. Toss together lightly.

In a small mixing bowl, combine the olive oil, vinegar, and salt & pepper. Mix well, then taste and adjust the seasonings, if necessary.

Pour the dressing over the salad in the large mixing bowl, then toss gently one more time.

Serve on a bed of lettuce leaves.

Lobster Salad

Yields 4 servings

— FROM "Kick the Tires and Light the Fires"
in A PIRATE LOOKS AT FIFTY / P. 119

Let me begin by stating my personal philosophy that the key ingredient in a LOBSTER SALAD should be lobster. *Not* mayonnaise, *not* celery, *not* avocado, *not anything else*. If there isn't a copious quantity of lobster, then it simply isn't LOBSTER SALAD, and you ought to shoot the cheap bastard who's trying to convince you that it is. That's just my bias from being raised along the New England coast.

INGREDIENTS:

1 lb cooked lobster meat, in ½-inch pieces
6 T mayonnaise
¼ c celery, chopped fine
¼ c fresh parsley, chopped fine
Cracked white pepper, to taste
3 T butter, melted
8 slices BIMINI BREAD

PREPARATION:

In a large mixing bowl, combine the mayonnaise, celery, and parsley.

Taste, then adjust the seasoning with fresh cracked white pepper.

Stir in the lobster meat until it is coated well with the mayonnaise mixture.

Brush the filling sides of each slice of BIMINI BREAD, then divide the lobster salad equally among the 4 sandwiches.

Serve immediately.

SOUTHERN-STYLE SALAD

Yields 4 servings

Okay, we're beginning to drift from the mooring a bit on this one. The sweet natural taste of the lobster begins to have a little competition with some of the other flavors in this list of ingredients, but it's still an acceptable variation. Remember, Jimmy likes his with a little hot sauce from Haiti.

INGREDIENTS:

> *1 lb cooked lobster meat, in ½-inch pieces*
> *½ c olive oil*
> *2 T red wine vinegar*
> *½ t salt*
> *¼ t dry mustard*
> *½ c mayonnaise*
> *2 c celery; sliced thin*
> *½ c red onion, minced*
> *Crystal®, to taste*
> *4 BAGUETTES*

PREPARATION:

In a large mixing bowl, combine the olive oil, red wine vinegar, salt, dry mustard, mayonnaise, celery, and red onion. Stir, taste, and adjust the seasoning with Crystal®.

Add the cooked lobster meat, then toss gently.

Cover the bowl tightly with plastic wrap and chill

the salad for at least 1 hour.

Split the baguettes lengthwise and divide the lobster salad equally among them.

If you wish, garnish with a dash of Crystal®, to taste.

CHEAPSKATE'S SALAD

Yields 4 servings

This salad's for those bastards who are too cheap to empty their pockets for more lobster, but still want to cover up their shortcomings with a little show of class.

INGREDIENTS:

> *1 c cooked lobster meat, in ½-inch pieces*
> *1 tomato, peeled, seeded & in ½-inch cubes*
> *1 ripened avocado, peeled & in ½-inch cubes*
> *Juice of ½ lime*
> *¾ c mayonnaise*
> *Salt & cracked black pepper, to taste*
> *1 hard-boiled egg, chopped fine for garnish*
> *Parsley sprigs, for garnish*

PREPARATION:

In a large mixing bowl, combine the lobster meat, tomato, avocado, fresh lime juice, and mayonnaise.

Toss together lighty, then taste, and adjust the seasoning with salt & pepper.

Cover the bowl tightly with plastic wrap and chill the salad for at least 1 hour.

Divide the lobster equally among your 4 salad plates.

Garnish with chopped egg and parsley.

GRILLED LOBSTER SALAD

Yields 4 servings

This is a great way to take your GRILLED LOBSTER on the road without being too obvious about it. After all, what would others say if you yanked a whole lobster out of your lunch box?

INGREDIENTS:

2 c GRILLED LOBSTER *meat, in ½-inch pieces*
2 t key lime juice
4 T mayonnaise
¼ c celery, chopped fine
¼ c red onion, chopped fine
Cracked black pepper, to taste
8 slices BIMINI BREAD

PREPARATION:

In a large mixing bowl, combine the key lime juice, mayonnaise, celery, and red onion.

Taste, then adjust the seasoning with fresh cracked black pepper.

Stir in the lobster meat until it is coated well with the lime-mayonnaise mixture.

Divide the lobster salad equally among the 4 sandwiches.

Serve immediately.

GALLEY NOTES:

POT COOKIN'

Callaloo & Melancholy Bouillabaise
Turtle Soup & Jambalaya & Gumbo
My Cups o' Chowder & Oyster Stew
Pumpkin Soup & Shrimp Étouffée
Chinese Claypot Duck & Barometer Soup

Callaloo

— FROM "Calaloo" on DON'T STOP THE CARNIVAL

Yields 4 servings

There's no coincidence in the lyric that "sooner or later, we're all in the stew." After all, what goes into this most famous of all the Creole soups pretty much depends not only upon where it's cooked up, but also what's in the cook's kitchen. Certainly, there must be some essential ingredients, such as the edible leaves of the callaloo plant; however, even that's not as simple as it sounds.

Almost as arguable as the spelling of CALLALOO (also known as *calaloo, callilu, calalou,* and *callau*) is the source of the leaves. One of these is the *taro*, which has an edible root, as well as edible elephant-ear leaves. The other source is so-called Chinese spinach, which can be found in Chinese markets as *yin-choi* or *hon-toi-moi,* or in Japanese markets as *hiyu.* The plant is also cultivated in India and Ceylon, where it is called *bhaji.* And because Jamaica and Trinidad have rather sizable Indian populations, *bhaji* is quite common in many West Indian markets. As a result, *callaloo* and *bhaji leaves* have become interchangeable in name and in stews.

Confusing as all this might be, the news is basically good. You might have more trouble finding the fresh taro leaves (canned *callaloo* is in Caribbean markets) than you will finding the Chinese spinach. When all else fails, you can do just as well with fresh spinach leaves. And while that might make Popeye happy, it would sure screw up the lyrics to the song!

The remaining ingredients are local variations.

CALLALOO/Trinidad

Yields 4 servings

Traditionally, this recipe is served in both Trinidad and Barbados with foo-foo, which are small, dumpling-like balls of green plantain.

INGREDIENTS:

> 1 lb callaloo leaves
> 6 c chicken or fish stock
> 1 onion, chopped fine
> 1 garlic clove, chopped
> 3 scallions (white & green parts), chopped
> ¼ t thyme
> 4 oz saltpork, in ¼-inch cubes
> 8 oz crab meat, cleaned & picked
> ½ c coconut milk
> 8 oz okra, sliced
> Salt & pepper, to taste
> Pickapeppa® or Crystal®, to taste

PREPARATION:

Wash and drain the callaloo. Remove the stems and chop the leaves.

In a large pot, place the chopped greens along with the stock, onion, garlic, scallions, thyme, and salt pork.

Bring the pot to the boil, then cover and reduce the heat. Simmer until the salt pork is tender.

Stir in the crab meat, coconut milk, and okra,

then simmer until the okra is tender, about 10 minutes.

Stir, taste, and adjust the seasonings.

Ladle into heated bowls.

LE CALALOU/Guadeloupe

Yields 4 servings

INGREDIENTS:

> 3 lbs callaloo leaves
> 8 oz okra, sliced
> 1 lb eggplant, peeled & chopped coarse
> 4 c water
> 4 T vegetable oil
> 4 oz lean salt pork, in ¼-inch cubes
> 3 green bananas, peeled & chopped
> 2 onions, chopped fine
> 2 garlic cloves, minced
> ½ t thyme
> ¼ t cloves, ground
> 2 T chives, chopped
> 1 hot pepper, seeded & chopped
> 1 T white vinegar
> Salt & pepper, to taste
> 1 c coconut milk

PREPARATION:

Wash and drain the callaloo. Remove the stems and chop the leaves.

In a large saucepan, place the chopped greens along with the okra, the eggplant, and the water.

Bring the pot to the boil, then cover and reduce the heat. Simmer until the vegetables are tender.

In a large pot, heat the oil. Add the salt pork and render the fat. Stir in the banana, onion, and garlic, then cover and cook until they are tender.

Remove and reserve any pieces of salt pork.

Force the banana, onion, and garlic mixture through a sieve, then return them to the pot.

Drain the cooked callaloo, okra, and eggplant, then add them to the pot as well.

Use an electric beater or immersible blender to create a light purée.

CAUTION: DO NOT EVEN THINK OF USING YOUR TRUSTY BAR BLENDER TO DO THIS. IT IS NOT THE KITCHEN TOOL TO BE USED WITH HOT LIQUIDS.

If you think the stew is too thick, you might want to add a little water or stock.

Return the reserved salt pork to the pot, stir, and bring to a simmer.

Ladle into heated bowls.

LE CALALOU/Martinique

Yields 4 servings

INGREDIENTS:

> 2 lbs callaloo leaves
> 8 oz okra, sliced
> 8 oz ham
> 1 hot green pepper, seeded & chopped
> ½ t thyme
> 1 garlic clove, chopped
> 4 scallions (white & green parts), chopped
> 1 T parsley, chopped
> Salt & pepper, to taste
> 4 c water

PREPARATION:

Wash and drain the callaloo. Remove the stems and chop the leaves.

In your pot place the callaloo, along with all the other ingredients.

Bring the pot to the boil, then cover, reduce the heat, and allow to simmer for 1 hour.

Remove and reserve the ham, then use a wire whisk to beat the stew into a light purée.

In some households, the ham is not eaten as part of the stew; in others, it is. If you do leave the ham in the pot, then purée the stew and ham together with an immersible hand blender.

CAUTION: DO NOT EVEN THINK OF USING YOUR TRUSTY BAR BLENDER TO DO THIS. IT IS NOT THE KITCHEN TOOL TO BE USED WITH HOT LIQUIDS.

Stir, taste, and adjust the seasonings.

Ladle into heated bowls.

LE CALALOU/Haiti

Yields 4 servings

INGREDIENTS:

> 2 oz salt pork, in ½-inch cubes
> 3 slices of lean bacon
> 8 oz fillet of whitefish, in 1-inch pieces
> 3 T flour
> 1 c okra, sliced
> 8 oz callaloo leaves, chopped coarse
> 1 t thyme
> 1 bay leaf
> Salt & pepper, to taste
> 6 c chicken or fish stock

PREPARATION:

In a frying pan, render the salt pork, then add the bacon and cook until crisp.

Remove the bacon and reserve on a paper towel to drain.

Coat the pieces of fish with a dusting of flour, then add the fish to the hot frying pan. Sauté to a golden brown.

Transfer the fish, along with any remaining pieces of salt pork, to a large pot. Add in any remaining fat from the frying pan.

Wash and drain the callaloo. Remove the stems and chop the leaves.

Into your pot, place the callaloo, okra, thyme, bay leaf, and stock. Stir, taste, and adjust the seasonings with salt & pepper.

Bring the pot to the boil, then cover and allow to simmer gently for about 30 minutes.

Ladle into heated bowls.

Garnish with crumbled bacon.

Callau/St. Lucia

Yields 4 servings

For an island whose possession has changed between the French and the British more than a dozen times, St. Lucia boasts a version of this stew that remains free of those faraway influences.

Ingredients:

> 1 lb callaloo leaves
> 12 small okras, whole
> 4 oz corned beef, sliced
> 4 oz salt pork, whole
> 8 oz crab meat, cleaned & picked
> 3 parsley sprigs
> 1 celery rib (with leaves), chopped
> 4 scallions (white & green parts), chopped
> ¼ t dried thyme
> Black pepper, ground fresh
> 1 hot red pepper, whole
> 6 c water

Preparation:

Wash and drain the callaloo. Remove the stems and cut the leaves in 1-inch pieces.

In your pot place the callaloo, along with all the other ingredients. Include a generous amount of the ground black pepper.

Bring the pot to the boil.

Cover, reduce the heat, then allow to simmer until the beef and the salt pork have become tender and the stew is somewhat thick.

Remove the meat from the pot and place on a clean dish.

Ladle the stew into heated bowls.

Cut the beef and pork into pieces, then use as a garnish for each serving.

Melancholy Bouillabaisse

— FROM "Lage Nom Ai"
on BAROMETER SOUP

Though you probably recognize this phrase from "Lage Nom Ai," it first took seed in the mind of Jim Harrison, Jimmy's longtime friend from the early Key West days, who wrote *Legends of the Fall*, as well as the novella, *The Man Who Gave Up His Name*. And as you know, "Lage Nom Ai" is based upon that novella.

Meanwhile, the true recipe for a *bouillabaisse* is made in only one place: Marseilles, France. And which of Jimmy's songs evokes more melancholy than "The Coast of Marseilles"? (Okay, so I'm stretching things a bit here.) The fact remains, all the other recipes remain only derivatives of this original, unique combination, which uses a minimum of 5 varieties of finfish and only a sparse amount of shellfish. Moreover, the true stock for this tasty bit of pot cookin' is not made from the customary frames and trimmings of large fish, but of tiny Mediterranean fish. (Yes, itsy-bitsy, teeny-weeny . . . *ooops!* That's no fish. It's a thong!)

Though the territorial waters of Margaritaville have no boundaries, let me note that the true recipe would include fish from this group available in U.S. waters: *baudroie* (goosefish), *congre* (conger eel), *dorade* (walleye), *grondin* (flying fish), *langouste* (spiny lobster), and *merlan* (kingfish), as well as fish from this other group that is generally unavailable in our coastal waters (approximate substitution in parentheses): *felian* (small eel), *galinette* (grouper), *rascasse* (sea bass), *rougier* (eel), *sard* (haddock or cod), and *turbot* (flounder).

As for a translation of *bouillabaisse* (that's always tough to spell), it roughly means "to stop the boil." So, if you should ever get that one right on *Jeopardy!*, I hope that you'll tell Alex where you heard it. But for now, *let's boil!*

Bouillabaisse/Marseilles

Yields 4 servings

INGREDIENTS:

For the stock:

> *Frames & trimmings, rinsed & chopped in 3-inch pieces*
> 3 T olive oil
> 6 garlic cloves, chopped
> 1 fennel bulb, chopped coarse
> 1 onion, chopped coarse
> 4 thyme sprigs
> 1 T orange zest
> 6 c water

For the bouillabaisse:

> 2 lbs assorted fish fillets
> 3 T olive oil
> 3 leeks (white & pale green), washed & chopped fine
> 8 tomatoes, peeled, seeded & diced
> ¼ c Pernod
> 6 c stock
> ½ T saffron threads, crushed
> 8 ½-inch slices of FRENCH BREAD
> 2 c ROUILLE

PREPARATION:

To make the stock:

In your pot, heat the olive oil, then sauté the garlic, fennel, onion, thyme, and orange zest for 10 minutes.

Stir the fish frames and trimmings into the pot, then sauté for another 10 minutes.

Add the water and simmer for 30 more minutes.

Remove the pot from the heat and strain the stock through a sieve into a heatproof bowl.

To make the pot of fish:

In your pot, heat the olive oil, then sauté the leeks until tender, about 10 minutes.

Stir in the tomatoes, Pernod, stock, and saffron, then simmer for 20 minutes.

Meanwhile, in a large skillet arrange the fillets in a single layer, then ladle just enough of the simmering stock to cover the fish. Bring the skillet to the simmer.

In a large bowl, place ½ c of the rouille, then spread each slice of French bread with rouille. Reserve some of the rouille for the garnish.

When the fillets just become opaque, whisk the stock from skillet into the bowl of rouille, then stir the mixture into the pot.

Place 2 slices of French bread in the bottom of each bowl.

Divide the fillets among each serving.

Ladle into the individual heated bowls.

Garnish with a dollop of rouille.

Rouille

Yields 2 cups

Though you will find this intense sauce used in the

finishing of some soups from Spain and Portugal, its origin is in the Provence. And while this recipe could be made with a food processor, using a mortar & pestle not only makes use of a traditional method, but also produces the traditional texture. Moreover, when extra virgin olive oil is processed or beaten, it can take on a bitter taste.

INGREDIENTS:

> ¼ t saffron threads, crushed
>
> 1 t warm water
>
> 3 roasted red bell peppers, peeled, seeded & chopped
>
> 3 jalapeño peppers, seeded & chopped fine
>
> 4 garlic cloves, minced
>
> 1 t kosher salt
>
> 4 ½-inch slices of FRENCH BREAD, no crust
>
> 2 c warm water
>
> ¾ c extra virgin olive oil

PREPARATION:

In a small mixing bowl, soak the saffron in the warm water for 20 minutes.

Meanwhile, in your mortar combine the red peppers, jalapeño peppers, and garlic.

Sprinkle in the salt to help release their oils, as well as to provide your pestle with some friction, then work the ingredients into a smooth paste.

In a large mixing bowl, soften the slices of bread in warm water. Squeeze the water out of each slice, then add the bread to the other ingredients in your mortar.

Add in the saffron and water, then continue to work the paste.

Gradually, add the olive oil into your mixture until all has been incorporated into the paste.

Cover tightly and reserve, or use as directed.

12v Bouillabaisse/The Baja

Yields 4 servings

To paraphrase Maurice Chevalier: "Thank heaven for *bouillabaise,* for without it what would other chefs do?" This particular variation comes from an old (but *not* aging!) chum of mine who (like the Twelve Volt Man) had taken up residence at the tip of that peninsula which parallels the Mexican mainland before dropping into the Pacific. Not quite qualifying as "a little latitude," Todos Santos appears to rival that of Havana and Key West in both climate and ambition. Unfortunately, he has since been thrown out of the country.

INGREDIENTS:

> 24 hardshell clams, scrubbed & in-shells
>
> 1 lb uncooked shrimp, peeled & deveined
>
> 8 oz red snapper fillets, in 1-inch pieces
>
> 8 oz crab meat, cleaned & picked
>
> 2 T olive oil
>
> 1 onion, chopped
>
> 4 green chili peppers, seeded & chopped
>
> 2 garlic cloves, minced
>
> 2 c dry white wine
>
> 1 T orange zest
>
> 2 c orange juice
>
> 3 c canned plum tomatoes, peeled & chopped, with juices
>
> 1 T sugar
>
> 1 T cilantro, chopped
>
> 1 T basil, chopped
>
> ½ T oregano, chopped

PREPARATION:

In your pot, heat the oil, then sauté the onion, green chili peppers, and garlic for 3 minutes.

Stir in the wine, orange zest, orange juice, tomatoes with their juices, sugar, cilantro, basil, and oregano, then bring to the boil.

Reduce the heat and simmer for 10 minutes.

Add the clams and mussels, then stir gently, cover, and simmer for 10 minutes.

Remove the pot from the heat. Coax open any clams and mussels with a tap of your fingers. Remove and discard any that do not open, then remove and discard any shells.

Add the red snapper, shrimp, and crab meat to the pot, then stir and simmer until the shrimp just turn pink.

Stir, taste, and adjust the seasonings with salt & pepper.

Ladle into individual heated bowls.

GULF COAST BOUILLABAISSE

Yields 4 servings

There might be a temptation to forego the rubbing and refrigerating by simply adding those ingredients directly into the pot, but the result is simply not the same. The fillets take on a distinctive flavor when allowed to absorb the essence of the rub.

INGREDIENTS:

1½ lbs assorted firm-fleshed fish fillets, cut in 1-inch pieces & rubbed with spices

8 oysters, shucked with liquor

2 crabs, cleaned & halved

8 uncooked shrimp, shells-on

For the rub:

1 garlic clove, crushed

2 whole cloves, crushed

3 allspice berries, crushed

½ T sea salt

12 black peppercorns, cracked

For the bouillabaisse:

1 T butter

1 T oil

1 onion, diced

2 celery ribs, diced

2 (more) garlic cloves, minced

2 tomatoes, peeled, seeded & diced

2 saffron threads, crushed

½ T red pepper flakes, crushed

4 c stock

1 lemon, sliced thin

Salt, to taste

Crystal®, to taste

2 T sherry

PREPARATION:

Before beginning this recipe, use a mortar & pestle to prepare a rub with the garlic, cloves, allspice berries, sea salt, and black peppercorns. Thoroughly coat the pieces of finfish with the rub, then place them in a bowl covered tightly with plastic wrap. Refrigerate at least 1½ hours.

In your pot, melt together the butter and oil, then sauté the onion, celery, and garlic for 10 minutes.

Place the refrigerated pieces of finfish on top of the sautéed vegetables in the pot.

Add the tomatoes, saffron, red pepper flakes, and stock, then bring to the boil.

Reduce the heat, cover, and simmer 15 minutes.

Add to the pot the oysters and their liquor, along with the split crabs and the shrimp.

Cover and simmer for 5 minutes.

Add the lemon.

Stir, taste and adjust the seasonings with salt & Crystal® sauce.

Stir in the sherry, then simmer 5 more minutes.

Ladle into individual heated bowls.

Turtle Soup

— FROM "Who's Eating Who?"
in WHERE IS JOE MERCHANT? / P. 126

Yields 4 servings

Now that the Turtle Kraals in Key West is but a restaurant surrounded by memorabilia of yesteryear's turtle harvests, you must order turtle meat through a gourmet shop.

INGREDIENTS:

1 lb turtle meat, chopped
1 T oil
2 celery ribs, chopped
2 carrots, chopped
1 onion, chopped
2 garlic cloves, chopped
2 cups cabbage, chopped
8 whole peppercorns
3 parsley sprigs
2 bay leaves
1½ t salt
5 c water
1 T oil
1 c water
½ c sherry

PREPARATION:

In your pot, heat the oil, then sauté the celery, carrots, onion, garlic and cabbage for 3 minutes.

Stir in the peppercorns, parsley, bay leaves, salt, and the 5 cups of water into the pot, then cover and bring to the boil.

Reduce the heat and simmer for 1 hour.

Meanwhile, in a saucepan heat the second 1 T of oil, then brown the turtle meat.

Add to the saucepan the 1 c of water, then bring that to the boil. Reduce the heat, cover, and simmer until the meat is tender.

After the kettle has simmered for the hour, remove it from the heat.

Strain the stock through a sieve into a heatproof bowl, then discard all the solids. Return the strained stock to the pot and bring to the simmer.

Add the turtle meat and its liquid to the pot, then stir in the sherry and simmer for 5 minutes.

Ladle into individual heated bowls.

Jambalaya

— FROM "Life is Just a Tire Swing" on A1A

Yields 4 servings

One of the most revered dishes in Louisiana, JAMBALAYA has roots claimed by Creoles and Cajuns alike; however, Cajuns are likely to stick-up for their rights on this one, and leave GUMBO to the Creoles.

Those who don't understand the difference between Creole and Cajun should know this. Creole cooking is very much city; Cajun is very much country. In fact, the very word *Creole* has its own Spanish and Portuguese roots that mean "white person born in the colonies." The word *Cajun*, on the other hand, comes from the generations of pronouncing *Acadians*, the name for French Catholics driven out of Acadia (Nova Scotia) in the late 18th century by British Protestants, who sent them to New Orleans. Being farmers, trappers, and fishermen, the 'Cadians felt uncomfortable in the city, so they moved to the outlying countryside of bayous and marshlands.

While wealthy French colonists brought chefs to New Orleans and hired free slaves as kitchen helpers, their cooks learned about local fare from the Choctaw Indians and introduced some of their own

African and Caribbean ingredients. To this city blend was added the influence of the Italian, Dutch, and Germans who immigrated to the Crescent City.

In the countryside, meanwhile, the Cajuns developed a hearty and simple cooking style, characterized by hot and spicy flavorings, as well as fish and game, cooked with rice and peppers. These are the ingredients that go into JAMBALAYA, a dish with humble beginnings as a poor man's catch-all for leftover meats, fish, sausages, and plenty of rice.

INGREDIENTS:

2 lbs chicken parts
½ lb shrimp, peeled & deveined, tails-on
½ t cayenne pepper
2 T vegetable oil
8 oz andouille sausage, in ¼-inch slices
1 onion, chopped
1 green bell pepper, seeded & chopped
1 celery rib, sliced
2 garlic cloves, minced
1 t dried thyme
1 c long-grain rice
1 16-oz can whole tomatoes, with juices
1 c fish stock or chicken broth
1 c water
1 bay leaf
4 green onions, sliced thin
Crystal® sauce, to taste

PREPARATION:

Pat the chicken dry, then sprinkle cayenne on all sides.

In a large skillet, heat the oil over medium-high heat. Add the chicken and cook on each side until browned, about 4 minutes.

Add the andouille and stir occasionally until it begins to brown, about 3 minutes.

With a slotted spoon, remove the chicken and andouille to a clean plate.

Add the onion, bell pepper, celery, and garlic to the skillet, then cook until the vegetables begin to soften. Stir frequently during this part to make sure that nothing burns, especially the garlic.

Stir in the thyme and the rice, then cook for another minute until the rice is coated with oil.

Add the tomatoes and their juices, then break them up with the side of your spoon.

Stir in the fish stock, ½ c of the water, and the bay leaf, then bring the mixture to a simmer over medium-high heat.

Return the chicken and sausage to the skillet, then cover and reduce the heat to low. Cook for another 15 minutes.

Being careful not to be burned by any escaping steam, remove the cover and distribute the shrimp over the top of your mixture, pressing the shrimp lightly into the rice.

Replace the cover once again and cook for 15 more minutes until the chicken and shrimp are cooked through, and the rice is tender. If the rice has absorbed all the liquid before it becomes tender, add up to ½ c more of water and cook a few minutes longer.

Remove the skillet from the heat.

Uncover and stir in the green onions.

Taste and adjust the seasoning with the Crystal®.

Serve hot.

Filé Gumbo

Yields 4 servings

Recipes for GUMBO reflect the tastes of a variety of ethnic groups that converged upon the Louisiana region over the centuries: the Native American Choctaw Indians thickened this stew with ground sassafras leaves (filé powder) and Africans — many of whom came as slaves — had included *ochingombo* (okra). The French refugees driven out of Nova Scotia brought their Acadian customs to the backcountry, while the Spanish and European French were bringing theirs into New Orleans. This GUMBO made in the Creole fashion with tomatoes and okra is a somewhat lighter pot cookin' dish preferred by the aristocratic settlers of the city, as opposed to that made by the Cajuns in the rural areas.

CREOLE GUMBO

Some maintain that *only* the CREOLE GUMBO is made with tomatoes, and this recipe reflects that style.

INGREDIENTS:

4 crabs, dressed
1 lb uncooked shrimp, peeled & deveined

12 oz firm fish fillets, cut in 1-inch pieces
12 oysters, shucked with liquor
8 oz andouille sausage, in ¼-inch pieces
2 bacon slices, diced
1 onion, minced
1 celery rib, diced
2 garlic cloves, minced
1 green pepper, seeded & minced
1½ c canned tomatoes, with juices
4 c stock
2 c okra, chopped
½ t salt
½ t fresh black pepper
2 dashes cayenne pepper
2 dashes Worcestershire
2 bay leaves
2 dashes Crystal® sauce
¼ t filé powder
3 c cooked rice, hot

PREPARATION:

In your pot, make a light brown roux by rendering the bacon fat.

Sprinkle in the flour and stir to incorporate with the fat. Continue to stir until the flour has cooked and the roux has become the color of peanut butter.

Slowly add the stock to your pot, stirring to mix with the roux.

Remove the pot from the heat, then pour the stock into a heatproof bowl and reserve.

Wipe clean your pot and render the andouille and bacon until crisp and browned.

With a slotted spoon, remove the andouille and bacon to a paper towel to drain.

Discard all but 2 T of the drippings, then sauté the onion, celery, garlic, and pepper 3 minutes.

Meanwhile, strain the tomatoes through a sieve and reserve the juices in a bowl.

Add the strained tomatoes to the pot, along with the stock and the okra, then cover the pot and simmer for 10 minutes.

Add the reserved tomato juices, as well as the salt, black pepper, cayenne pepper, Worcestershire, bay leaves, and Crystal® sauce to your pot, then stir and bring to the boil.

Reduce the heat, cover, and simmer for 2 hours.

After the 2 hours, add the crabs, then simmer for another 10 minutes.

Stir in the shrimp and fish, along with the reserved andouille and back, then simmer 10 more minutes.

Meanwhile, in a saucepan cook the rice according to directions on the package.

Stir the gumbo, taste, and adjust the seasonings. Add the oysters and their reserved liquor to your pot, then simmer until the edges of the oysters just begin to curl.

Use a custard cup or similar small dish to mold each serving of hot rice, then turn into individual heated soup bowls.

Dust the rice with filé powder, then ladle the gumbo into each bowl.

Divide the seafood equally among them.

CAJUN GUMBO

CAJUN GUMBO is a darker, richer dish that reflects the tastes and provisions of the 'Cadian refugees in the rural areas. Some will debate whether the Cajun recipe ought to contain tomatoes, and this one does not. If you wish to do so, then simply adjust the Creole recipe to be made with a dark roux.

INGREDIENTS:

4 crabs, dressed
1 lb uncooked shrimp, peeled & deveined
12 oz firm fish fillets, cut in 1-inch pieces
12 oysters, shucked with liquor
1 T bacon fat
2 T flour
6 c stock
8 oz andouille sausage, in ¼-inch pieces
2 bacon slices, diced
1 onion, minced
1 celery rib, diced
2 garlic cloves, minced
1 green pepper, seeded & minced
2 c okra, chopped
½ t salt
½ t black pepper
2 dashes cayenne pepper
2 dashes Worcestershire
2 bay leaves
2 dashes Crystal®
¼ t filé powder
3 c cooked rice, hot

PREPARATION:

In your pot, make a dark brown roux by rendering the bacon fat.

Sprinkle the flour into the pot and stir to incorporate with the fat. Continue to stir until the roux is the color of milk chocolate.

Slowly add the stock, stirring to mix with the roux. Remove the pot from the heat, then pour the stock into a heatproof bowl and set aside.

Wipe the pot clean and render the andouille and bacon until crisp and brown.

Remove the andouille and bacon to a paper towel to drain.

Discard all but 2 T of the drippings, then sauté the onion, celery, garlic, and pepper for 3 minutes.

Return the reserved stock to the pot and bring to the simmer.

Add the okra; cover and simmer for 10 minutes.

Stir in the salt, black pepper, cayenne pepper, Worcestershire, bay leaves, and Crystal®, then cover and simmer for 2 hours.

Add the crabs, then simmer for 10 minutes.

Stir in the shrimp and fish, along with the reserved andouille and bacon, then simmer another 10 minutes.

Meanwhile, in a saucepan cook the rice according to directions.

Stir the gumbo, taste, and adjust the seasonings. Add the oysters and their reserved liquor, then simmer until the edges of the oysters just begin to curl.

Use a custard cup or similar dish to mold each serving of hot rice, then turn into individual heated bowls.

Dust the rice with filé powder, then ladle the gumbo into each bowl.

Divide the seafood as equally as possible among them.

My Cups o' Chowder

— FROM "Honey Do"
on ONE PARTICULAR HARBOUR

— FROM "I Must Confess,
I Could Use Some Rest"
in TALES FROM MARGARITAVILLE / P. 208

Conch is readily available from the Honduras. Your local fish market can order you a 5-pound box of conch meat that comes all cleaned so you can use only what you need and keep the rest in your freezer.

As with a great many other recipes in this collection, any attempt to present any recipe for chowder as the *definitive* one would only ignite a debate on the subject. Please, then, accept these next three only as variations upon a theme.

BO's CHOWDER/Key West

Yields 4 servings

If not the best conch chowder in Key West, then certainly one of the best in Key West is at B.O.'s Fish Wagon, which is located — as of this writing — at the corner of Caroline & William, not far from where the shrimpboats once tied up to the pilings. While you won't find B.O. (Buddy Owen) or his fish wagon mentioned in any of Jimmy's stories, you'll see it all right there in the credits for all the albums produced at Shrimpboat Sound.

INGREDIENTS:

1 lb conch steak, chopped
6 c water
¼ c key lime juice
1 T salt
½ c olive oil
1 green pepper, seeded & diced
1 onion, diced
3 celery ribs, diced
2 garlic cloves, chopped
½ t red pepper flakes, crushed
¼ t thyme
1 c parsley, chopped
½ c rice, uncooked

PREPARATION:

Prepare the conch steak by placing it upon a plate, rubbing it with the salt, and allowing it to stand for 15 minutes.

Rinse the conch steak well. Using a sharp knife, dice the conch into small pieces.

In your pot, combine the conch meat, water, lime juice, and salt, then bring to the boil.

Cover, reduce the heat, and simmer for 30 minutes.

In a small skillet, heat the oil, then sauté the pepper, onion, celery, garlic, thyme, and ½ c of parsley for 5 minutes.

Stir the sautéed vegetables into the pot, then simmer for 1 hour.

Add the rice to the pot, stir, and simmer another 30 minutes.

Stir in the remaining parsley.

Ladle into individual heated bowls.

CONCH SOUP/Big Pine

Yields 4 servings

Barley is one of those ingredients we often associate with all kinds of soups, but seldom with pot cookin'. Unlike corn, which — we are reminded time and time again — was a new concept to settlers when they arrived upon these shores, barley was something they brought *to* this continent from the Old World. Given the taste and texture of conch, barley does make a fine complementary ingredient to this thicker recipe.

INGREDIENTS:

1 lb conch steak, chopped
1 c barley, uncooked
2 T salt
4 oz salt pork, diced
2 onions, chopped
1 sweet red pepper, seeded & chopped

PREPARATION:

Prepare the conch steak by placing it upon a plate, rubbing it with the salt, and allowing it to stand for 15 minutes.

Rinse the conch steak well. Using a sharp knife, dice the conch into small pieces.

In your pot, cook the barley according to directions on the package.

Remove the pot from the heat, then pour the cooked barley and water into a heatproof bowl.

Wipe clean the pot, then render the salt pork until crisp and brown.

Discard all but 2 T of the drippings, then sauté the onions and pepper for 5 minutes.

Add the conch to the pot, along with the barley and its liquid.

Stir well, then cover and bring to the simmer until the conch meat is cooked.

Ladle into individual heated bowls.

CHOWDER/The Bahamas

Yields 4 servings

Generally, you come upon 2 basic variations of a chowder made with conch. One is white; the other, red. Sound familiar? If so, then you already know the main difference among the ingredients.

INGREDIENTS:

> *1 lb conch steak, chopped*
> *4 oz salt pork, diced*
> *1 onion, diced*
> *1 sweet red pepper, diced*
> *1 t flour*
> *2 tomatoes, peeled, seeded & chopped*
> *6 c water*
> *2 potatoes, peeled & diced*
> *4 T butter, garnish*

PREPARATION:

Prepare the conch steak by placing it upon a plate, rubbing it with the salt, and allowing it to stand for 15 minutes.

Rinse the conch steak well. Using a sharp knife, dice the conch into small pieces.

In your pot, render the salt pork until crisp and brown.

Discard all but 2 T of the drippings, then sauté the onion and pepper for 5 minutes.

Sprinkle the flour into the pot and stir to incorporate with the drippings and vegetables.

Stir in the tomatoes and water, then bring to the simmer for 5 minutes.

Add the conch and potatoes to your pot and bring to the boil.

Reduce the heat and simmer for 1 hour.

Ladle into individual heated bowls.

Garnish each with a pat of butter.

QUAHAUG CHOWDER

Yields 4 servings

Though Jimmy writes of Nantucket chowder, there is no such item, *per se.* The two most popular ones on the island would have to be Quahaug (KO-hog) Chowder, or else Scallop (rhymes with "call up") Stew. Quahaugs are the hard-shelled clams, known also as Mahogany Clams or Manilla Clams.

INGREDIENTS:

> *24 quahaugs, shucked & chopped (liquor reserved)*
> *4 oz salt pork, cubed*
> *1 onion, chopped*
> *2 c stock*
> *4 potatoes, peeled & diced*
> *2 c evaporated milk*
> *8 crackers*
> *2 c cream*
> *Salt & pepper, to taste*
> *2 T butter, for garnish*

PREPARATION:

In a large pot, render the salt pork until crisp and brown, then remove and reserve the pieces.

Discard all but 2 T of the drippings, then sauté the onion for 3 minutes.

Stir in the stock and bring to the simmer.

Add the potatoes and cook until they are tender.

In a small bowl, soak the crackers in the 2 c of

evaporated milk until they are soft, then stir in the cream, browned salt pork, clams, and juices.

When the potatoes have become fork tender, add the mixture from the bowl to the pot.

Stir, taste, and adjust the seasonings with salt & pepper.

Add the butter and simmer until it has completely melted.

Ladle into individual heated bowls.

SCALLOP STEW

Yields 4 servings

So compact that it is a town, a county, and an island all in one, Nantucket had long been the largest scallop fishery along the entire eastern seaboard of the United States. But in recent years, island development has damaged some of its fragile shoreline environment, and the shellfish itself has become nothing less than gold in this economy.

As for this bit of pot cookin', it remains the island's treasure. As you work your way through its 3 deliberate stages, take your time and do not allow anything to boil except the potatoes.

INGREDIENTS:

1 lb bay scallops, shucked
6 T butter
1 onion, sliced thin
2 c milk
2 c cream
1 c water
1 T salt
1 potato, peeled & in ½-inch cubes
Salt & fresh cracked black pepper, to taste
4 T butter, for garnish
Paprika, for garnish

PREPARATION:

In a large pot, melt 4 T of the butter, then sauté the onion for 10 minutes.

Stir in the milk and the cream, then partially cover and bring to the simmer for 15 minutes.

Remove the pot from the heat.

Strain the stock through a fine sieve into a heatproof bowl. Discard the solids.

In a saucepan bring the water to the boil. Add the salt and potatoes, then cook until the potatoes are tender.

Drain the potatoes and reserve them on a plate.

Wipe clean your pot, then melt the remaining 2 T of butter and sauté the scallops on each side until they are opaque.

Add the potato and the stock to the pot, then bring to the simmer.

Taste and adjust the seasoning with salt & pepper.

Simmer for 5 more minutes.

Ladle into individual heated bowls.

Garnish each with a pat of butter and paprika.

TUCKERNUCK STEW

Yields 4 servings

Just west of Madaket Harbor at the western tip of Nantucket, lies tiny Tuckernuck Island. Aside from the fact that Madaket is where Jimmy's Widgeon went into the drink, these waters also are home to the most succulent of the island's small scallops. This is the recipe which the Nantucket Angler's Club uses to create its version of SCALLOP STEW.

INGREDIENTS:

4 T butter

1 garlic clove, halved
2 c bay scallops
2 c milk
Crown pilot® crackers

PREPARATION:

In a small saucepan, melt the butter over medium heat.

Add the halved garlic clove, then gently sauté so that it does not burn, about 5 minutes.

Remove and discard the garlic, then add the scallops to the saucepan.

Sauté the scallops until they are just translucent, about 4 minutes.

Add the milk to the saucepan, then bring just to the simmer. Be careful that you do not allow the milk to come to the bowl.

Ladle the stew into heated bowls and top with broken Crown pilot® crackers.

Oyster Stew

Yields 4 servings

— FROM "Boomerang Love"
in TALES FROM MAGARITAVILLE / P. 98

— FROM "I Wish Lunch Could Last Forever"
in TALES FROM MARGARITAVILLE / P. 146

Don't ever, ever, *ever* get into an argument with anyone about whose waters produce the best oysters. You'd be much better off (and live a much longer life) if you were to keep your conversation to religion and politics. That said, there is not a true oysterman anywhere who will not vouch for the tasteful simplicity of this recipe. Angel Beech adds a garnish of fresh chives, then a dash of Tabasco® sauce.

INGREDIENTS:

24 oysters, shucked & drained (liquor reserved)
2 T butter
6 c milk
Salt & pepper, to taste

PREPARATION:

In your pot, heat the reserved oyster liquor and bring to the simmer.

Add the oysters and cook just until the edges begin to curl.

Remove and reserve the oysters on a warm plate.

Add to the saucepan the butter and milk, then bring to the simmer for 5 minutes.

Stir, taste, and adjust the seasonings with salt & pepper.

Return the oysters to the pot and simmer for 3 more minutes.

Ladle into individual heated bowls.

SAN PADRE OYSTER STEW

Yields 4 servings

I continue to be amazed at the number of people who forget the fact that the Lone Star State indeed has a coastline. It's not that those people never knew, but more a result of the fact that so much of the Texas lore is based upon the western aspects of the state's culture. Still, this is a pleasant reminder that Texas sits upon the bountiful Gulf of Mexico.

INGREDIENTS:

24 oysters, shucked & drained (liquor reserved)

3 c stock

3 red-skinned potatoes, diced

1 onion, chopped

1 bay leaf

6 jalapeño peppers, seeded & diced

1 c kernel corn

1 roasted red bell pepper, seeded & chopped

2 c cream

Salt, to taste

1 T butter

1 t marjoram, chopped for garnish

PREPARATION:

In your pot, bring 2 c of the stock to the boil, then add the potatoes.

Reduce the heat and simmer the potatoes until they are fork tender.

Remove and reserve the potatoes in a clean bowl.

Add the remaining stock to the pot, along with the chopped onion and bay leaf, then simmer for 15 minutes.

Remove and discard the bay leaf.

Stir in the jalapeño peppers and corn, then simmer for 5 minutes.

Add the cream and reserved liquor, then bring to the simmer for 5 minutes.

Stir, taste, and adjust the seasonings with salt.

Add the butter and oysters, then simmer until the butter has melted and the edges of the oysters just begin to curl.

Ladle into individual heated bowls.

Garnish each with marjoram.

ROCKEFELLER OYSTER SOUP

Yields 4 servings

Contrary to popular opinion, the original recipe for "Oysters à la Rockefeller" — created a century ago by Jules Alciatore for Antoine's in New Orleans — never included spinach among its ingredients. At that time, snails from Europe were becoming more difficult to import, and the chef hoped to create a dish from the local abundance of oysters. To make his oysters different from all the others being served, he created a secret sauce from scallions, celery, chervil, tarragon leaves, bread crumbs, Crystal®, and butter. The flavor of his well-guarded recipe proved to be so rich that he named his dish after the man he believed to be the richest in the world. In the years since, however, the recipe has changed somewhat to include both spinach and bacon, neither of which was part of his secret.

In addition, Alciatore became an oyster pioneer of yet another sort. With the exception of oyster stew, this shellfish generally had been served uncooked.

INGREDIENTS:

> ½ pt shucked oysters, liquor reserved
> 2 slices bacon
> 1 scallion (white part), chopped
> 1 potato, peeled & diced
> 2 c stock
> 1 t lemon juice
> ½ t tarragon
> 1 c evaporated milk
> 1 c water
> 5 spinach leaves, washed & stemmed
> Salt & pepper, to taste
> Dash of Pernod

PREPARATION:

In your pot, render the bacon until crisp and brown.

With a slotted spoon, remove and reserve the bacon on paper towel to drain. Remove and discard all but 1 T of the drippings.

Add the chopped scallion to your pot and sauté for 3 minutes.

Stir in the stock and bring to the boil.

Add the diced potato to the pot, reduce the heat, and simmer until the potato is fork tender.

Stir in the lemon juice, tarragon, and evaporated milk, then continue to simmer.

Meanwhile, in a small saucepan bring the water to the boil and blanch the spinach for 3 minutes.

Drain the spinach, chop, then add to the pot.

Wipe clean your saucepan and bring the reserved liquor to the simmer. Add the oysters and simmer just until the edges begin to curl.

Add the oysters and liquor to the pot.

Stir, taste, and adjust the seasonings with salt & pepper.

Simmer for 3 more minutes.

Ladle into individual heated bowls.

Garnish each with chopped bacon.

CAPE FEAR OYSTER STEW

Yields 4 servings

Dumplings are still not an usual item in many regions along the eastern U.S. shoreline, and this variation takes full advantage of that.

INGREDIENTS:

For the stew:

> 24 oysters, shucked with their liquor
> 4 oz salt pork, ½-inch cubes
> 1 c water
> Salt & black pepper, to taste

For the dumplings:

> 4 eggs
> 1½ cups milk
> 6 T butter, melted
> 1½ c corn meal

PREPARATION:

In your pot, render the salt pork until crisp and brown.

Add the water and the oyster liquor.

Stir, taste, and adjust the seasonings with salt & pepper.

Bring the pot to the boil.

In a large mixing bowl, beat together the eggs, milk, and melted butter.

Reduce the heat of the pot to the simmer, then stir in the oysters.

Spoon the dumplings on top of the stew, cover, and steam until the dumplings are cooked.

Ladle into individual heated bowls.

Pumpkin Soup

Yields 4 servings

— FROM "I Wish Lunch Could Last Forever"
in TALES FROM MARGARITAVILLE / P. 155

Leave it to Bubba to remind us that pumpkins are not something reserved for goblins and Pilgrims, but are a common vegetable in the islands. *Calabaza*, the West Indian or green pumpkin, is not the same as the North American pumpkin, but almost as large. Though it's okay to use our more familiar pumpkin in this recipe, you'd find a flavor more like *calabaza* if you substitute a butternut or Hubbard squash.

INGREDIENTS:

2 lbs soup bones
4 qts water
8 oz pickled pork (optional)
2 scallion stalks
1 sprig thyme
1 garlic clove
1 green pepper, seeded & whole
2 lbs pumpkin, peeled & seeded
1 lb yams, peeled
1 T ginger root, peeled & minced

PREPARATION:

In a large pot, place the soup bones, pork, and 4 qts of cold water, then cover and bring to the boil.

Once the meat in the pot has cooked, add the scallion, thyme, garlic, green pepper, yams, and pumpkin. Cover and bring to the boil. Cook until the pumpkin and yams are tender.

With a slotted spoon, remove the cooked pumpkin from the pot and allow to cool for 5 minutes.

Reduce the heat and allow the pot to simmer.

Purée the cooled pumpkin pieces in a food processor, then return to the pot.

Remove and discard the green pepper.

Stir, taste and correct the seasoning with salt & pepper.

Divide the minced ginger among the heated soup plates, then ladle the soup.

Shrimp Étouffée

Yields 4 servings

— FROM "I Wish Lunch Could Last Forever"
in TALES FROM MARGARITAVILLE / P. 155

Pronounced AY-too-fay, this traditional New Orleans pot cookin' is well worth the time it takes to bring together its various, but simple stages. You'll recognize that some ingredients make it a bit like JAMBALAYA or GUMBO, but are just different enough to own up to its own special billing.

Essentially, you're going to make a stock from the shrimp shells, then a roux with the vegetables, and then bring them together to go with the rice and the shrimp. Again, it's not at all difficult, just another slow process that requires a good 5 minutes of strict attention while you're making the roux.

This ÉTOUFFÉE can be made ahead of time, then reheated when the rice is made. The recipe can also be made with crawfish, with the fillets of any whitefish, or even with a combination of shrimp, crawfish, and whitefish. In any event, you'll want to have on the table a large basket of FRENCH BREAD and a bottle of Crystal®.

INGREDIENTS:

2 lbs shrimp, uncooked & with shells

6 c water
¼ c vegetable oil
½ c flour
½ t salt
½ t cayenne
½ t fresh black pepper
½ t fresh white pepper
½ t dried basil
½ t dried thyme
½ c onion, chopped
½ c celery, chopped
½ c green bell pepper, chopped
8 T butter
½ c scallions (entire), chopped fine
2 c uncooked rice (not instant)

PREPARATION:

In a large saucepan, combine 6 c water with ¼ t of salt and bring to the boil over medium heat.

Peel the shells from the shrimp and add the shells to the boiling water. Cover, reduce the heat, and simmer for 30 minutes.

Devein and butterfly the shrimp. Rinse them under cold water, drain them, then place them in the refrigerator until needed.

Take a few minutes to bring together all of the ingredients and tools for making the roux.

Mix together the salt, cayenne, black and white peppers, basil, and thyme, then reserve 1 t of this seasoning mixture to put into your rice.

In a small mixing bowl, combine the onion, celery, and green bell pepper, then reserve ½ c of this "trinity" to mix into your rice.

After the shrimp shells have simmered for 30 minutes, strain the stock into a heatproof bowl and discard the shells.

Now devote your attention to making the roux. If you get distracted, you might either burn yourself, or burn the flour. So, turn up the heat, turn on the stove exhaust, send everyone else out of the kitchen, and take the phone off the hook.

In a large, cast iron skillet, heat the oil until it is so hot that a pinch of flour dropped into the skillet will sizzle upon contact.

Carefully whisk into the hot oil all of the flour and continue to stir over the medium-high heat. Paying close attention, cook the flour in the roux until it becomes the rich brown of peanut butter, about 4 to 5 minutes.

Reduce the heat to low and mix your seasonings into the roux.

Add the "trinity" of vegetables to the thickening roux and continue to stir with a wooden spoon over low until the vegetables have wilted.

Gradually add some of the shrimp stock to the skillet until the roux and vegetables are no longer a paste.

Remove the skillet from the heat and replace it with your pot.

Transfer the thinned roux from the skillet to the pot and continue to stir once again with a whisk over medium-low heat. If necessary, add more stock and continue to whisk until the roux has thoroughly mixed with the stock. If it becomes too thick at any time, you can add a little water, chicken stock, or even flat beer, because you want to reserve 2½ c of the stock to use in making the rice. At this point, you can either remove this étouffée sauce from the heat and serve the meal later, or else simmer this sauce over low heat and continue to finish the meal.

In a large saucepan, bring the reserved 2½ c of

the stock to the boil. Stir in the reserved seasonings and the reserved "trinity."

Stir the rice into the boiling stock. Cover, reduce the heat to low, and cook the rice 18 minutes without lifting the lid and letting the steam escape.

Remove the rice from the heat, then fork the rice to keep the grains from sticking. Replace the lid and allow the rice to rest for 20 minutes.

Cut the butterflied shrimp into bite-sized pieces.

In a large skillet, melt the butter over medium heat.

Add the chopped scallions and shrimp, then stir gently until the shrimp is just cooked.

Serve by placing on each dish a helping of rice, topped with the buttered scallions and shrimp, then smothered with the étouffée sauce.

Chinese Claypot Duck

Yields 4 servings

— FROM "A Strange Array of Feelings" in A PIRATE LOOKS AT FIFTY / P. 58

Two-quart claypot are words with rhythm and rhyme in my homeport on Cape Cod, but that doesn't diminish the mouth-watering taste of this slow-cooked duck. In the event that you don't own a claypot, this recipe can be prepared with a Dutch oven; however, the claypot does make this recipe one of the ultimate in the category of pot cookin'.

INGREDIENTS:

1 2-lb duck
2 garlic cloves, minced
2 t fresh ginger, grated
½ t sugar
3 T dry sherry
3 T soy sauce
2 whole star anise
2 dried Chinese chili peppers, broken into halves
1 c chicken broth, low salt
12 large cabbage leaves, whole
½ c lemon juice

½ c brown sugar, packed
1 T cornstarch
2 T cold water
2 T vegetable oil
1 scallion, in 1-inch pieces for garnish

PREPARATION:

Soak your 2-quart claypot as directed by the manufacturer.

Whether you wish to leave the skin on the duck or remove it remains your choice, but you should remove as much of the fat from the bird as possible. Leaving the bone in for flavor, cut the duck into serving pieces.

In a small mixing bowl, combine the garlic, ginger, sugar, sherry, soy sauce, star anise, Chinese chili peppers, and chicken stock. Allow this to stand at room temperature for the flavors to mix.

Line your claypot with the cabbage leaves, then add ½ c of cold water.

In a small saucepan, combine the lemon juice and brown sugar over medium heat. Stir until the sugar has dissolved.

Mix together the cornstarch and 2 T of water, then stir half of this mixture into the saucepan. Continue to stir until the sauce has thickened.

Remove the thickened lemon sauce from the heat and set aside.

In a wok, heat the vegetable oil over a high temperature.

When the oil is hot, add the pieces of duck and brown them on all sides.

With a pair of tongs, transfer each browned piece of duck from the wok to the claypot lined with cabbage leaves. When done, remove the wok from the stove.

Add to the claypot the small mixing bowl of seasonings.

Place the claypot over medium heat and gradually bring it to the near boil.

Stir gently, cover, and simmer for 45 minutes.

Add the remaining cornstarch mixture, as well as the lemon sauce. If this is too thick, then add a little water; if too thin, add a little cornstarch.

With oven mitts and a trivet, place the claypot on your table.

Garnish the Chinese duck with the scallion.

Barometer Soup

Yields 0 servings

— FROM "Barometer Soup"
on BAROMETER SOUP

— FROM "The Ballad of Skip Wiley"
on BAROMETER SOUP

Snowdrifts can be melted down for this recipe if it's not the rainy season; however, they do tend to lose their flavor should a gravity storm occur.

INGREDIENTS:

4 c fresh rainwater
2 c fresh drizzle
½ c sunshine
¼ c storm cloud
3 T tradewinds
3 t squall
Little latitude, for garnish

PREPARATION:

In a small bay, combine the rainwater and drizzle, then swirl in a tidal motion.

Stir in the sunshine, storm cloud, tradewinds, and squall.

Serve in a seashell and garnish with a little latitude.

CARNIVOROUS HABITS

Cheeseburgers in Paradise
Brisket Sandwich 🍔 Chicken Adobo
Boliche 🍔 Chili Cheese Dog
Roast Chicken 🍔 Fried Chicken
Country Ham 🍔 Chicken Fried Steak
Cuban Pork 🍔 Meatloaf Sandwich
Picadillo 🍔 Jamaican Jerk Roasts
Cuban Sandwich 🍔 Tampico Broil

Cheeseburgers

Yields 4 half-pound burgers

— FROM "Brand New Country Star"
on LIVING AND DYING IN ¾ TIME

— FROM "Cheeseburger in Paradise"
on SON OF A SON OF A SAILOR

Now's the time to get a bit more serious about your CHEESEBURGER; especially since there are some people out there who actually look down upon those of us who sing about them. To such other people, the CHEESEBURGER is not the quintessential American food item, but a culinary cliché. Well, shame on them. They are what they eat!

So, let us (did someone say *lettuce?*) revisit the origins of the CHEESEBURGER and consider how the CHEESEBURGER (and *you!*) can earn some deserved respect. To do that, we must begin at the beginning and borrow some original aspects of Steak Tartare. No, I'm *not* going to suggest that you not cook the beef; however, I am going to advocate relentlessly that your CHEESEBURGER begin with beef that is *chopped* in a food processor rather than *forced into mush* through the holes of a meat grinder. And I also think you must combine various cuts of beef in each burger. (There ain't no ham in hamburger.)

My friend, Karen, thinks I'm crazy to believe that anyone would bother doing this, but by chopping the meat, you'll discover a much more appetizing texture. Sort of like that English muffin that has all those nooks and crannies, the texture of chopped beef allows the cheese to ooze a bit between the pieces of meat, rather than to flow toward the edges and into the flame. And by including various cuts of beef, you'll be able to take advantage of the subtle flavors that each part of a steer has to offer. Believe me, you'll savor the *very little extra* effort and cost that are involved.

I am assuming, of course, that you not only ignore those prefabricated burgers in the freezer section of your grocery store, but that you also have been paying some attention to the percentage of fat in whatever ground beef you've been using. Always keep in mind that the leanest beef isn't necessarily the tastiest and that the cheapest isn't always the best buy. When all is said and done with this recipe, you'll have the best of both worlds, and that can only be paradise.

Finally, let me add a couple of words about the variables of cheese and bread. The cheddar cheese and bun in this recipe are merely suggestions, and they are not as important as that meat that makes the burger itself. So, let's *moooo*ve on and earn some respect.

INGREDIENTS:

1 lb chuck neck meat (approx 4 lbs of chuck neck bones)
8 oz bottom chuck, boneless
8 oz sirloin tips
4 oz short rib meat (approx ½ lb of short ribs)
4 oz filet mignon
8 oz suet (beef fat)
Salt
Black pepper, cracked fresh
8 oz extra sharp cheddar cheese, in 4 slices
1 tomato, sliced
1 Bermuda onion, sliced
4 large lettuce leafs, washed & dried

Stone-ground mustard
4 CHEESEBURGER BUNS, *split*

PREPARATION:

Though you might not be familiar with the chuck neck bones, don't be afraid to ask a butcher or the meat-cutter in your grocery store. This ingredient is nothing new to those folks behind the two-way mirrors, but I wouldn't ask them to trim the bones. *Ka-ching!* Do it yourself, or pay the price.

Okay, so look over the neck bones and trim as much meat as you can from them. If you avoid any fat, you should have about 1 lb of meat from the chuck neck. But, remember, fat is flavor.

Trim the meat from the short ribs, then cut all the pieces of meat into chunks no larger than 1-inch cubes. Anything larger might stop the blade of your food processor.

Cut your filet mignon into 1-inch cubes.

If it appears that the meat-to-fat ratio is greater than 4:1, cut enough suet so that your final mixture will be 15% to 20% fat. Cut the suet into ½-inch cubes.

Add the chunks of meat to the bowl of your food processor, then pulse until you can see the pieces of meat begin to break up.

Add the pieces of suet to your meat mixture and continue pulsing.

If necessary, use a rubber spatula to scrape down the sides of your processor, then continue to pulse.

Though it's not likely to happen if you pay attention to what you're doing, do not over-pulse so that your mixture becomes a mush. Remember: texture is a key element of this recipe.

Divide the meat mixture into 4 equal portions, then use your hands to form each portion into a patty that is loose enough to retain the coarse texture of the chopped meat. Be careful not to overwork a portion or to press too hard to lose that desired coarseness. Place the formed burgers on a clean platter.

Lightly season both sides of each burger with salt & pepper.

Because a burger of this size cooked to medium doneness will take about 5 minutes per side, you'll have to adjust the cooking/cheese times accordingly for rare and well-done burgers.

For medium/rare burgers (as the song says), cook each about 5 minutes on the first side.

Flip each burger, then cook another 2 minutes.

Place a slice of cheddar atop the center of each burger.

Cook another 3 minutes.

Meanwhile, split the buns. (There's still time for any who want the roll toasted.) Spread mustard on each. (Just like the song says.)

Place a cheeseburger atop each bun and garnish with onion, lettuce & tomato.

Best served with FRENCH FRIED POTATOES, big KOSHER PICKLE, and cold, draft beer.

BAHAMA BURGER

Yields 4 half-pound burgers

In *The Parrot Head Handbook*, Jimmy lists among his favorite cheeseburgers those at Ruby's on Harbour Island in the Bahamas and served on BAHAMA BREAD.

INGREDIENTS:

1 lb beef, ground
1 lb pork butt, ground
½ c fresh bread crumbs
2 large eggs
½ c ketchup
¼ c Bermuda onion, chopped
¼ t white pepper, cracked
¼ t salt
¼ c milk
2 T fresh parsley, chopped
8 oz extra sharp cheddar cheese, in 4 slices
4 large lettuce leafs, washed & dried
8 slices BAHAMA BREAD

PREPARATION:

In a large mixing bowl, combine the meat, bread crumbs, eggs, ketchup, onion, pepper, salt, milk, and parsley. Use your hands to mix just enough to combine the ingredients.

Divide the meat mixture into 4 equal portions, then use your hands to form each portion into a patty. Place the burgers on a clean platter.

Because a burger of this size cooked to medium doneness will take about 5 minutes per side, you'll have to adjust the cooking/cheese times accordingly for rare and well-done burgers.

For medium/rare burgers (as the song says), cook each about 5 minutes on the first side.

Flip each burger and cook another 2 minutes.

Place a slice of cheddar atop the center of each burger.

Cook another 3 minutes.

Place a cheeseburger atop a slice of BAHAMA BREAD and garnish with onion, lettuce & tomato. Top with the second slice of bread.

Best served with FRENCH FRIED POTATOES, big KOSHER PICKLE, and cold, draft beer.

'BURGER WITH TUNA

Yields 4 half-pound burgers

Hold the pickle! Having a carnivorous habit doesn't mean that you can't eat a cheeseburger made with fresh tuna (red meat). To savor the tuna, select a mild cheese; to complement the flavor, select a smoked cheese. For a condiment, use a ROUILLE.

INGREDIENTS:

> 4 8-oz fresh tuna steaks
> 2 T olive oil
> White pepper, cracked fresh
> 8 oz cheese, in 4 slices
> 4 large lettuce leaves, washed & dried
> 4 T ROUILLE
> 4 MUFFALATTA BUNS

PREPARATION:

Follow the very same directions for the burger made with chopped beef, but omit the need for fat. Instead, brush each burger with olive oil, then season with cracked white pepper.

Brisket Sandwich

Yields 6 servings

— FROM "Take Another Road"
in TALES FROM MARGARITAVILLE / PP. 34 & 39

One of the landmarks followed to the sea by Tully Mars was the legendary Tujague's, which has been on Decatur Street in New Orleans since 1856. In addition to this famous sandwich, you'll also find at the restaurant a picture of Bubba, himself, just to prove that he's been there and done this sandwich, complete with their HORSERADISH SAUCE.

INGREDIENTS:

> 4 lbs beef brisket, trimmed
> 2 onions, sliced
> 2 celery ribs, chopped
> 2 garlic toes (cloves), mashed
> 3 parsley sprigs
> 2 bay leaves
> ½ t thyme
> 2 T salt
> 12 black peppercorns, whole

PREPARATION:

Trim any excess fat from the brisket.

In your pot, place the brisket along with the onions, celery, garlic, parsley, bay leaves, thyme, salt, and peppercorns.

Add enough water to cover the brisket, then bring to the boil.

Reduce the heat, cover, and simmer slowly until the brisket is tender, about 2½ to 3 hours.

When the brisket is ready, remove it from the pot and drain any excess liquid.

Slice the brisket on the bias, then serve on a BAGUETTE with HORSERADISH SAUCE.

HORSERADISH SAUCE

Yields 2 cups

INGREDIENTS:

½ c horseradish
½ c Creole mustard
1 c ketchup
Dash of Worcestershire sauce

PREPARATION:

In a small mixing bowl, blend all the ingredients.

Refrigerate at least 1 hour.

Chicken Adobo

Yields 4 servings

— FROM "The Pascagoula Run"
in TALES FROM MARGARITAVILLE / P. 133

All that Jimmy mentions is a deboned chicken breast, but I thought I'd go one step further by using ADOBO, a fragrant Cuban paste that's so often used when grilling fish, poultry, or meat.

INGREDIENTS:

4 8-oz chicken breasts, skinned & boned
3 garlic cloves, chopped
¼ c onion, minced
½ t cumin seeds, toasted & ground
½ t fresh oregano, crushed
1½ T fresh cilantro, chopped
1 T fresh parsley, chopped
Juice of 1 lime
2 T extra virgin olive oil
Salt & black pepper, cracked fresh

PREPARATION:

In the bowl of a small food processor, combine the garlic, onion, cumin seeds, oregano, cilantro, parsley, lime juice, and olive oil, then purée.

Transfer the purée to a glass baking dish.

Place the chicken breasts in the marinade and turn to coat each side well.

Cover the dish and refrigerate for 1 hour, turning the chicken once or twice to marinate evenly.

Prepare your grill or skillet for medium heat.

Remove the baking dish from the refrigerator and transfer the chicken breasts to a clean platter.

Salt & pepper each side of the breasts.

Grill the chicken over medium heat until cooked, but juicy, about 5 minutes per side.

Serve hot or serve cold as a sandwich.

Boliche

— FROM "The Wind is in from Africa"
in WHERE IS JOE MERCHANT? / P. 119

Atop the stove behind the counter at La Taza de Oro, near the intersection of Miami's First Avenue and First Street, the big aluminum pots of BLACK BEANS and BOLICHE were about all that Trevor Kane could see from her perch at the counter. Hungry as she was, she should have ordered some of this as she waited for her shyster cousin, Hackney Brimstone III, but she didn't. And that's her loss. To say that this dish is like a Cuban pot roast is to deny the meal its due.

For starters, the cut of beef is much better than that used in a Yankee Pot Roast; the spices in the chorizo cannot be duplicated by themselves; and the potatoes do more to thicken the pot than to remain as potatoes. This is generally served with YELLOW RICE.

INGREDIENTS:

2 lbs eye of the round cut of beef
3 links of chorizo sausage
1 T olive oil
2 24-oz cans of tomato sauce
2 bay leaves
1 t oregano

½ T basil

¼ c olive oil

1 garlic clove, mashed

4 red potatoes, skins on & quartered

¼ c green olives

PREPARATION:

With a sharp knife, cut several slits in the beef, then stuff each slit with the chorizo.

In a large pot, heat the 2 T of olive oil, then brown all sides of the beef.

When the meat has been browned, add the tomato sauce, bay leaves, oregano, basil, ¼c of olive oil and the mashed garlic, but be certain to place the potatoes and the green olives on top.

Add just enough water to cover the potatoes, then bring the pot to the boil.

Reduce the heat, cover, and simmer the boliche over low heat until the meat is completely tender, at least 4 hours.

Carefully transfer the meat and potatoes to a large serving platter.

Chili Cheese Dog

Yields 24 servings.

— FROM "Take Another Road"
in TALES FROM MARGARITAVILLE / P. 42

See, I told you there was more to Paradise than 'burgers and 'ritas. So, now it's time to belly up to a beer and grab yourself a CHILI CHEESE DOG. Once you've got this CONEY ISLAND SAUCE made, then the rest is relatively easy. Perhaps the most difficult step in this whole procedure is making certain that you've ground your ground beef a full 3 times in order to get the right sawdust-like consistency that yields all the flavor of the beef in a much smoother sauce.

Generally speaking, these hot dogs are steamed, then served in a steamed bun with the cheese, chopped onion, and mustard on the side.

This sauce can also be used for the CHILI CHEESE-BURGER that Jimmy writes about.

INGREDIENTS:

1½ lbs lean beef, ground 3 times

3 T chili powder

1 T salt

1 t black pepper, cracked fresh

2 onions, minced

1½ t garlic powder

4 drops Crystal® sauce
1 23-oz can tomato juice

PREPARATION:

Let me repeat the fact that you absolutely *must* have the beef ground 3 times in a grinder, not a food processor.

In a pot, brown the ground beef over high heat.

Stir in the chili powder, salt, pepper, onion, garlic salt, Crystal®, and tomato juice.

Reduce the heat and cook the sauce slowly for at least 2 hours.

To serve, slather all over a steamed hot dog in a steamed bun.

Garnish with onions and mustard.

Roast Chicken

Yields 4 servings

— FROM "Sometimes I Feel Like A Rudderless Child"
in TALES FROM MARGARITAVILLE / P. 218

First impressions can sometimes be deceiving, and that's the case with this recipe. If you're looking here for a lot of razzle-dazzle herbs, spices, oils, sauces, and rubs, then you're going to be disappointed. But this chicken not only tastes wonderful, but also remains crispy on the outside and juicy on the inside. It's great served hot, or packed cold for those sails when the wind just dies.

INGREDIENTS:

1 3-lb chicken
Salt & fresh cracked black pepper
2 small limes, washed well and dried
2 garlic cloves, peeled

PREPARATION:
Preheat your oven to 350° F.

Thoroughly wash, drain, and dry the chicken.

Remove any excess pieces of fat, then season the chicken inside and out with salt & pepper.

Roll the limes back and forth under pressure of your palm to release the juices and oils within. With a knife, poke each lime in at least 20 places.

Insert the limes and the garlic into the cavity of the chicken, then seal the cavity with toothpicks. Tie the leg knuckles together with butcher's twine. All this trussing and sealing causes the crispy skin to puff up and separate from the meat.

Set the chicken breast-side down in a roasting pan, then place the pan in the upper third of the oven and roast for 30 minutes.

With an oven mitt, remove the pan from the oven, then turn the chicken carefully onto its back. Do not baste the chicken. Return the pan to the oven and roast another 30 minutes.

Increase the oven temperature to 400° F, then roast the chicken 20 more minutes.

With an oven mitt, remove the roasting pan from the oven. Spoon the juices over the chicken and allow the bird to rest for 10 minutes before carving.

Serve hot or cold.

Fried Chicken

Yields 4 servings

— FROM "Life is Just a Tire Swing" on A1A

— FROM "Folly Chasing Death" in A Pirate Looks at Fifty / p. 36

There are 3 key aspects to making *true* Southern FRIED CHICKEN. The first is to have 2 large seasoned, cast iron skillets. The second is to have buttermilk. And the third is to have the patience and foresight to prepare this traditional recipe with care. If you can bring all of these into your galley, then all of your guests will leave with a smile on their faces.

INGREDIENTS:

2 c buttermilk
¼ t salt
½ t black pepper, ground fresh
¼ t cayenne, ground fresh
1 chicken, dissembled into 2 wings, 2 thighs, 2 legs, 4 pieces of breast*
1¼ c all-purpose flour
1½ t salt
1¼ t black pepper, ground fresh
1¼ t cayenne, ground fresh
Solid vegetable shortening for frying

PREPARATION:

At least 10 hours before frying:

In a shallow, non-metal baking dish, combine the buttermilk, salt, ½ t of black pepper, and the ¼ t of cayenne. Mix well with your fingers.

Add the chicken to the mixture and toss with your fingers to coat the pieces well.

Cover the dish tightly with plastic wrap and refrigerate at least 8 hours. During this time, you should turn the pieces over once or twice.

Two hours before frying:

Remove the baking dish from the refrigerator and place the pieces of chicken on a rack to drain. They should remain moist enough to allow the next dry ingredients to stick to the chicken.

In a large plastic bag, combine the flour, salt, 1¼ t black pepper, and the 1¼ t cayenne.

Toss each piece in the bag of dry ingredients until it is well coated, then set the pieces on a clean, dry rack.

When you've coated each piece, repeat the procedure again to give each piece a second coating. This time, shake off any excess flour.

Allow the coated chicken to sit for 2 hours at room temperature.

For frying:

Place enough solid vegetable shortening in each skillet to create a ½-inch depth when it melts and reaches 360° F.

Keeping in mind that the temperature of the oil will drop dramatically if you add too much chicken too soon. And keeping in mind that it will take the pieces of thigh and leg meats longer to fry, carefully add the chicken to each skillet.

The temperature of the oil should remain between 300° F and 320° F.

Plan to cook the chicken for 10 to 12 minutes per side and to use tongs to turn the pieces only once.**

Cooked chicken should be a crispy dark brown and the juices from inside should run clear when the crust is pierced.

With the tongs, remove each piece from the skillet and place on clean paper towels to drain.

Serve hot, warm, or cold.

* If you're too damn lazy to keep track of all those parts and bones, then just use 2 lbs boneless chicken breasts that still have their skin; no skin, no crispy. This is not healthy sh*t.

**The boneless pieces will need only 4 to 5 minutes per side.

Country Ham

— FROM "Dreamsicle"
on VOLCANO

— FROM "Mambo on the Wind"
in WHERE IS JOE MERCHANT? / P. 302

Yields 4 servings

Urban ham is cured rather quickly and simply in great quantities, and the taste of the meat is quite bland; however, a COUNTRY HAM is one that's endured a long and deliberate process to earn that "country" label. In the rural sections of Virginia, Tennessee, Kentucky, and Georgia it's not uncommon for a ham to be first coated with salt and sugar, then refrigerated for 5 days; salted again and refrigerated a day for each pound of meat; washed and refrigerated yet another 2 weeks; smoked for 10 days; and finally aged for 6 to 12 months. By then, you don't need to read any label, you can taste that it's a COUNTRY HAM.

INGREDIENTS:

2 1-lb slices of country ham, ¼-inch-thick center cut
2 c milk
8 T black coffee
1 t sugar

PREPARATION:

Overnight, soak slices of COUNTRY HAM in the 2 c of milk to remove some of the saltiness.

Rinse the milk from the ham slices and pat the meat dry. Trim any outside fat from the slices, then dice the fat.

In a large skillet, render the diced fat over medium-high heat until the remaining pieces are brown and crisp.

Drain the fat from the skillet and reserve the browned cracklings.

Place the slices of COUNTRY HAM in your skillet and fry them until they are browned on both sides.

Remove the ham slices from the skillet and transfer them to a warm platter.

Add the black coffee to the skillet and deglaze the pan. Allow the coffee to come to the boil, then reduce the heat and add the sugar and the cracklings to the skillet.

Cover and cook another 2 minutes.

Serve the ham and RED EYE GRAVY hot with GRITS and BISCUITS.

Chicken Fried Steak

Yields 4 servings

— from "Take Another Road"
IN TALES FROM MARGARITAVILLE / P. 28

Tell me this meal isn't the best of all worlds: red meat fried in a nice heavy batter, then topped with gravy! Whenever I eat this I do believe that I've sunk into heaven, because I'd never be able to float anywhere with this in my gullet.

More often than not, CHICKEN FRIED STEAK (aka COUNTRY FRIED STEAK) is *not* served with FRENCH FRIED POTATOES, but with mashed potato, as well as BISCUITS to soak up that great WHITE GRAVY. It's a sure way of losing one's religion.

INGREDIENTS:

4 8-oz cube steaks
4 T meat tenderizer
½ c all-purpose flour
Salt & cracked pepper, to taste
½ c vegetable oil

For the gravy:
2 T all-purpose flour
4 c milk

PREPARATION:

Under cold running water, rinse the cube steaks clean of any packaging juices, but do not dry.

Place the steaks on a dish, then sprinkle each side of the steaks with the meat tenderizer.

In a large skillet, heat the oil over medium-high temperature so that it becomes hot without smoking.

In a shallow bowl, combine the flour, salt & pepper.

Dredge each steak in the flour mix to coat them generously.

Carefully place the steaks in the oil and fry until golden brown on each side. Turn each steak only once.

Cover your skillet and allow the steaks to cook through, about 4 minutes.

Remove each steak from the skillet and drain on paper towels.

Drain all but 1 T of the oil from the skillet and take care not to remove any particles of flour or meat.

Sprinkle the flour into the oil and stir until the oil has absorbed the flour and made a roux.

Gradually add the milk to the roux and continue to stir.

For the gravy to thicken, you *must* allow the milk to come to the boil, then reduce the heat and allow it to cook the flour, about 5 minutes.

Continue to add milk to maintain the consistency you wish.

Keeping in mind that this gravy is close to the boiling point, carefully taste the gravy, then adjust the seasonings with salt & pepper.

To serve, place a fried steak on each plate along with a good mound of mashed potatoes, then smother it all with gravy.

Cuban Pork

— FROM "The Skies Over Cuba"
in A PIRATE LOOKS AT FIFTY / P. 130

Yields 4 servings

Most people who haven't tasted any Cuban cuisine tend to assume that it is the same as Mexican, but this recipe should put an end to that misconception. This is the way they make CUBAN PORK at the New Orleans Margaritaville Cafe, where it's served up alongside BLACK BEANS and YELLOW RICE, then topped with SPANISH ONION RINGS. I guarantee that you'll never forget the meal.

INGREDIENTS:

5 lbs pork loin, boneless
¼ c vegetable oil
1 c onion, chopped
2 garlic cloves, minced
1 c orange juice
½ c lime juice
4 T fresh parsley, chopped
1 T oregano
¼ t salt
¼ t cracked black pepper
¼ c clarified butter

PREPARATION:

Trim any excess fat from the pork loin, then slice into ¼-inch thick medallions.

In a glass baking dish, combine the vegetable oil, onion, garlic, orange juice, lime juice, parsley, oregano, salt & pepper. Stir well.

Place the pork medallions in the baking dish and coat well with the marinade. Allow the pork to marinate for 2 hours.

In a hot skillet, sear the pork in clarified butter for 1½ to 2 minutes per side.

Serve hot with BLACK BEANS, YELLOW RICE, and SPANISH ONION RINGS.

Meatloaf Sandwich

Yields 1 loaf

— FROM "Shelter in the Storm"
in WHERE IS JOE MERCHANT? / P. 103

The Margaritaville Cafe at Universal Studios in Orlando draws upon Jimmy's own recipe for MEATLOAF, which is actually another Cuban dish. Large enough to be served with side dishes as an entree, this recipe will provide you at least 4 good-sized sandwiches.

INGREDIENTS:

>   2½ lbs beef, ground
>   2½ lbs pork butt, ground
>   1 c fresh bread crumbs
>   4 large eggs
>   ½ c ketchup
>   ½ c onion, chopped
>   ½ t white pepper, cracked
>   1 t salt
>   1 oz Tony's seasoning
>   ¼ c milk
>   ¼ c fresh parsley, chopped
>   8 slices CUBAN BREAD

PREPARATION:

Preheat your oven to 350° F.

In a large mixing bowl, combine the meat, bread crumbs, eggs, ketchup, onion, pepper, salt, Tony's seasoning, milk, and parsley. Mix only enough to combine the ingredients.

Lightly oil a 9-inch loaf pan.

Transfer the mixture from the bowl to the pan, then cover the pan with aluminum foil.

Place the pan on the center rack of your oven and bake for 1½ hours.

With an oven mitt, remove the meatloaf from the oven and cool to room temperature.

When the meatloaf has cooled, transfer it to a cutting board and slice to desired thickness.

Serve on CUBAN BREAD.

Picadillo

— FROM *"The Skies Over Cuba"*
in A PIRATE LOOKS AT FIFTY / P. 129

Yields 4 servings

Though it has several variations, a recipe for this Cuban-style hash (pronounced: PEEK-a -DEE-yo) *must* include beef (either shredded or ground), as well as tomatoes and garlic. This second recipe has a sweet & sour taste, but BLACK BEANS and YELLOW RICE are natural side dishes for both.

PICADILLO I

Yields 4 servings

INGREDIENTS:

¼ c olive oil
1 large onion, diced
1 large green bell pepper, seeded & chopped fine
2 garlic cloves, minced
½ t cayenne
2 lbs beef, ground
3 tomatoes, peeled, seeded & chopped
½ t ground cumin
2 T capers
Salt & cracked black pepper, to taste

PREPARATION:

In a large saucepan, heat the oil.

Add the onion, green pepper, garlic, and cayenne, then sauté until the onions are soft, about 5 minutes.

Add the beef to the saucepan and mash in with the other ingredients.

When these first ingredients begin to resemble a Sloppy Joe, add the tomatoes and cumin.

Cover, reduce the heat, and simmer 15 minutes.

Stir the capers into the saucepan and simmer 5 more minutes.

Taste and adjust seasonings with salt & pepper.

Serve hot.

PICADILLO II

Yields 4 servings

INGREDIENTS:

¼ c olive oil

3 c potatoes, peeled & diced

2 onions, chopped

1 green pepper, seeded & diced

2 lbs ground round

3 c tomatoes, peeled, seeded & diced

2 garlic cloves, minced

2 t salt

Fresh cracked black pepper, to taste

¼ c pimento-stuffed green olives, chopped

1 T brown sugar

¼ c vinegar

1 T capers

½ c red wine

PREPARATION:

In a large saucepan, heat the oil.

Add the potatoes and sauté until lightly browned.

With a slotted spoon, remove the potatoes and allow to drain on a paper towel.

Add the onion and pepper, then sauté until brown.

Add to the saucepan the ground round of beef, tomatoes, salt, garlic, and black pepper. Cook until the meat has browned and broken into smaller pieces.

Return the potatoes to the saucepan, along with the green olives, brown sugar, vinegar, capers, and red wine.

Stir, then reduce the heat and simmer until the meat is tender, about 30 minutes.

Serve hot.

Jamaican Jerk Roasts

Yields 4 servings

— FROM "Jamaica Mistaica"
on BANANA WIND

— FROM "Let's Blame It All on the Weather"
in WHERE IS JOE MERCHANT? / P. 34

As amazing as the French language sometimes appears to me, nothing delights me more than the flexibility of English. When it gets exported to the Caribbean, though, it tends to lose a bit in the translation. For example, at home Americans are very comfortable interchanging the words "jerk" and "dope." In Jamaica, though, the words exist in a world of their own. I can assure you that this JAMAICAN JERK contains no Jamaican dope. Then, again, I suppose it *could* happen.

INGREDIENTS:

¼ c allspice berries, toasted
1½-inch piece of cinnamon, broken
1 t fresh nutmeg, milled
6 whole scallions, sliced
1 Scotch bonnet pepper, seeded
Salt
Fresh cracked black pepper
1 T dark Jamaican rum

PREPARATION:

In a small skillet, shake the allspice berries over medium-high temperature until they are toasted, about 10 minutes.

When the berries are toasted, remove the skillet from the heat and transfer them to a spice mill. Add the broken piece of cinnamon and the nutmeg, then grind together the 3 ingredients.

Transfer the milled spices to the bowl of your food processor, along with the scallions and the Scotch bonnet pepper.

Add salt & pepper to the ingredients, then process into a paste.

Transfer the paste to a small mixing bowl, then mix in the rum.

Allow this paste to sit at least 1 hour before using, or else cover tightly and refrigerate.

Because of the Scotch bonnet pepper, you might want to wear rubber gloves whenever you apply the rub to a meat.

JERK PASTE II

4 garlic cloves, chopped
12 scallions (entire), chopped
4 Scotch bonnet peppers, seeded & diced
1 T black pepper, cracked fresh
1½ t salt
1 T fresh ginger, grated
2 sprigs of fresh thyme
¾ t allspice (pimento beans)
½ t nutmeg, grated
1 T Worcestershire sauce
4 T fresh squeezed lime juice
4 T cane vinegar
3 T brown sugar

PREPARATION:

Add all of the ingredients to the bowl of your food processor, then process into a paste.

Transfer the paste to a small mixing bowl, then allow to sit at least 1 hour before using, or else cover tightly and refrigerate.

BECAUSE OF THE SCOTCH BONNET PEPPER, YOU MIGHT WANT TO WEAR RUBBER GLOVES WHENEVER YOU APPLY THE RUB TO A MEAT.

JERK PORK

Yields 4 servings

INGREDIENTS:

JAMAICAN JERK *paste*
1 4-lb boneless pork loin

PREPARATION:

Wearing rubber gloves, rub the jerk seasoning over the entire surface of the pork.

Place the pork in a glass baking dish, then cover with plastic wrap and allow to marinate at room temperature for at least 1 hour.

Preheat your oven to 400° F.

Transfer the marinated pork to a roasting pan, then place the pan on the center rack of your oven and roast the pork for 30 minutes.

Reduce your oven temperature to 350° F, baste the pork, and roast for another 1½ hours. Baste the pork every 30 minutes.

With an oven thermometer, check the internal temperature of the pork.

When the pork is roasted to your liking, use an oven mitt to remove the baking dish.

Allow the pork to rest 5 minutes before carving.

JERK CHICKEN

Yields 4 servings

INGREDIENTS:

4 halved frying chickens, skin on
JAMAICAN JERK *paste*

PREPARATION:

Wearing rubber gloves, rub the jerk seasoning over the entire surface of the 4 pieces of chicken.

Place the chicken in a glass baking dish, then cover with plastic wrap. Refrigerate overnight.

Preheat your oven to 350° F.

Transfer the chicken to a roasting pan, then place the pan on the center rack of your oven and roast for 1 hour or until the juices in the chicken run clear when the skin is pierced. Baste the chicken every 30 minutes

When the chicken is roasted to your liking, use an oven mitt to remove the roasting pan from your oven.

Serve hot or warm.

Cuban Sandwich

Yields 4 sandwiches

— FROM "Islands in the Stream"
in A PIRATE LOOKS AT FIFTY / P. 133

While restaurants do have a special press to make these CUBAN MIX sandwiches, you can make them either with the griddle portion of a waffle iron, or else with two frying pans. If you use the latter method, one of the two *must* be a heavy cast iron pan heated to toast the top of the sandwich. Without question, however, this sandwich can only be made with CUBAN BREAD, which also comes in a small size, not unlike a BAGUETTE.

INGREDIENTS:

4 individual loaves of CUBAN BREAD
4 T butter
1 lb CUBAN ROAST PORK, *shaved*
1 lb smoked ham, shaved
½ lb Swiss cheese, sliced
1 c sliced dill pickles

PREPARATION:

Assuming that you do not have a sandwich press available, preheat both of your 2 frying pans.

Slice each loaf of bread lengthwise and generously butter the insides *and* the outsides.

On each loaf, place a layer of pork, then ham, then cheese, and then pickles.

Fold each loaf closed.

Place the loaves in one heated frying pan, then place the other heated pan on top to flatten them.

Grill them until each is golden brown, about 2 to 3 minutes, then turn them over and grill the other side. Though the top pan will not grill the top for you, it will flatten and toast it enough to prepare it to be flipped.

Remove the sandwiches from the pan, slice, and serve hot.

Tampico Broil

Yields 4 servings

— FROM *"Boomerang Love"*
in TALES FROM MARGARITAVILLE / P. 98

INGREDIENTS:

1¼ lbs sirloin steak
½ c gold tequila
½ c orange juice concentrate
½ c lime juice
1 T fresh ginger, grated
¼ fresh cilantro, chopped
1 garlic clove, chopped
¼ t red pepper flakes, crushed

PREPARATION:

In a glass dish, combine the tequila, orange concentrate, lime juice, ginger, cilantro, garlic, and pepper flakes. Place the sirloin in the marinade, turn to coat well, then refrigerate overnight.

Preheat your oven to broil, then cook the sirloin to the desired doneness.

Slice the steak thinly against the grain and serve with PAPAYA-PEPPER SALSA.

CATCH OF THE DAY

Crab Farci ✤ Flying Fish Sandwich
Shark Sandwich ✤ Po'boy Sandwich
Oyster Loaf ✤ Oyster & Bacon Casserole
Grilled Lobster ✤ Shrimp Boil
Trout Meunière ✤ Pompano en Papillote
Snapper Fried Light ✤ Lobster & Coconut
Fried Grouper Fingers ✤ Crab Cakes
Fried Shrimp ✤ Grilled Salmon
Striped Bass with Lobster Sauce
Sushi in the Mall

Crab Farci

— FROM "I Wish Lunch Could Last Forever"
in TALES FROM MARGARITAVILLE / P. 155

Yields 4 servings

Yes, this is the way the French say "stuffed crab," or *Crabes Farcis* on Martinique, the homeland of Isabella Rivière. It's no surprise, then, that the dish made its way onto her menu at Chéz Bar-B-Q Hill. When/if you do get to Martinique or Guadeloupe, be certain to bring home a bottle of *rhum vieux* for the crowning touch to this dish.

INGREDIENTS:

4 2-lb hardshell crabs, cooked
1½ c fresh bread crumbs
1 Scotch bonnet pepper, seeded & chopped
3 T fresh chives, chopped
2 T fresh parsley, chopped
2 garlic cloves, crushed
1 T lime juice
¼ t allspice
3 T good dark rum or rhum vieux
Salt & fresh cracked black pepper, to taste
4 T butter

PREPARATION:

Remove the legs and claws from the cooked crabs. Crack the shells of the legs and claws, remove the meat, and reserve in a clean mixing bowl. Discard the shells.

Remove and discard the soft belly shells and the spongy gills from the crab bodies. Remove the meat from the backs and place in the bowl with the reserved leg and claw meat.

Scrub the empty back shells and rinse them clean. Set them aside to dry.

In a large mixing bowl, combine the bread crumbs, pepper, chives, parsley, garlic, lime juice, allspice, and dark rum. Set aside.

Preheat your oven to 350° F.

Chop fine the crabmeat and add to the bowl of other mixed ingredients.

Mix, taste, and adjust the seasonings with salt & pepper.

Divide the crab mixture equally among the 4 clean shells, then top each with 1 T of butter.

Place on a baking sheet, then place on the middle rack of your oven.

Bake until golden brown, about 30 minutes.

With an oven mitt, remove the baking sheet from the oven.

Serve hot.

BEACH FIRE STUFFED CRABS

Yields 4 servings

Essentially the same as CRAB FARCI, these are a treat worth preparing for any throwback shell beach party. Another bad habit, they go well with rum, cooked animals, and bullsh*t by the ton.

INGREDIENTS:

> 4 2-lb hardshell crabs, cooked
> 1 c celery, chopped fine
> ½ c onion, chopped fine
> 1 c green bell pepper, seeded & chopped fine
> 2 jalapeño peppers, seeded & chopped fine
> ½ c mayonnaise
> Juice of 1 key lime
> Salt and fresh black pepper, to taste
> ½ c seasoned bread crumbs
> 1 c cheddar cheese, shredded

PREPARATION:

Remove the legs and claws from the cooked crabs. Crack the shells of the legs and claws, remove the meat, and reserve in a clean mixing bowl. Discard the shells.

Remove and discard the soft belly shells and the spongy gills from the crab bodies. Remove the meat from the backs and place in the bowl with the reserved leg and claw meat.

Scrub the empty back shells and rinse them clean. Set them aside to dry.

In a large mixing bowl, combine the celery, onion, green bell pepper, jalapeno pepper, mayonnaise, and lime juice. Set aside.

Light your fire/grill and bring to a medium hot heat.

Chop fine the crabmeat and add to the bowl of other mixed ingredients.

Mix, taste, and adjust the seasonings with salt & pepper.

Divide the crab mixture equally among the 4 scrubbed shells, then cover each equally with the bread crumbs and shredded cheese.

Wrap each crab loosely in aluminum foil with a small steam vent on the top.

Place the wrapped crabs, vent side up, on your grill, then allow them to cook for 20 minutes.

With an oven mitt or a pair of tongs, remove the crabs from the grill. Be careful that you do not burn yourself with any steam escaping from the wrapped foil.

Serve hot.

Flying Fish Sandwich

Yields 4 sandwiches

— FROM "Are You Ready for Freddy?"
in TALES FROM MARGARITAVILLE / P. 179

Okay, so you didn't have much luck on the water today and your fish market is all out of flying fish. Jeez, I hate when *that* happens. But if you need to improvise, any white, flaky fish fillet will be a worthy substitute.

INGREDIENTS:

4 flying fish fillets
1 onion, sliced thin
1 green pepper, seeded & chopped
1 blade of chive, chopped
1 T fresh thyme, chopped
1 T fresh parsley, chopped
Salt & fresh cracked black pepper
Juice of ½ lime
1 c all-purpose flour
1 egg, beaten
3 c fresh bread crumbs
Solid vegetable shortening, for frying
8 slices BAHAMA BREAD
1 lime, quartered

PREPARATION:

In a small mixing bowl, combine the onion, pepper, chive, thyme, parsley, salt & pepper, and lime juice.

Place the fish fillets in a shallow glass baking dish, then cover them with the ingredients from the bowl. Turn once to coat the fillets well.

Allow this to stand 1 hour at room temperature.

In a heavy skillet, melt enough solid shortening over medium heat to create ¼ inch of hot oil.

Dredge each fillet in the flour, then shake to remove any excess.

Dip each fillet in the beaten egg, then dredge in the bread crumbs.

Fry the fillets gently in the oil until both sides are a light golden brown, about 10 minutes.

Serve each fillet as a sandwich, garnished with a lime wedge.

Shark Sandwich

Yields 4 sandwiches

— FROM *"Que Pasa?"*
in TALES FROM MARGARITAVILLE / P. 327

While I love MAKO SHARK as a sandwich served on BAHAMA BREAD, there's no reason why you couldn't just serve it up as a dinner entrée, along with RICE & BEANS or even FRENCH FRIED POTATOES. But that just means you need to dirty-up some dishes and tableware, and that always tends to confuse me. Is it *forks to the left* or *forks to the right?*

INGREDIENTS:

> *Juice of 2 limes*
> *6 T olive oil*
> *2 T fresh ginger, peeled & grated*
> *4 garlic cloves, minced*
> *4 scallions, chopped*
> *Salt & fresh black pepper, to taste*
> *4 6-oz mako shark steaks*
> *8 slices* BAHAMA BREAD

PREPARATION:

In a glass baking dish, combine the lime juice, olive oil, ginger, garlic, and scallions. Stir together well, then taste and adjust the seasonings with salt & fresh ground pepper.

Place the mako steaks in the baking dish and turn several times to cover well with the marinade.

Allow the shark steaks to marinate for 30 minutes at room temperature.

Prepare your grill or cast iron skillet. If you use hardwood, allow the embers to gray before placing your steaks on the grill. If you use a skillet, allow it to become hot over medium heat.

Remove the shark steaks from the marinade and place on your grill or in your skillet.

Allow the steaks to cook for 3 minutes on the first side, before you turn them to cook for 3 minutes on the other side.

Serve each mako steak on fresh BAHAMA BREAD.

Po'boy Sandwich

Yields 4 sandwiches

— FROM "The Pascagoula Run"
in TALES FROM MARGARITAVILLE / P. 132

Don't let anyone tell you otherwise. In New Orleans, a PO'BOY is a sandwich of fried oysters, dressed and served on FRENCH BREAD or a BAGUETTE. Anything else, might be a hoagy, a hero, or a sub, but a PO'BOY *must* be oysters! This is the way they make a PO'BOY at Margaritaville Cafe in New Orleans, then they serve it with FRENCH FRIED POTATOES.

INGREDIENTS:

40 large oysters, shucked
2 c corn meal
4 T blackening seasoning
4 BAGUETTES or 4 8-inch lengths of FRENCH BREAD
2 c lettuce, shredded
1 tomato, sliced
3 c vegetable oil
4 T olive oil

PREPARATION:
In a heavy skillet, heat the vegetable oil to 350° F. and heat another skillet to grill the bread.

In a shallow dish, mix together the cornmeal and seasonings.

In small batches, dredge the oysters in the seasoned cornmeal, then shake them to remove any excess.

Carefully add small batches of the dredged oysters to the hot oil and fry until golden brown. Use a slotted spoon to turn the oysters in the oil, as well as to remove each batch to drain on paper towel.

Split each BAGUETTE and brush with olive oil, then grill them on your second skillet until the face of the bread is lightly golden.

Remove the split BAGUETTES from the skillet, place 10 oysters on the bottom half of each loaf, then dress each top half with lettuce and tomato.

Serve warm.

Oyster Loaf

— FROM "The Pascagoula Run"
in TALES FROM MARGARITAVILLE / P. 129

— FROM "J.D. and Me"
in A PIRATE LOOKS AT FIFTY / P. 161

Just as fine as that line between Saturday Night and Sunday Morning, so remains the slender one between an OYSTER LOAF and a PO'BOY. As you'll see below, there are some allowed variations. But if you stray too far, you've made something else altogether.

OYSTER LOAF I

Yields 4 servings

INGREDIENTS:

    24 oysters, shucked
    4 BAGUETTES
    ½ c butter, melted
    Crystal®, to taste
    Salt & fresh black pepper, to taste
    ½ c heavy cream

PREPARATION:

Preheat oven to 425° F.

Cut BAGUETTES lengthwise and remove the tops. With your fingers, hollow out the bottoms and leave about a ¼-inch shell of bread within the crust.

Brush the insides of the BAGUETTES with melted butter, then place them on a cookie sheet and bake in the oven until toasted golden, about 10 minutes.

In a medium skillet, add the remaining melted butter and sauté the oysters just until their edges curl, about 2 to 3 minutes.

Stir into the skillet the heavy cream, along with the Crystal® and the salt & pepper, to taste.

With an oven mitt, remove the toasted rolls from the oven.

Fill each hot BAGUETTE bottom with 6 oysters and as much cream sauce as you wish.

Cover the oysters with the tops of the BAGUETTES.

Serve hot.

OYSTER LOAF II

Yields 4 servings

INGREDIENTS:

1 *loaf* FRENCH BREAD
¼ c butter, melted
24 oysters, shucked
½ c all-purpose flour
2 eggs
1 c toasted bread crumbs
1 c vegetable oil

PREPARATION:
Preheat your oven to 400° F.

Slice the FRENCH BREAD lengthwise and remove the top. With your fingers, hollow out the bottom and leave about a ¼-inch shell of bread within the crust.

Brush the insides of the top and bottom of the bread with melted butter, then place it on a cookie sheet and bake in the oven until toasted golden, about 10 minutes.

In a cast iron skillet, heat the oil to 375° F.

Drain the oysters, then coat them with the flour, dip them in the egg wash, and dredge them in the bread crumbs.

Shake any excess crumbs from the oysters, then carefully place in oil. Fry them until they are a golden brown, about 3 to 4 minutes. Use a slotted spoon to turn them in the oil.

With a slotted spoon, remove the oysters from the hot oil and drain them on paper towel.

With an oven mitt, remove the toasted bread from the oven.

Fill the bottom of the loaf with the oysters, then cover them with the toasted top of the loaf.

Slice or break the loaf into 4 equal servings.

Serve hot.

Oyster & Bacon Casserole

— FROM "I Wish Lunch Could Last Forever"
in TALES FROM MARGARITAVILLE / P. 155

Yields 4 servings

Whether you serve this as an entrée with a salad and bread, or simply as an appetizer, you'll know why Jimmy finds it worth mentioning.

INGREDIENTS:

8 bacon slices, browned & crumbled
2 pts oysters, shucked & in their liquor
Dash of fresh cracked black pepper
4 c unsalted cracker crumbs
1½ c heavy cream
1 c unsalted butter, melted
½ c oyster liquor
1 t salt
½ t Worcestershire sauce

PREPARATION:

In a large skillet, render the bacon over medium-hot heat until browned and crisp.

With a slotted spoon, remove the bacon from the skillet and set aside on paper towel to drain.

Preheat your oven to 350° F.

Lightly butter a glass casserole, then spread the crumbs across the bottom.

Drain the oysters and reserve their liquor.

Spread a layer of oyster across the bottom of the casserole. Crumble the bacon and spread a layer atop the oysters. Spread the remaining crumbs, then season with pepper.

In a small mixing bowl, combine the cream, melted butter, Worcestershire sauce, salt & pepper.

Pour the combined liquids over the casserole.

Place the uncovered casserole on the center rack of your oven and bake for 40 minutes.

With an oven mitt, remove the casserole from your oven.

Serve hot.

Grilled Lobster

Yields 4 servings

— FROM "A Gift for the Buccaneer"
in TALES FROM MARGARITAVILLE / P. 213

— FROM "Kick the Tires and Light the Fires"
in A PIRATE LOOKS AT FIFTY / P. 117

Perhaps the most difficult part of grilling a lobster is not in the cooking, but in the splitting of the lobster before grilling. If you are squeamish about cutting into a live lobster, the crustacean can be put out of its perceived misery just before the splitting by inserting a sharp knife about 1 inch deep between the eyes. If that bothers you, too, then I suggest you not make this recipe.

INGREDIENTS:

> 4 1½- to 2-lbs lobsters
> 1 c butter, softened
> Juice of 2 key limes
> ½ t Crystal®
> 2 t scallion (white part only), chopped
> 1 t fresh chive, chopped
> ¼ t fresh paprika
> Sea salt, to taste
> Fresh cracked black pepper, to taste
> 2 t cayenne

PREPARATION:

At least 6 hours before grilling the lobsters, prepare the lime butter that will be used to finish the lobster on the grill.

In a small mixing bowl, combine the softened butter with the lime juice, Crystal®, scallion, chives, paprika, sea salt, and pepper.

Transfer the butter mixture to the center of a square piece of plastic wrap, then wrap tightly into the shape of a hockey puck and chill in the refrigerator for at least 6 hours.

Prepare a medium-hot grill.

With a sharp chef's knife, split the lobster lengthwise, then separate the halves. Dust the cut side of each half with cayenne pepper.

Place the 8 halves, shell side up, on the grill and cook until the meat is white, about 10 minutes.

With tongs or an oven mitt, turn the lobster halves over and place slices of the chilled lime butter upon the exposed sections of cooked meat. Grill the lobsters another 3 minutes.

Serve hot.

Shrimp Boil

— FROM *"Margaritaville"*
on CHANGES IN LATITUDE, CHANGES IN ATTITUDE

Yields 4 servings

Of course, this one's right out of the national anthem, so you ought to know how it's done at the Margaritaville Cafe. There are those who will argue whether shrimp ought to be boiled or steamed, but the focus should be upon this simple truth: cooked shrimp should not be *over*-cooked shrimp. This recipe is based upon a 26/30 count shrimp, meaning there are 26 to 30 shrimp in a pound.

INGREDIENTS:

> 4 dozen uncooked shrimp, shell-on
> 1 c cabernet
> 2 qts water
> 3 celery ribs
> 1 onion, quartered
> 1 lemon, halved
> 1½ t cayenne
> 1½ t red pepper flakes, crushed
> 1 T kosher salt
> 2 garlic cloves, crushed

PREPARATION:

In a large pot, combine the cabernet, water, celery, onion, lemon, cayenne, red pepper flakes, salt, and garlic, then bring to the boil.

Carefully add all of the shrimp to the pot, then cook until they begin to float on the boiling surface, their shells turn pink, and the meat is just translucent.

With potholders, carefully drain the shrimp with a colander, then place in a large, heatproof bowl.

Serve hot.

Trout Meunière

— FROM "I Wish Lunch Could Last Forever"
IN TALES FROM MARGARITAVILLE / P. 151

Believe it or not, Julia Child showed me how to make this dish. One Saturday morning at 7, I just happened to see a PBS re-run (*ca.* 1960s) of Julia preparing TROUT MEUNIÈRE. My reaction was mixed: so *that's* the way it's done, but nothing could be more simple. Meanwhile, I also had a Dan Ackroyd *Saturday Night* flashback (*ca.* 1970s) when the Not Ready for Prime Time Player was cooking up a riotous send-up of Julia one minute, then pitching the *Bass-O-Matic* the next. Talk about classics!

So, here's a variation of this classic French dish presented more in the mode of Julia than *a la* Ackroyd. *Bon appètit!*

INGREDIENTS:

> 4 whole 8-oz trout, dressed
> Salt & fresh cracked black pepper
> ½ c all-purpose flour
> ¾ c clarified butter
> Juice of ½ lemon
> ¼ c fresh parsley, chopped

PREPARATION:

Whether you leave the heads and tails on each trout is your personal decision; however, most chefs do leave them on.

Rinse each dressed trout under cold running water, then pat dry.

Sprinkle the insides of each with salt & fresh black pepper, then close the body cavity. Dust the outside of the fish with flour.

In a large skillet, heat the clarified butter on a medium stove until bubbling hot. It is important that you be able to maintain this heat without browning the butter.

Place the dusted trout in the skillet and slowly sauté them about 5 minutes per side. Use a spatula to carefully turn each trout only once. When done, the trout should have no rosy red color deep in the body cavities, but they should still be juicy.

Place a trout on each dinner plate, then squeeze lemon juice upon the fish and dust with parsley. Drizzling the hot butter remaining in the skillet over the trout should make the parsley sizzle.

Pompano en Papillote

Yields 4 servings

— FROM "I Wish Lunch Could Last Forever"
in TALES FROM MARGARITAVILLE / P. 151

Once again, we must pay homage to the father & son team of chefs, Antoine and Jules Alciatore, who not only created this dish, but have made it a signature of New Orleans.

Created by son Jules to honor the Brazilian balloonist Alberto Santos-Dumont, this popular recipe for POMPANO EN PAPILLOTE is a variation of his father Antoine's Pompano Montgolfier, which was originally created to honor two French brothers, Joseph Michel and Jacques Étienne Montgolfier, who invented ballooning in 1783 when they filled a linen bag with hot air. In fact, famed movie director Cecil B. DeMille so loved this dish that he managed to write it into his script for his 1937 motion picture, *The Pirate's Lady*. Food and movie critics alike are quick to point out that the movie was set in a New Orleans that was well ahead of the founding of Antoine's restuarant. Still, you'll give this one four thumbs up.

INGREDIENTS:

4 8-oz fillets of pompano

For the sauce:

    3 T butter

    1 c scallion, chopped

    1 c uncooked shrimp, peeled & deveined

    1 c white wine

    1 c crab meat, cleaned & picked

    2 c fish velouté sauce

    Salt & fresh black pepper, to taste

    Cayenne

For the poaching liquid:

    2 c water

    1 onion, sliced

    2 t salt

    5 black peppercorns, whole

    ½ c white wine

    2 bay leaves

    Juice of 1 lemon

For the papillotes:

    4 10- by 14- inch pieces of parchment

PREPARATION:

Of the sauce:

In a large skillet, melt the butter over medium heat, then add the chopped scallion and sauté until wilted, about 3 minutes.

Add the shrimp and the white wine, then bring to the boil.

Stir in the crab meat, fish velouté sauce, then add a dash of salt, fresh black pepper, and cayenne.

Reduce the heat and allow to simmer 10 minutes.

When the sauce has finished simmering, remove it from the heat and allow it to cool.

Of the poaching liquid:

In a separate skillet, combine the water, sliced onion, salt, peppercorns, wine, bay leaves, and lemon juice, then bring to the boil.

Reduce the heat and add the pompano, then cover and allow the fillets to poach for 5 minutes.

Of the papillote:

Preheat your oven to 400° F.

Lightly butter the 4 pieces of parchment paper.

Place 1 fillet on each sheet of parchment paper.

Spread equal portions of the sauce atop each fillet, then fold the parchment paper and seal tightly, crimping the edges all around to keep the envelope airtight.

Place the papillotes on a baking sheet, then bake on the center rack of your oven until the paper turns brown, about 15 minutes.

With an oven mitt, remove the baking sheet from your oven.

Place 1 papillote on each dinner plate, along with lemon wedges for garnish.

Snapper Fried Light

Yields 4 servings

— FROM "Landfall"
on CHANGES IN LATITUDE, CHANGES IN ATTITUDE

The taste of SNAPPER FRIED LIGHT is what you get with this recipe for the delicate flavor of this fish. Keeping the skin on each fillet will not only help you handle the fish in the pan, but also enhance the flavor. The thickness of the fillets will determine the temperature for cooking. A ½-inch thick fillet needs only 4 minutes in the pan and should be turned after the first 2 minutes.

INGREDIENTS:

> 4 8-oz red snapper fillets
> Salt & fresh cracked black pepper, to taste
> 4 t pure olive oil
> 3 T sherry vinegar
> 3 T extra virgin olive oil
> 1 T fresh parsley, chopped
> 1 T fresh chives, chopped

PREPARATION:

Inspect each fillet for bones, scales, or anything else you don't want to eat.

Season both sides of each snapper fillet with salt & pepper.

In a large sauté pan, heat the pure olive oil over medium temperature.

Add the snapper fillets, then adjust the heat. Thicker fillets will require lower heat.

After the 4 minutes of frying, remove the fillets to a heated platter and keep warm.

Wipe clean your sauté pan with a paper towel, then add the sherry vinegar, extra virgin olive oil, and herbs. Increase the heat until this sauce comes to the rapid boil, then remove the pan from the heat.

Place a fillet of red snapper on each plate, then spoon sauce over each.

Serve hot.

Lobster & Coconut

Yields 4 servings

— FROM "That Time-Bomb Look"
IN WHERE IS JOE MERCHANT? / P. 272

Though I doubt that the local Indians on Little Lorraine who served Frank Bama coconuts and lobster did so in this manner, you could always just get yourself a coconut and a lobster, then eat them on the beach. But if you're going to be in a kitchen, I suggest you give this version a try.

INGREDIENTS:

4 1½-lb lobsters, cooked, cleaned & cut in pieces
½ c milk
1 c cream of coconut
1 small onion, chopped fine
2 scallions, chopped fine
2 sprigs fresh thyme
2 T curry powder
Salt & fresh cracked white pepper, to taste
Dash of cayenne
½ c fresh Parmesan cheese, grated
1 lime, quartered

PREPARATION:

Preheat your oven to 400° F.

In a large saucepan, combine the milk and cream of coconut over medium heat, then add the onion, scallions, thyme, and curry powder, then stir.

Continue to stir as you cook this mixture for 5 minutes.

Add to the saucepan the lobster meat, salt, pepper, and cayenne, then cook another 7 minutes so that the flavors can blend.

Transfer the mixture to a baking dish, then top with grated cheese.

Place the dish on the center rack of your oven and bake until the top is browned, about 15 minutes.

With an oven mitt, remove the baking dish from your oven.

Serve hot.

Fried Grouper Fingers

Yields 4 servings

— FROM "Let's Blame It All on the Weather"
in WHERE IS JOE MERCHANT? / P. 38

— FROM "Stand by Your Passenger"
in WHERE IS JOE MERCHANT? / P. 155

— FROM "I'd Rather Watch Paint Dry"
in WHERE IS JOE MERCHANT? / P. 218

— FROM "Time to Come Home, Cowboy"
in WHERE IS JOE MERCHANT? / P. 263

This recipe covers two food references: FRIED GROUPER and GROUPER FINGERS. The latter are nothing more than the grouper fillets cut into strips, rather than left whole. They can be served as either an entree or an appetizer. (At B.O.'s Fish Wagon in Key West they're cut into smaller pieces and known as GROUPER NUTS. It's a great use of odd-sized pieces you might find in your fish market as "chowder fish.") In any case, FISH FINGERS should not be confused with FISH STICKS. In FISH STICKS, the fish is flaked or pulverized and often mixed with some other ingredient before fried. In short, a FISH STICK is more of a FISH CAKE formed into a different shape.

INGREDIENTS:
For the fish:

> 3 lbs of grouper fillet, whole or in strips
> 1 c lemon juice
> 1 T Worcestershire sauce
> ¼ t salt
> ¼ t fresh cracked white pepper

For the batter:

    ¾ c cornstarch

    2 ½ c flour

    1 t salt

    3 t sugar

    ¼ t fresh cracked white pepper

    1¾ c water

    2 egg yolks

    ½ c flat beer

    2 t baking powder

    Vegetable oil, for frying

PREPARATION:

Of the fish:

Cut the grouper into the size pieces you wish to serve.

In a glass baking dish, combine the lemon juice, Worcestershire sauce, salt & pepper.

Add the grouper to the baking dish and coat well with the marinade.

Place the grouper in the refigerator to marinate for 1 hour, turning every 15 minutes to keep the fish coated.

Of the batter:

In a large mixing bowl, combine the cornstarch, flour, sugar, salt & pepper.

In a small mixing bowl, whisk together the water, egg yolks, and beer.

Gradually whisk the wet ingredients into the bowl of dry ingredients until the batter is smooth.

Whisk in the baking powder.

Of the fried grouper:

In a large cast iron skillet, heat the oil over medium-high temperature.

Remove the dish of marinated grouper from the refrigerator.

Drain and discard the marinade.

Without dredging the grouper in flour, dip the fish into the batter

Carefully place each fillet in the hot oil and fry until they are golden brown on each side, about 5 minutes.

With a slotted spoon or tongs, remove the fried grouper from the hot oil and drain on paper towel.

Serve hot with TARTAR SAUCE.

Crab Cakes

— from "I Wish Lunch Could Last Forever"
in TALES FROM MARGARITAVILLE /P. 148

About the only advice I can offer for this recipe is that you use fresh lump crab meat and not anything less that will disappear among the other ingredients. In other words, you ought to be able to recognize the crab meat and not have this look like a fish cake. Other than that, choose whatever sort of crab best suits your tastes.

INGREDIENTS:

1 lb fresh crab meat, picked & cleaned
2 T butter
1 onion, diced
1 red bell pepper, seeded & diced
2 celery ribs, diced
2 t dried basil
2 t dried thyme
2 t dried tarragon
½ t cayenne
½ T Creole mustard
2½ T mayonnaise
1 T Worcestershire

½ T Crystal®
Salt & fresh cracked black pepper, to taste
4 T butter
2 c all-purpose flour
2 eggs, beaten
2 c bread crumbs

PREPARATION:

In a small skillet, melt the butter over medium heat, then sauté the onion, bell pepper, and celery for 5 minutes.

Add to you skillet the basil, thyme, and tarragon, as well as the Worcestershire and the Crystal®. Stir together well.

Remove your skillet from the heat and allow the mixture to cool.

In a large mixing bowl, combine the crab meat with the cooled vegetable mixture.

Stir in the mustard, mayonnaise, and the salt & pepper with enough of the bread crumbs to be able to shape the mixture into crab cakes.

Wet your hands, then form 8 crab cakes of approximately the same size.

Preheat your oven to 400° F.

In a large skillet, melt the 4 T of butter over medium heat.

In separate dishes, arrange in sequence the flour for dredging, the beaten egg for washing, and the remaining bread crumbs for coating.

Dredge, wash, and coat each crab cake, then place in the large skillet.

Pan fry the crab cakes until they are golden on each side, then transfer them to an ungreased baking sheet.

Place the baking sheet on the center rack of your oven and bake the crab cakes until they are browned and heated through.

With an oven mitt, remove the baking sheet from the oven.

Serve the crab cakes hot with either ROUILLE, KEY WEST HOT SAUCE, or TARTAR SAUCE.

Fried Shrimp

Yields 4 servings

— FROM "When My Ship Comes In, I'll Be at the Airport" in WHERE IS JOE MERCHANT? / P. 14

Shrimp remain one of the food items that not only hold up well under the batter and hot oil, but also keep their distinctive taste. They don't require any fancy tools for frying. A cast iron pan will do just fine.

INGREDIENTS:

> 2 lbs uncooked shrimp, peeled & deveined, tails on
> 1 c all-purpose flour
> 1 T paprika
> ½ t salt
> 12 oz flat beer
> ½ t Worcestershire sauce
> ¼ t Crystal®
> Vegetable oil, for frying
> All-purpose flour, for dredging

PREPARATION:

In a medium mixing bowl, combine the 1 c of flour, paprika, and salt.

Whisk into those ingredients the flat beer, as well as the Worcestershire and Crystal® sauces.

Cover the mixing bowl tightly with plastic wrap, then allow the batter to stand at room temperature for at least 1 hour.

In a deep, cast iron skillet, heat 2 inches of vegetable oil to 375° F.

Dredge the cleaned shrimp in flour, then dip in the batter.

Carefully place the shrimp into the hot oil a few at a time.

Using a slotted spoon to turn them once, fry the shrimp until they are golden brown, about 2 to 3 minutes.

Use your slotted spoon to remove the fried shrimp from the hot oil, then drain on a paper towel.

Serve hot with CREOLE TARTAR SAUCE or KEY WEST HOT SAUCE.

COCONUT BEER SHRIMP

Yields 4 servings

INGREDIENTS:

2 lbs uncooked shrimp, peeled & deveined, tails on

For the seasoning:
  1 T red pepper flakes, ground
  1½ t sweet paprika
  1½ t cracked black pepper
  1¼ t garlic powder
  ¾ t onion powder
  ¾ t thyme
  ¾ t oregano

For the batter:
  2 eggs

  1¾ c all-purpose flour
  ¾ c flat beer
  1 T baking powder
  3 c unsweetened coconut, grated
  Vegetable oil, for frying

For the dipping sauce:
  1 c orange marmalade
  ¼ c prepared horseradish

PREPARATION:

In a small mixing bowl, prepare the seasoning by combining the red pepper flakes, paprika, black pepper, garlic and onion powders, thyme, and oregano. Transfer to a clean dish.

In a large mixing bowl, combine 2 t of the seasoning with 1¼ c of the flour, the baking soda, and the flat beer.

In another small mixing bowl, combine the remaining ½ c of flour with another 2 t of the seasoning.

In a deep, cast iron skillet, heat 2 inches of vegetable oil to 375° F.

Coat each shrimp by dredging in the dish of seasoning mix, then in the flour-seasoning mixture.

Dip each shrimp in the batter, then dredge in the shredded coconut.

Carefully place the shrimp into the hot oil a few at a time.

Using a slotted spoon to turn them once, fry the shrimp until they are golden brown, about 1 to 2 minutes.

Use your slotted spoon to remove the shrimp from the hot oil, then drain on paper towel.

Serve hot with DIPPING SAUCE.

Of the dipping sauce:

In a small mixing bowl, combine the orange marmalade with the prepared horseradish. Mix together well, then refrigerate for 1 hour.

Transfer the dipping sauce to a small dish.

CARIBBEAN SHRIMP

Yields 4 servings

INGREDIENTS:

>*2 lbs uncooked shrimp, peeled & deveined, tails on*
>
>*1½ c all-purpose flour*
>
>*1 t salt*
>
>*¼ t cracked white pepper*
>
>*2 egg yolks, beaten*
>
>*¾ c flat beer*
>
>*1 T dark rum*
>
>*1 c unsweetened coconut, shredded*
>
>*Vegetable oil for frying*

PREPARATION:

In a large mixing bowl, combine the flour, salt, pepper, and egg yolks.

Gradually stir in the flat beer and rum.

Cover the bowl tightly with plastic wrap, then allow to rest in the refrigerator for 1 to 2 hours.

In a deep, cast iron skillet, heat 2 inches of vegetable oil to 350° F.

Rinse the shrimp thoroughly and pat dry.

Dip each shrimp in the batter, then dredge in the shredded coconut.

Carefully place the shrimp into the hot oil a few at a time.

Using a slotted spoon to turn them once, fry the shrimp until they are golden brown, about 1 to 2 minutes.

Use your slotted spoon to remove the fried shrimp from the hot oil, then drain on paper towel.

Serve hot with DIPPING SAUCE.

Grilled Salmon

Yields 4 servings

— FROM "At Arm's Length"
in WHERE IS JOE MERCHANT? / P. 307

Remember that hinged rack your father used to have for cooking burgers over a fire? Well, that same rack (or something similar to it) is an ideal utensil to have for grilling a flaky fish, such as salmon. Aside from making the fish much easier to handle in one piece, it also makes the basting a bit easier.

INGREDIENTS:

> 4 4-oz salmon steaks, 1 inch thick
> 1 c dry white wine
> ½ c olive oil
> 3 garlic cloves, mashed
> 4 T melted butter
> 1 t dried thyme

PREPARATION:

In a glass baking dish, place the salmon steaks and pour the wine over them. Turn the steaks once to give them a good coating of wine, then refrigerate for at least 2 hours.

Prepare a hot barbecue grill. If you're cooking with charcoal, prepare an area that will enable you to later cook with a medium heat.

Remove the salmon steaks from the refrigerator, then drain and discard the wine.

In a small mixing bowl, mix a basting sauce with the olive oil, garlic, melted butter, and dried thyme.

Place the salmon steaks on your hot grill and baste the upper side with your sauce.

After grilling the salmon for 3 minutes, turn the steaks over and baste this upper side.

After grilling the salmon for 4 minutes, cook them over medium heat until they are tender and flaky, but be very careful that you do not allow them to overcook and become dry.

Striped Bass with Lobster Sauce

Yields 4 servings

— FROM "The Perfect Day"
in A PIRATE LOOKS AT FIFTY / P. 50

Jimmy's idea of a "small" bass is actually a striper big enough to feed you and your friends until you're all stuffed to the gills (so to speak). Throughout the northeast, where he and a jillion others pray they'll hook up with a "keeper" (which is *not* the same as keeping-up with a hooker!), the legal size is usually something 28 inches or longer, depending upon whose waters the bass is in.

If you're just a hard-working landlubber, though, you might find it easier to buy yourself striped bass (skin on!) at your local fish market and save yourself the sort of obsession that makes Capt. Ahab seem like a slacker. Ask your fishmonger for an entire section of the fish, dressed so that you have two sides with the skin, as well as a cleaned body cavity. In other words, you're not getting a fillet with skin on just one side, and you're getting something much more than a 1-inch steak.

This recipe is the way Jimmy says that Jane would want her GRILLED BASS: with a LOBSTER SAUCE, RISOTTO and WHITE TRUFFLES. That's okay, but this is something you won't prepare on a whim. All at the same time, you'll be boiling water, melting butter, and reducing a sauce, and to add to the excitement you'll be burning-off of some Cognac. Of course, somewhere a bass will be grilling, too. So, be sure to let everyone know what you're doing before you begin. Make certain you're not wearing any loose-fitting clothing that might catch on fire and that you do have either a long wooden match, or a long butane lighter. And keep in mind that the flame of the alcohol might be so rich in oxygen that it's not visible to the casual bystander.

INGREDIENTS:

For the grilled bass:

> 2 lbs striped bass fillets, skin on
> 2 T olive oil

For the lobster sauce:

> ½ lb melted butter
> 1 1¼-lb lobster, cooked & cleaned
> ¼ c butter
> Salt & fresh cracked white pepper, to taste
> 3 T Cognac
> 1 c heavy cream
> 3 egg yolks
> 2 T water

PREPARATION:

Of the grilled bass:
Prepare a medium-hot fire under your grill. If you're using charcoal, be certain that you let the coals go to gray before beginning to cook.

With a sharp knife, score the skin of the bass so that it does not curl while cooking. Brush both sides of the fish with the oil to prevent it from sticking to your grill, then place the fish, skin side down, on the hot grill and cook for 5 minutes on the first side.

After the first side has cooked, carefully turn the bass and cook for 5 minutes on the second side.

When the bass is done, it should flake quite easily with your fork.

Of the lobster sauce:
In a small saucepan, melt the ½ lb of butter.

In the bottom portion of a double boiler, bring 2 c of water to the boil.

Slice the meat of the lobster claws and tail.

In a medium skillet, melt the ¼ c of butter, then add the lobster meat. Season with salt and fresh cracked white pepper.

Pour the Cognac into the skillet, then ignite it to burn off the alcohol.

Add the heavy cream to the skillet, then bring the sauce just to the boil.

In the top portion of the double boiler, add together the 3 egg yolks and 2 T of water, then place the top over the base of the double boiler. With a whisk, beat the yolks vigorously until they are pale yellow and thickened.

Gradually, spoon the clear liquid of the melted butter into the thickening egg yolks and continue to whisk the eggs. Do not use the solid, milky portion of the melted butter.

Transfer the egg sauce from the double boiler to the skillet with the rest of the ingredients.

Reduce the heat beneath the skillet and stir the mixture well.

For the finish:
Remove the bass from the grill and transfer to a large platter.

With a spoon, gently scrape away the cooked skin, as well as any fins that might be on the fish.

Place a serving of bass on each dish, then top with the LOBSTER SAUCE.

Sushi in the Mall

— FROM "Fruitcakes"
on FRUITCAKES

Without a doubt, trying to explain to the uninitiated about SUSHI and how to prepare it opens up a whole new can of worms, which reminds me of fish bait, which (in turn) reminds me of SUSHI! Quite frankly, I was going to slide over Jimmy's reference to "sushi in the mall" only because there are so many variables.

And then, just when I thought this project was finished, I made landfall in Key West for a brief respite. The fact that the Cuban Coffee Queen had become an all-you-can-eat SUSHI bar didn't sway me to include these pages. No, it was the shock of discovering that the renovations at Fausto's Food Palace now included "sushi made fresh daily." *Ouch!* (Which aisle has the chocolate milk?)

Anyway, to make these recipes the right way you not only need to have some appreciation of the food and cultural etiquette, but also a unique shopping list, along with a special set of kitchen utensils.

For starters, you're supposed to serve SUSHI with tea, sake, or beer; that means, no rum, no tequila, no Bloody Mary. Next, you're supposed to dip SUSHI *only* into soy sauce; that means, no Crystal® sauce, no tartar sauce, no Heinz 57®. When you dip, you're supposed to dip with the fish side down, then stick it in your mouth the same way. (I'm not sure whether or not double-dipping is allowed.) Finally, between courses you're allowed to eat some pickled ginger (GARI) or shredded DAIKRON (not Dacron®!) to refresh your taste buds. Of course, I think you've heard that rules are meant to be broken, right?

Aside from picking up some gari and daikron at the store, you'd better stock up on . . .

VEGETABLES: Any of these can be combined in the recipes that follow with the rice and/or fish for a variety of SUSHI that suits your taste.

> *Carrots, steamed & in ¼-inch thick sticks*
> *Avocado, in ¼-inch thick sticks*
> *Pickled daikon, ¼-inch thick sticks*
> *Other pickled vegetables*
> *Fried tofu, ½ inch thick strips*

FRESH FISH: The key word in this phrase is "fresh," because you're mostly going to serve these items uncooked. If you are afraid of bacteria, you can always freeze the fish for 2 hours, then slice it.

> *Clams, smoked whole*
> *Crab meat, picked & cleaned*
> *Eel, grilled*
> *Flounder, 1- by 2- by ¼-inch pieces*
> *Halibut, 1- by 2- by ¼-inch pieces*
> *Octopus, cooked & sliced thin*
> *Oyster, smoked whole,*
> *Red snapper, 1- by 2- by ¼-inch pieces*
> *Roe*
> *Salmon, 1- by 2- by ¼-inch pieces*
> *Sea bass, 1- by 2- by ¼-inch pieces*
> *Shad, 1- by 2- by ¼-inch pieces*
> *Shrimp, poached & butterflied*
> *Squid, grilled or raw & sliced*
> *Tuna, 1- by 2- by ¼-inch pieces*

WASABI: A horseradish grown only in Japan that's grated to a fine pulp just to hide the fishy smell of the sushi and to make your nose tingle. (You eat it, not snort it!) Fresh wasabi is expensive, but the powdered or paste form is more affordable. Still, don't overstock this stuff.

VINEGAR: In this case, it's rice vinegar and not far removed from sake. In fact, you could substitute a dry white wine if you want. (See, you *can* break the rules!) Because SUSHI is a lot of raw seafood, the vinegar helps to destroy bacteria, as well as to break down some of the proteins. In that regard, it's a bit like the acid in a ceviche. And though you put some rice vinegar into the SUSHI RICE, you're also supposed to add some sugar to hide the taste of the vinegar.

I don't know about you, but I'm beginning to get the sense that there's a lot of hiding in SUSHI. Horseradish hides the smell of the fish; sugar hides the taste of the vinegar; and ginger kills the taste of the SUSHI. I don't recall all the illusion with PEANUT BUTTER, do you?

SOY SAUCE: Japanese soy sauce is not as dark and heavy as the Chinese recipe. A natural alternative to sugar and salt, the Japanese variety is reddish, but clear, and gives off a definite aroma.

GARI: A pickled ginger root that refreshes your mouth between bites of SUSHI.

NORI: Sold in standardized thin sheets, this is a dried seaweed which has been toasted to hold together various other ingredients. Generally, you need to give it one more very quick toasting on your stove top just before preparing the SUSHI.

RICE: As important an ingredient to SUSHI as the quality of the fish, SUSHI RICE has a somewhat harder texture than other rices. It should never be refrigerated or kept for more than a day. Each SUSHI roll requires about 1 c of SUSHI RICE.

As for kitchen utensils, you're supposed to use these.

HANGIRI: A wooden vessel for the cooked SUSHI RICE.

SHAMOJI: A spatula for separating grains of hot rice.

MAKISU: A small bamboo mat for rolling the SUSHI.

SUSHI RICE

Yields 8 cups cooked rice

INGREDIENTS:

> 3½ c short-grain rice, uncooked
>
> 4 c water

For the seasoning:

> 5 T rice vinegar
>
> 5 T sugar
>
> 4 t salt

PREPARATION:

In a medium saucepan, bring the water to the boil over medium heat. Stir in the rice, cover, and allow the rice to cook for 2 minutes.

Reduce the heat and simmer until all the water has been absorbed, about 15 to 20 minutes.

Remove the saucepan from the heat and take off the cover. Spread a clean kitchen towel across the top of the saucepan, then replace the cover. Allow this to stand for 10 to 15 minutes.

Of the seasoning:

In a small skillet, bring a cup of water to the boil.

In a heatproof glass measuring cup, combine the rice vinegar, sugar, and salt. Carefully place the measuring cup into the water and stir until the sugar has dissolved.

With an oven mitt or a pair of canning tongs, carefully remove the measuring cup from the water and set aside to cool. (If you wish, you can place the cup in a dish of ice cubes.)

Transfer the cooked rice from the saucepan to the hangiri, then separate the grains of rice by making slicing motions with your shamoji. Continue to slice and fan the sushi rice until it is at room temperature. Cover the hangiri with a clean cloth and set the rice aside.

MAKI SUSHI

Yields 8 uncut rolls

Maki ingredients are first wrapped together in a roll, then sliced into 1-inch sections

INGREDIENTS:

> 8 c sushi rice
>
> ½ c vinegar water
>
> 8 sheets of nori, toasted
>
> 1 t powdered wasabi
>
> 1 small Japanese cucumber, julienned
>
> 4 oz fresh raw tuna, julienned
>
> ½ oz salmon roe

PREPARATION:

Place 1 sheet of nori, shiny side down, on a mat.

Wet your right hand with vinegar water, then pick up 2 T of rice and spread it evenly over the left half of the nori.

Spread a string of wasabi lengthwise down the middle of the rice, then arrange strips of cucumber and tuna along the string of wasabi. Dot with roe.

Lift the edge of your makisu that is on the rice half of your nori, then gently roll the nori over the rice and other ingredients. Pressing to compact the rice, continue to roll the nori forward until you approach the portion that has no other ingredients.

Use your fingers to apply a thin coat of vinegar water to the remaining nori so that the completed roll will be sealed.

With a sharp knife, cut the roll into 4 1-inch slices and serve while the nori remains crispy.

NIGIRI SUSHI

Yields 4 servings

Rather than wrapping in nori, you wrap the ingredients together in the rice, which requires some dexterity to keep the rice in even proportion to its filling.

INGREDIENTS:

> ½ c water
> ¼ c rice vinegar
> 8 c sushi rice
> 1 t powdered wasabi
> 1 small Japanese cucumber, julienned
> 4 oz smoked salmon, sliced thin

PREPARATION:*

In a small bowl, combine ½ c of water and ¼ c of vinegar, then dip your fingers into the water/vinegar bowl to prevent the rice from sticking to them.

In your left hand, place about 2 T of rice, then use the first 2 fingers of your right hand to press the rice firmly into an oval pad.

With the tip of your right index finger, place a dab of wasabi in the center of the rice pad.

With your right hand, pick up a topping of cucumber and salmon, then cradle it in your hand.

Transfer the pad of rice onto the cradled topping, then roll the sushi along your right hand until the topping is once more on the top. (Whew!)

Gently press together the top and sides of rice to give the sushi a firm shape.

Place the sushi on a clean plate and start all over.

These directions are for a right-handed Occidental; if you're left-handed, then do what you do best.

TEMAKI SUSHI

Yields 8 cones

This is a cone-shaped sushi which you could make right in your hand; however, you might find it somewhat easier to do with the bamboo mat. These ingredients are for the so-called "California roll," so I expect you'd find it in the mall.

INGREDIENTS:

> 8 c sushi rice
> ½ c vinegar water
> 8 sheets of nori, toasted
> 1 t powdered wasabi
> 1 small avocado, julienned
> 4 oz fresh crab meat, picked & cleaned

PREPARATION:

Place a sheet of nori, shiny side down, on your makisu.

Wet your right hand with vinegar water, then pick up 2 T of rice and spread the rice evenly over the left half of the nori.

Spread a string of wasabi lengthwise down the middle of the rice, then arrange strips of avocado and crab meat along the string of wasabi.

Lift the edge of the makisu that is on the rice half of your nori, then gently roll the nori over the rice and other ingredients.

Pressing to compact the rice, roll the nori into the shape of a cone until you approach the portion that has no other ingredients.

Use your fingers to apply a thin coat of vinegar water to the remaining nori so that the completed cone will be sealed.

Serve while the nori remains crispy.

SIDE DISHES

French Fried Potatoes 🍟 Hushpuppies
Red Beans & Rice 🍟 Yellow Rice
Popcorn Rice 🍟 Black Beans
Zucchini Fettucine 🍟 Rasta Pasta
Risotto & White Truffles 🍟 Onion Rings
Oyster Dressing

French Fried Potatoes

Yields 4 servings

— FROM "Cheeseburger in Paradise"
on SON OF A SON OF A SAILOR

Success in this recipe comes not only in your careful selection of the potatoes, but also in the two stages of frying at specific heats. Though a deep-fryer is a helpful bit of kitchenware for this recipe, you can do just as well with a cast-iron frying pan, an electric frying pan (with a temperature control), or even a wok. In fact, a wok can provide you more depth with less oil. In any case, you might best cook these in batches.

I like to season my fries with sea salt, which is a coarser granule available in most markets.

INGREDIENTS:

3 large russet potatoes, peeled & cut lengthwise in ¼-inch strips
6 c vegetable oil
4 T cornstarch
Sea salt, to taste

PREPARATION:

After you have peeled the russets and sliced them lengthwise into strips that are ¼-inch thick, refrigerate them in a bowl of cold water overnight.

Drain the potatoes and pat them dry. Sprinkle the cornstarch over the potatoes, then toss them to coat thoroughly, but lightly.

In a deep, cast iron skillet, bring the oil to 325° F, then carefully add your first batch of potatoes. Fry them about 3 to 5 minutes until they are soft and begin to brown.

Line a tray with paper towels. Transfer the first pre-cooked batch to the paper towels to drain.

Allow the oil to heat again and repeat the process until you have pre-cooked all the potatoes.

When you are ready to serve the potatoes, heat the oil to 400° F. Again, add each batch of potatoes to your fryer and cook about 1 minute until golden brown.

Remove each batch to drain on fresh paper towels.

Season with sea salt.

Hushpuppies

Yields 2 dozen

— FROM "Come Monday"
on LIVING AND DYING IN ¾ TIME

— FROM "Squalls Out on the Gulf Stream"
in WHERE IS JOE MERCHANT? / P 15

Well before there were the soft leather loafers that bear this brand name, folks from the Outer Banks of the Carolinas south to the Gulf Coast were serving up this deep-fried cornmeal that's nothing short of a gastronomic tradition.

By legend — and this is perhaps a true one — HUSHPUPPIES got their name as Southern cooks prepared the evening meal. Hungry hounds would hang around the kitchen and bark for their share of the meal being prepared. And the harried cooks, trying to get a meal completed for a waiting family, attempted to appease the dogs with bits of corn bread batter dropped into the hot frying fat. The little fried dough balls were thrown out the kitchen door with the admonishment, "hush puppy!"

On the other hand, *Morris Dictionary of Word and Phrase Origins* gives yet another account — based on a Southern reader's letter — that in the South the aquatic reptile called the salamander was often known as a *water dog* or *water puppy* or even *mud puppy*, because of their squat stout legs. In the period of scarcity following the Civil War, these reptiles were deep fried with cornmeal dough and formed into sticks They were called HUSH PUPPIES, because eating such lowly food was not something a Southern wife would want known to her neighbors.

Whatever the origin of the term, it's apparently not that old, appearing in print for the first time only in 1918. Nonetheless, they surely are a tasty treat, often served alongside fried fish. And in the case of Frank Bama, still served up fresh to his own dog, Hoagy, awaiting him in the parking lot of Bobalou's.

Whether or not the HUSHPUPPIES should be fried in the same oil as the fish, as well as whether or not grated onion should be an ingredient remains very much a regional matter, as might be the ratio of flour and sugar. Along the Outer Banks, for example, they forego the onion in favor of more sugar, and they insist that the hushpuppies not have the fishy taste of the oil. The result is almost a cake-like bread. The choice is all yours, but I think Frank Bama would prefer them this way.

INGREDIENTS:

    1½ c cornmeal
    ¼ c all-purpose flour
    ¼ c sugar
    2 t baking powder
    ½ t salt
    1 egg
    ¼ cup milk
    1 onion, grated (optional)
    Oil for frying

PREPARATION:

In a deep skillet, bring the oil to 350° F.

Sift together into a bowl the cornmeal, flour, baking powder, and salt.

In a separate, small bowl beat the egg into the milk. (Add the grated onion.)

Pour the blended wet ingredients into the bowl of sifted cornmeal, flour, and sugar, then stir together to form a medium thick batter.

Carefully drop a tablespoon of batter at a time into the hot fat until you have 6 or 8 hushpuppies frying.

Fry until golden brown.

Use a slotted spoon to remove each hushpuppy to a paper towel to drain; then repeat those last 2 steps until you have enough to serve hot.

Red Beans & Rice

Yields 4 servings

Without a doubt, it can be said that there are as many subtle variations of this dish as there are islands in the Caribbean. Also known in Jamaica as PEAS & RICE when fresh "pigeon peas" (gungo peas) are in season, this recipe more often than not relies upon dried red or pink beans.

INGREDIENTS:

5 c water

1 c unsweetened coconut milk

4 garlic cloves, chopped

3 T thyme, chopped

½ Scotch bonnet pepper, stemmed, seeded & chopped

¼ t allspice, ground

2 c long-grain rice, uncooked

3 c red beans, cooked, rinsed & drained

1 c scallions, sliced (including green tops)

3 T butter

1 t salt, plus some extra for adjusted seasoning

Fresh black pepper, cracked to taste

PREPARATION:

Before you can begin to cook this meal, you must first remove the starch from the rice, otherwise it will simply cook into a merciless lump. To do this, place the uncooked rice in a large bowl and cover with cold water. When the water has turned white, drain the rice and discard the water. Repeat this process until the water no longer turns white.

In a large pot, bring to the boil the 5 c of water. Stir in the coconut milk, garlic, thyme, hot pepper, and allspice. Reduce the heat and simmer uncovered for 5 minutes.

Add to the pot the cleaned rice, red beans, scallions, butter, and 1 t of salt.

Cover partially and cook over low heat until the rice is tender and the liquid is absorbed, about 40 to 45 minutes. Occasionally stir the pot to prevent the rice and beans from sticking. If the liquid should be absorbed before the rice becomes tender, add either more coconut milk or more water.

When the rice is cooked, taste and adjust the seasonings with salt & pepper.

Yellow Rice

YELLOW RICE is a popular dish not only in the Latin American nations, but also in Africa and India; however, they are not all the same recipe. This version is Cuban and the proper accompaniment to the popular combination of BLACK BEANS & RICE.

INGREDIENTS:

2 T olive oil
2 t cumin seeds
¼ t saffron thread, crumbled
2 c unconverted long-grain rice
4 c water
¾ t salt

PREPARATION:

In a large saucepan, heat the olive oil until it is hot, but not smoking.

Add the cumin seeds, then sauté them until they darken and become fragrant, about 10 seconds.

Stir into the saucepan the saffron and the rice.

Sauté the rice in the olive oil until it is coated well with the saffron, about 1 to 2 minutes.

Add the water to the saucepan, along with the salt. Without stirring the ingredients or covering the saucepan, bring the water to the boil until the top

grains of rice appear dry and steam holes cover the surface, about 8 to 10 minutes.

Remove the saucepan from the heat, cover, and allow the rice to stand for 5 minutes.

With a fork, fluff the rice and serve hot.

Popcorn Rice

Yields 4 servings

— FROM "I Will Play for Gumbo"
ON BEACH HOUSE ON THE MOON

Bill Wharton is not only the "Sauce Boss" whom Jimmy mentions in this song, but also a superb blues guitarist, as well as creator of his own line of *Liquid Summer*® pepper sauces. None of which has any more to do with rice than does popcorn, except that these facts all come together in Jimmy's lyrics, sort of like a GUMBO.

INGREDIENTS:

1 T unsalted butter
½ onion, diced fine
1 bay leaf
1 t salt
¼ t dried thyme
Fresh white pepper, cracked to taste
2 c basmati rice
3¼ c stock

PREPARATION:

In a saucepan, melt the butter over medium-high heat, then add the onion and bay leaf.

Stir and sauté until the onion is soft, about 2 minutes.

Reduce the heat to low, then stir in the salt, thyme, and white pepper. Continue to stir and cook for 30 seconds, then add the rice. Still stirring, cook the onion and rice another whole minute.

Add to the saucepan the stock, then increase the heat to medium and bring to the boil. Reduce heat to very low, cover, and cook for 17 minutes.

Remove the saucepan from the heat and serve the rice immediately.

Black Beans

— FROM "I'm Clean"
in WHERE IS JOE MERCHANT? / P. 119

Yields 8 servings

There is no such thing as a "small" batch of BLACK BEANS, but you shouldn't be afraid of this recipe. As with most that involve dry beans, this one requires an overnight soaking . . . of the beans.

INGREDIENTS:

1 lb black beans, dry
1 head of garlic, chopped fine
1 onion, chopped
1 green pepper, chopped
1 bay leaf
¼ t cumin
¼ t oregano
¾ c olive oil
3 t salt
2 t vinegar
4 t dry wine
2 T sugar
¼ c tomato ketchup
15 c water
½ c salad olives

PREPARATION:

Place the dry beans in a colander, remove any that don't suit your liking, then rinse them well.

In a large pot, combine the 15 c of water with half of the green pepper, as well as the rinsed beans, then soak them overnight to soften.

Bring the water to the boil over medium-high heat and simmer the beans for 45 minutes.

In a large skillet, heat the oil, then stir in the garlic, onion, and the remaining green pepper.

Cook these about 3 minutes, then add them to the pot of beans, along with the salt, oregano, bay leaf, black pepper, ketchup, and sugar.

Simmer the beans over medium heat until they are soft.

Into a heatproof bowl, ladle 2 c of the beans, mash them well, then return them to the pot.

Stir in the wine, vinegar, and olives, then reduce the heat and simmer 1 more hour.

Just before serving, stir in 1 more T of olive oil.

Zucchini Fettucine

Yields 4 servings

— FROM *"Cheeseburger in Paradise"*
on SON OF A SON OF A SAILOR

Sure, I could lead you down that kitchen path and have you make fettucine with zucchini right in the pasta dough. But I've wasted a lot of my own time through the years making red pepper pasta, tomato pasta, spinach pasta, carrot pasta, and even pasta with that useless ink from a squid. And what's it all taste like? Whatever sauce I've made to go with it! So, I'll spare you the kneading and the rolling and the cutting of dough and opt to put the zucchini in the sauce.

INGREDIENTS:

1 zucchini
1 c fresh peas
1½ T olive oil
¾ c shallots, chopped coarse
1 lb fresh fettucine, uncooked
3 T fresh basil, chopped
Salt & fresh black pepper, cracked to taste
4 T fresh Parmesan cheese, grated

PREPARATION:

In a large pot, bring to the boil enough water to cook the fettucine.

Trim the ends from the zucchini, then julienne the zucchini in 1½-inch strips.

In a large skillet, heat the olive oil over medium heat, then add the shallots and sauté until soft, about 3 minutes. Stir the zucchini into the skillet and reduce the heat to low.

Place the fresh peas into a heatproof bowl, then ladle 2 c of the boiling water atop the peas. Set aside.

Add the fettucine to the pot of boiling water and cook until the pasta is *al dente*, about 3 minutes.

Drain the fettucine and the peas together in a colander, then transfer to a large mixing bowl.

Add to the bowl the warm zucchini and shallots, as well as the basil, salt & pepper. Toss lightly, then taste and adjust the seasoning.

Grate the Parmesan cheese into the bowl, then toss again lightly.

Divide the fettucine among 4 warm plates and serve warm.

Rasta Pasta

— FROM *"Reggae Accident"* on MARGARITAVILLE LATE NIGHT MENU

Yields 4 servings

Pasta, as you and I have come to know it, is not a staple of the Caribbean diet. Friends of mine in the Dominican Republic, however, do make this recipe with pasta when they can get it; with rice when they cannot.

INGREDIENTS:

> 4 slices of bacon, chopped coarse
> 1 onion, peeled & chopped fine
> 2 garlic cloves, chopped fine
> 1 T fresh hot pepper, seeded & chopped
> 2 c macaroni shells, uncooked
> 4 tomatoes, peeled, seeded & chopped
> 3 c chicken stock
> Salt & fresh cracked black pepper
> 2 T unsalted butter
> 1½ lbs raw shrimp, peeled, deveined & in ½-inch pieces
> 2 T fresh parsley, chopped fine
> Fresh Parmesan cheese, grated

PREPARATION:

In a large skillet, render the bacon slices over medium heat until they are crisp. With a slotted spoon, remove the bacon and keep it warm.

In the remaining bacon fat, sauté the onion, garlic, and hot pepper until the onion is tender, but not brown. Add the uncooked macaroni to the skillet and cook until the remaining bacon fat has been absorbed, about 3 minutes.

Stir the tomatoes and the chicken stock into the mixture in the skillet, then taste and adjust the seasonings with salt & fresh black pepper.

Bring the stock to the boil, then cover and reduce the heat to its lowest setting.

When the pasta has simmered for 10 minutes, melt the butter over medium heat in a separate skillet. Add the shrimp and sauté until they just turn pink, about 5 minutes.

After the pasta has absorbed the liquid, stir in the shrimp, the bacon, and the parsley. Cover and cook until all the ingredients are warmed.

Transfer the pasta to a large heatproof bowl and serve family style with the fresh Parmesan served on the side.

Risotto & Truffles

Yields 4 servings

— FROM *"The Perfect Day"*
in A PIRATE LOOKS AT FIFTY / P. 50

This is meant to accompany the STRIPED BASS with LOBSTER SAUCE, the way that Jimmy says Jane would want it, garnished with WHITE TRUFFLES. So, here it is, with a couple of variables. First, you could use a chicken stock, or a lobster stock (which might go best with the sauce). Second, you can make RISOTTO with long grain rice, but the true dish is with arborio rice. The final secret is your undivided attention. RISOTTO is not a rice which you cover and leave unattended. There is a lot of stirring to this recipe unless you're making paste.

INGREDIENTS:

> 4 c stock
> 4 T butter
> 3 T olive oil
> 2 T shallots, chopped fine
> 2 c arborio rice, uncooked
> ½ c dry white wine
> ¼ c Parmesan cheese, grated
> Salt & fresh cracked black pepper, to taste
> 2 oz fresh white truffles, shaved

PREPARATION:

In a medium saucepan, bring your stock to the simmer over medium heat.

In a large saucepan, melt 2 T of the butter with the 3 T of olive oil over medium heat, then sauté the chopped shallots until they are translucent.

Stir in the rice until it is coated thoroughly with the butter and oil, then sauté the rice 2 to 3 minutes and stir in the dry white wine.

When the wine has been almost completely absorbed by the rice, add ½ c of the simmering stock and continue stirring.

As the rice absorbs the stock, repeat the process of adding another ½ c, then frequently stirring until the rice is cooked *al dente* and the risotto is creamy. This should take about 20 to 25 minutes, and you might have some stock left over.

Remove the saucepan from the heat, then stir in the grated cheese and the remaining 2 T of butter.

Taste and adjust the seasonings with salt & cracked black pepper.

Garnish the risotto with shaved white truffles.

Onion Rings

Yields 4 servings

Through the kitchen exhaust fan of the Island Hotel, the aroma of onion rings wafted into Bubba's Key West apartment in the days that the only remittance man he knew was Lance Larrimoore III. Now, whether that's a fictional fact or factional fiction, I do not know; however, these ONION RINGS are good enough for the Margaritaville Cafe.

INGREDIENTS:

> *2 large Spanish onions, peeled & sliced into ½-inch rings*
> *12 oz beer, warm*
> *1 c all-purpose flour, sifted*
> *Salt*
> *Cayenne*
> *Crystal® sauce*
> *1 c all-purpose flour, for dredging*
> *Oil*

PREPARATION:

Cut off the ends of the onions, then peel and slice them into rings.

omeultult

Place the onion rings into a large bowl of ice water and set aside.

In a large skillet or deep fryer, heat your vegetable oil to 375° F.

In a large mixing bowl, combine the beer and flour, along with the salt, cayenne, and Crystal® sauce, then whisk these together well.

Drain the ice water from the onion rings, then pat the rings dry with paper towel.

Dredge the dried rings in the flour, then shake them to remove any excess.

Dip the floured rings into the batter, then carefully place them in small batches into the hot oil.

Fry the onion rings until brown and crisp.

Remove the rings from the oil and drain on paper towel.

Serve hot.

Oyster Dressing

Yields 3 cups

— FROM "I Will Play for Gumbo"
on BEACH HOUSE ON THE MOON

Jimmy sings of TURKEY WITH OYSTER STUFFING, but 9 times out of 10 you'll discover that oysters are used in dressing, not stuffing. Stuffing goes into the turkey and makes it taste somewhat fishy; dressing is baked and served on the side.

INGREDIENTS:

2 doz medium oysters, shucked & in their liquor
1 c cold water
4 t seasoning (see recipe below)
1 t garlic, minced
½ c onion, chopped
12 T margarine
½ c fresh parsley, chopped fine
3 bay leaves
1 c celery, chopped
1 c very fine dry bread crumbs
1 c green bell pepper, chopped
2 T unsalted butter, softened
½ c scallion, chopped

For the seasoning:

> 2½ T paprika
>
> 2 T salt
>
> 2 T garlic powder
>
> 1 T black pepper
>
> 1 T onion powder
>
> 1 T cayenne pepper
>
> 1 T dried oregano
>
> 1 T dried thyme

PREPARATION:

In a small mixing bowl, combine the oysters and their liquor with the cold water. Refrigerate at least 1 hour.

Strain the oysters and reserve the liquor and water. Refrigerate the oysters for another hour.

In a large skillet, melt 4 T of the margarine over high heat.

Add ¼ c of the onion, ½ c of the celery and ½ c of the green bell pepper. Stirring frequently, saute over high heat until the onion is dark brown, but not burned, about 8 minutes.

Reduce the heat to medium, then stir 2 t of the seasoning, as well as the garlic into the skillet. Cook another 5 minutes and stir occasionally.

Add to the skillet the remaining ¼ c of onion, ½ c celery, ½ c green bell pepper and 8 T of margarine, as well as ¼ c of the scallion, ¼ c of the parsley, and the bay leaves. Stir altogether until the margarine is melted.

Cook this mixture another 10 minutes and stir occasionally.

Add the reserved oyster liquor and water to the skillet, then increase the heat to high. Stirring occasionally, cook for 10 minutes.

Stir the remaining 2 t of seasoning into the skillet, along with enough of the dry bread crumbs to make the dressing just moist, but not runny.

Remove the skillet from the heat, then stir the oysters into the dressing.

Preheat your oven to 350° F.

Spoon the dressing into an 8 by 8 baking dish, then bake uncovered for 30 minutes.

With an oven mitt, remove the baking dish from the oven.

Remove and discard the bay leaves, then stir in the butter, along with the remaining ¼ c of scallion and ¼ c parsley.

Serve hot.

BREADS, BUNS & BISCUITS

French Bread & Baguettes
Muffalatta Bun ❧ Cheeseburger Buns
Bimini Bread ❧ Garlic Cheese Bread
Biscuits & Syrup ❧ White Bread
Raisin Bread ❧ Coconut Bread
Monkey Bread ❧ Cuban Bread

French Bread & Baguettes

Yields 2 loaves or 6 baguettes

— FROM "Take Another Road"
in TALES FROM MARGARITAVILLE / P. 39

— FROM "I Wish Lunch Could Last Forever"
in TALES FROM MARGARITAVILLE / P. 151

— FROM "Sometimes I Feel
Like A Rudderless Child"
in TALES FROM MARGARITAVILLE / P. 218

— FROM "I'd Rather Watch Paint Dry"
in WHERE IS JOE MERCHANT? / P. 218

Whether you envision Tully Mars and Donnakay, eating BRISKET SANDWICHES at Tujague's with FRENCH BREAD and HORSERADISH SAUCE, or Slade and Isabella at Galatoire's with FRENCH BREAD and lots of butter, or maybe even Jimmy himself sopping up his GUMBO, these are a couple of recipes you should try.

As with most rustic breads, these can be baked on a breadstone, in a brick oven, or else on a cookie sheet lined with parchment. In an ideal world, you'd also have a bread peel to help get from your pastry cloth to your oven without much effort.

INGREDIENTS:

½ c plus 2 c water (100° F to 110° F)
2 T active dry yeast
1 T granulated sugar
1 T salt
7 c bread flour

PREPARATION:
Proof the yeast by combining the warm water

and sugar in a large mixing bowl. Stir the yeast into the water until it has dissolved. Allow this to stand until bubbles appear in the surface foam.

Add to the yeast mixture the 2 other c of water and 1 T salt. Stir these together, then add 2 c of flour and stir into a smooth batter.

Gradually add 4 more c of flour to your bowl and stir until it becomes very difficult to work the mixture.

Turn your dough onto a clean, floured surface.

Knead the dough, adding enough of the remaining flour as you work until the dough has almost no stickiness. If you add too much flour, your loaves of bread will be a bit tough. You can stop kneading when your dough has no lumps, is somewhat elastic, and has an almost satiny appearance.

Lightly oil a large mixing bowl.

Form the dough into a ball. Place the ball of dough into the bowl, then turn the dough until its entire surface is oiled.

Place a damp towel over the bowl and place the bowl in a warm place for 1¼ to 1½ hours.

When the dough has doubled in bulk, punch it down to its original size. Cover once more with a damp towel, then allow it to rise in a warm place until it has doubled again, about 1 hour.

Punch down the dough one more time and divide it into two equal pieces.

Form each of these pieces into a long loaf, but don't be surprised if the dough is very elastic and doesn't easily stretch into the length you want. There's enough dough here to make 2 long loaves, so be aggressive! You've already kneaded it, and

punched it twice, so don't feel bad about pulling the dough or even slapping it against your counter.

Then, again, if you feel more comfortable in being less aggressive, you can divide the dough into 6 equal pieces and work toward making baguettes.

Dust your bread peel with cornmeal, or place a sheet of parchment atop a cookie sheet and dust the paper with cornmeal.

Place your loaves on the peel or cookie sheet, then cover them with a damp towel. Allow them to double in volume, about 20 minutes.

Preheat your oven to 375° F. If you're using a baking stone, now is the time to place it in the oven.

When the loaves have doubled in volume, place them in the oven.

They need to bake for about 40 minutes. During the first 20 minutes, creating steam in the oven will improve the quality of the crust.

When the bread becomes a golden brown, use an oven mitt to remove the loaves from oven. Turn them over and gently tap the bottoms. If they do not sound somewhat hollow, they should be baked a bit longer.

Cool slightly on a wire rack; however, these loaves are best when served hot.

Muffalatta Bun

— FROM "Boomerang Love"
in Tales from Margaritaville / p. 94

Yields 1 10-inch loaf

To make a true MUFFALATTA sandwich, you're going to need (knead?) a true bun. Just remember: this 10-inch beauty is *not* you're CHEESEBURGER'S BUN!

INGREDIENTS:

> *1 c water (110° to 115° F)*
> *1 T sugar*
> *1 T active dry yeast*
> *3 c bread flour*
> *1½ t salt*
> *2 T vegetable shortening*
> *Sesame seeds*

PREPARATION:

You'll probably find that a food processor will make this recipe a bit easier to execute.

Proof the yeast by combining the warm water and sugar in a small bowl. Stir the yeast into the water until it has dissolved. Allow this to stand until bubbles appear in the surface foam.

Meanwhile, fit the steel blade into your food processor. Add the flour, salt, and shortening to the bowl of the processor, then pulse for about 30 seconds.

When the yeast has proofed, pour that mixture into your food processor.

Process the ingredients about 5 seconds until the dough forms a ball. Stop the machine and check to see if your dough is smooth and satiny. If it is too dry, add more warm water, 1 T at a time, then process just enough to blend. If dough is too sticky, add more flour, 1 or 2 T at a time, then process just enough to blend.

Once your dough is smooth and satiny, process another 20 seconds to knead.

Lightly oil a large mixing bowl.

Form the dough into a ball. Place the ball of dough into the bowl, then turn the dough until its entire surface is oiled.

Place a damp towel over the bowl and place the bowl in a warm place for 1¼ to 1½ hours.

Lightly grease a baking sheet.

When the dough has doubled in bulk, punch it down to its original size, then turn it out onto a lightly floured surface.

Form your dough into a loaf about 10 inches in diameter.

Dust your bread peel with cornmeal, or place a sheet of parchment atop a cookie sheet and dust the paper with cornmeal.

Place your loaf on the peel or cookie sheet, then sprinkle the top with sesame seeds and gently press them into the surface. Cover very loosely with plastic wrap and let rise until almost doubled in volume, about 1 hour.

Before you preheat your oven to 475° F, place the oven rack in the center. If you're using a baking stone, this is the time to allow it to heat in the oven.

Remove the plastic wrap from the loaf and put the bread in the oven.

Bake the bread for 10 minutes, then reduce the heat to 375° F and allow it to bake for another 25 minutes.

When the bread appears a golden brown, use an oven mitt to remove it from oven. Turn the loaf over and gently tap the bottom. If it doesn't sound somewhat hollow, it should be baked a bit longer

Cool completely on a rack before slicing.

Cheeseburger Buns

Yields 12 large buns

These might well be your CHEESEBURGER'S buns; however, for the sake of accuracy I must note that Jimmy sings not of them. All he craves is a big hunk of bread, and I suggest the WARM BEER IN BREAD. For the minors in the family, though, give 'em one of these.

INGREDIENTS:

2 T active dry yeast
2 c water (110° to 115° F)
½ c vegetable oil
½ c sugar
4 c all-purpose flour
1 T salt
3 eggs
4 c bread flour

PREPARATION:

Proof the yeast by combining ½ c of the warm water and sugar in a large mixing bowl. Stir the yeast into the water until it has dissolved. Allow this to stand until bubbles appear in the surface foam.

Add to the yeast mixture the other 1½ c of water, the oil, and the T of salt.

Combine the 4 c of all-purpose flour and sugar in a mixing bowl, then gradually stir into the larger bowl of liquid ingredients.

Add the eggs, then beat the mixture at low speed for 30 seconds.

Scrape the bowl, then beat another 3 minutes at high speed.

By hand, stir in 4 c bread flour to make a soft dough.

Turn your dough onto a clean, floured surface.

Knead the dough, adding enough of the remaining flour as you work until the dough has almost no stickiness. You can stop kneading when your dough has no lumps, is somewhat elastic, and has an almost satiny appearance.

Lightly oil a large mixing bowl.

Form the dough into a ball. Place the ball of dough into the bowl, then turn the dough until its entire surface is oiled.

Place a damp towel over the bowl and place the bowl in a warm place for about 1 hour. When the dough has doubled in bulk, punch it down to its original size.

Divide the dough into 3 equal portions, then cover it once more with a damp towel and allow it to rest for 5 minutes.

Divide each portion of the dough into 4 balls.

Shape each ball of dough into a circle by pulling the ball slightly outward, then folding the outer edges back and under. Place each circle on a greased baking sheet, then press them gently into 3½-inch circles.

Cover with a damp towel one more time and allow the buns to rise until they have doubled in volume, about 30 minutes.

Preheat your over to 375° F.

Bake the buns until the tops are golden brown, about 10 minutes.

With an oven mitt, remove the baking sheet from oven and allow the buns to cool on a wire rack.

Bimini Bread

Yields 4 loaves

— FROM "Why I Love My Seaplane"
in THE PARROT HEAD HANDBOOK / P. 20

Part of the reason Jimmy loved his Widgeon so much, he says in *The Parrot Head Handbook*, is that he could fly solo along the coastline from Florida to Long Island at "see level." Among his favorite foods he liked to pack for "Air Jimmy" were CONCH SALAD, as well as GRILLED LOBSTER on BIMINI BREAD. I might add that this menu tastes quite good at ground level, too. Sometimes called BAHAMA BREAD, this is just a bit sweeter than most other pan breads. And yet, it is definitely not a dessert or coffee bread, such as COCONUT BREAD.

INGREDIENTS:

2 T active dry yeast

½ c plus 1½ c water (100° to 110° F)

½ c instant nonfat dry milk

¾ c sugar

½ c vegetable oil

1 t salt

2 eggs

1½ c warm water

7½ c all-purpose flour

PREPARATION:

Proof the yeast by combining the warm water and sugar in a large mixing bowl. Stir the yeast into the water until it has dissolved. Allow this to stand until bubbles appear in the surface foam.

Add to the yeast mixture the dry milk powder, sugar, oil, salt and eggs. Mix well, then stir in the other 1½ c of warm water.

Add 2 c of flour and stir this altogether into a smooth batter.

Gradually add the remaining flour to your bowl and stir until it becomes very difficult to work the mixture.

Turn your dough onto a clean, floured surface.

Knead the dough, adding enough of the remaining flour as you work until the dough has almost no stickiness. If you add too much flour, your loaves of bread will be a bit tough. You can stop kneading when your dough has no lumps, is somewhat elastic, and has an almost satiny appearance.

Lightly oil a large mixing bowl.

Form the dough into a ball. Place the ball of dough into the bowl, then turn the dough until its entire surface is oiled.

Place a damp towel over the bowl and place the bowl in a warm place for 2½ hours.

Grease two 8- by 4-inch loaf pans.

When the dough has doubled in bulk, punch it down to its original size. Divide the dough into 4 equal pieces, then shape each into a loaf.

Place each loaf into a greased loaf pan, then cover once more with a damp towel. Allow them to rise in a warm place until they have doubled again in volume, about 1 hour.

Preheat your oven to 350° F.

Place the loaf pans on the center rack of your oven and bake the loaves until they are browned, for about 40 minutes.

With an oven mitt, remove the pans from the oven and the loaves from their pans, then allow them to cool on wire racks.

You can freeze any loaves you don't plan to use within the next couple days.

Garlic Cheese Bread

Yields 2 loaves

— FROM "I'd Rather Watch Paint Dry"
in WHERE IS JOE MERCHANT? / P. 218

INGREDIENTS:

1½ c milk
½ c warm water
3 T butter
6½ to 7½ c all-purpose flour
2 T sugar
1 T salt
2¼ t active dry yeast
2 c shredded sharp cheddar cheese
4 garlic cloves, minced
2 T butter, melted

PREPARATION:

In a small saucepan, warm the milk, water and butter over low heat until they reach 105° F to 115° F. Remove the pan from the heat and stir in the yeast. Allow this to stand until the yeast has proofed and bubbles appear in the surface foam.

In a large mixing bowl, combine 4 c of the flour with the sugar and salt.

Mix in the cheese, then add the warm liquids and the proofed yeast. Stir well with your fingers and gradually add the remaining flour.

Turn the dough out onto a lightly-floured work surface and knead the dough until it is smooth and elastic. If the dough feels stiff or dry, knead in additional cool water, 1 T at a time.

Lightly oil a large mixing bowl. Form the dough into a ball and place in the oiled bowl. Turn the dough until the entire surface is greased, then cover and let this rest until it doubles in size.

Grease two 9- by 5-inch loaf pans.

Punch the doubled dough down and divide into 2 loaves. Place a loaf in each greased pan, then cover and let rise until it again doubles in size.

Preheat your oven to 375° F. Place the pans on the center rack of your oven and bake until the crust is a deep golden brown, about 40 minutes.

In a small saucepan, melt the remaining 2 T of butter with the minced garlic.

With an oven mitt, remove the pans from the oven, brush the tops of the loaves with garlic butter and allow them to cool on a wire rack.

Biscuits & Syrup

Yields 1 dozen

— FROM "Take Another Road"
in TALES FROM MARGARITAVILLE / P. 35

— FROM "Boomerang Love"
in TALES FROM MARGARITAVILLE / P. 98

Syrup, in this instance, is cane syrup, but there's nothing wrong with maple syrup or (*yahoo!*) gravy. Then, again, you could always use good old butter.

INGREDIENTS:

3 c all-purpose flour
2½ t baking powder
1 t salt
3 t sugar
¾ c shortening
1¼ c buttermilk

PREPARATION:

Into a large mixing bowl, sift together the flour, baking powder, salt, and sugar.

With your fingertips, cut in the shortening until you have a coarse mixture.

Add the buttermilk to the mix, then stir with a fork until you form a very stiff dough.

Turn the dough out onto a lightly floured board.

Knead the dough about 20 times with your hands, and NEVER, EVER use a rolling pin.

Cover the dough with a towel and allow it to rest for 10 minutes.

Preheat your oven to 450° F.

Lightly oil a baking sheet.

Pat the dough with your hands and fingers until it is about an inch thick.

Cut the biscuits with a floured cutter (or the floured mouth of a drinking glass).

Place the biscuits on the baking sheet and bake on the center rack of your oven for 12 to 15 minutes.

With an oven mitt, remove the baking sheet from the oven.

Biscuits should be served as hot as possible with butter and cane syrup.

White Bread

— FROM "Paradise Lost"
in WHERE IS JOE MERCHANT? / P. 173

Yields 2 loaves

While it's true that Jimmy's written reference to WHITE BREAD is really about that sliced stuff wrapped in cellophane that goes well with packaged baloney and yellow mustard, it also appears as HOT TOASTED BREAD at the Café Creola. So, whether you want to upgrade your baloney sandwich, or traipse off on the difficult route to hot toast, this is the way it should be done.

INGREDIENTS:

½ c water (105° to 115° F)
3½ t active dry yeast
1 t Sugar
9 c unbleached all-purpose flour
4½ t Kosher salt
1½ c plus 4 T cool water (75° F)

PREPARATION:
Proof the yeast by combining the ½ c of warm water and sugar in a large mixing bowl. Stir the yeast into the water until it has dissolved. Allow

this to stand until bubbles appear in the surface foam.

Add to the yeast mixture the 4½ t Kosher salt and the 1½ c plus 4 T cool water.

Gradually add the flour into the larger bowl of liquid ingredients and use your fingers to stir the dough.

When all of the flour has been incorporated, turn the dough out onto a lightly floured work surface and knead for 4 minutes. The dough should be sticky and will not look smooth. If the dough feels stiff or dry, knead in additional cool water, a T at a time.

Lightly dust a large mixing bowl with flour. Put the dough in the bowl, cover, and allow it to rest for 20 minutes.

Return the dough to your lightly-floured surface and knead it for another 7 to 8 minutes. The dough will go from being sticky to smooth and then will become supple, but not too firm.

Lightly dust another large mixing bowl with flour. Divide the dough into two equal balls. Place a ball of dough into each dusted bowl, then turn each ball until its entire surface is dusted.

Place a damp towel over each bowl and place them in a warm place for about 2 to 2½ hours. When the dough has doubled in bulk, punch them down to their original size.

Once again, turn a dough ball out onto a very lightly floured surface. Gently deflate the dough and pat it into a rectangle. The short sides should be the top and bottom edges; the long sides should be left and right.

Starting with a short side, fold the top edge down and the bottom edge up so that you can slightly overlap them. Turn the dough a quarter turn, then fold the top down and the bottom up once again to form an envelope.

Shape the dough into a loaf by rolling it down 2 or 3 times. Seal the seam with the heel of your palm, then roll the loaf on the table to smooth it out.

Lightly oil two 9- by 5-inch loaf pans.

Place the loaf (seam side down) in a pan, then gently press the loaf to fill the corners of the pan.

Repeat this procedure for the other ball of dough.

Cover each loaf with oiled plastic wrap and allow them to double in volume, rising about an inch above their pans.

Preheat your oven to 425° F.

Gently place the pans on the center rack of the oven.

Bake for 10 minutes, then reduce the oven temperature to 400° F and bake another 30 minutes longer, or until the top is a deep golden brown.

With an oven mitt, remove the bread pans from the oven and allow them to sit atop the stove for 5 minutes.

Wearing oven mitts, remove the loaves from their pans and allow them to cool on a wire rack.

Raisin Bread

Yields 2 loaves

— FROM "An Appointment with the Moon"
in WHERE IS JOE MERCHANT? / P. 335

Say what you will about Frank Bama's nemesis, the sinister Colonel Cairo, at least he had the decency to know that Desdemona's RAISIN BREAD was pretty damn good. Still, there's no truth to the rumor that he said: "I'd give my right arm to be able to bake bread this good!" (Don't you just love literary humor?) If not, you'll still love this bread toasted. A loaf will remain fresh for a couple of days or else freeze it without any problem.

INGREDIENTS:

> ½ c water (105° to 115° F)
> 3½ t active dry yeast
> 1 t sugar
> 9 c unbleached all-purpose flour
> 4½ t Kosher salt
> 1½ c plus 4 T cool water (75° F)
> 3 t fresh cinnamon, grated
> 6 T sugar
> 3 c dark raisins
> 4 T unbleached all-purpose flour

PREPARATION:

Proof the yeast by combining the ½ c of warm water and sugar in a large mixing bowl. Stir the yeast into the water until it has dissolved. Allow this to stand until bubbles appear in the surface foam.

Add to the yeast mixture the 4½ t Kosher salt and the 1½ c plus 4 T cool water.

Gradually add the flour into the larger bowl of liquid ingredients and use your fingers to stir the dough.

When all of the flour has been incorporated, turn the dough out onto a lightly floured work surface and knead for 4 minutes. The dough should be sticky and will not look smooth. If the dough feels stiff or dry, knead in water, a T at a time.

Lightly dust a large mixing bowl with flour. Put the dough in the bowl, cover, and allow it to rest for 20 minutes.

Return the dough to your lightly floured surface and knead it for another 7 to 8 minutes. The dough will go from being sticky to smooth and will become supple, but not too firm.

Lightly dust another large mixing bowl with flour. Divide the dough into two equal balls. Place a ball of dough into each dusted bowl, then turn each ball until its entire surface is dusted.

Place a damp towel over each bowl and place them in a warm place for about 2 to 2½ hours. When the dough has doubled in bulk, punch them down to their original size.

Once again, turn a dough ball out onto a very lightly floured surface. Gently deflate the dough and pat it into a rectangle. The short sides should be the top and bottom edges; the long sides should be left and right.

In a cup, mix together the cinnamon and sugar, then sprinkle half of this mixture evenly over the dough. Reserve enough for the second loaf.

Drain the raisins and toss them with 4 T flour. Spread half of these raisins evenly over the dough and gently press them into it. Reserve enough raisins for your second loaf.

Starting with a short side, fold the top edge down and the bottom edge up so that you can slightly overlap them. Keep your eyes open for renegade raisins that might try to escape. Tuck them back in. Turn the dough a quarter turn, then fold the top down and the bottom up once again to form an envelope. Make another bedcheck of the raisins.

Shape the dough into a loaf by rolling it down 2 or 3 times. Seal the seam with the heel of your palm, then roll the loaf on the table to smooth it out. Last call for runaway raisins!

Lightly oil two 9- by 5-inch loaf pans.

Place the loaf (seam side down) in a loaf pan, then gently press the dough to fill the corners of the pan.

Repeat this procedure for the other ball of dough.

Cover each loaf with oiled plastic wrap and allow them to double in volume, rising about an inch above their pans.

Preheat your oven to 450° F.

Gently place the pans on the center rack of the oven.

Bake for 15 minutes, then reduce the oven temperature to 375° F and bake another 20 to 30 minutes longer, or until the top is a deep golden brown. Watch this carefully. Because of the cinnamon, the crust might darken more quickly than with the plain WHITE BREAD recipe. If the bread is browning too fast for your liking, cover the loaves loosely with aluminum foil.

With an oven mitt, remove the bread pans from the oven and allow them to sit atop the stove for 5 minutes.

Wearing oven mitts, remove the loaves from their pans and allow them to cool on a wire rack.

Coconut Bread

Yields 2 loaves

— FROM "Changing Channels" in WHERE IS JOE MERCHANT? / P. 282

Stranded in the Caribbean with Frank Bama nowhere to be found, Trevor Kane had her spirits lifted when Desdemona served her up a breakfast of a CHEDDAR CHEESE OMELET and toasted COCONUT BREAD. Simple? Yes, but also *tres* elegant. (I think I've been reading too many of these French recipes.) Though packaged coconut can be used, there is nothing that compares to fresh coconut grated especially for this recipe. You'll need at least 2 coconuts, but more likely 3. So, stop monkeying around and fetch some coconuts; there'll be enough monkeying in the next recipe.

INGREDIENTS:

2 c all-purpose flour
1 T baking powder
1 t salt
1 c sugar
2 c fresh coconut, grated fine
1 egg, beaten well
1 c evaporated milk
1 t vanilla

4 oz unsalted butter, melted & cooled
Sugar

PREPARATION:

Sift into a large mixing bowl the flour, baking powder, and the salt. Add the sugar and the coconut, then mix well.

In a small mixing bowl, beat the egg well, then add the milk, vanilla, and melted butter.

Mix the liquid ingredients lightly, but thoroughly into the bowl of dry ingredients.

Preheat your oven to 350° F.

Grease two 9- by 5-inch loaf pans, then divide the batter equally between the two pans, about two-thirds full. Sprinkle sugar across the top of the batter.

Bake the bread for about 55 minutes, or until an inserted toothpick comes out clean.

With an oven mitt, remove the bread from the oven and allow them to cool partially in the pans before turning them out onto a cake rack to complete cooling.

Monkey Bread

Yields 1 loaf

— FROM "Iguana Sit Right Down and
Write Myself A Letter"
in WHO IS NATALIE MERCHANT? / P. OOO

Mocking the notion that he'll never work in dis bidness again, Jimmy sings that he told it to the MONKEY BREAD, but it didn't talk back. I mention that just to piss off that one get-a-lifer out there who just can't wait to write me a note about some picayune mistake I've made in this book. Well, I'm certain I've made more than a couple in this project, but you and I know damn well that Bubba *never* says a thing about MONKEY BREAD. Still, the get-a-lifers won't have read this far to know that the joke's on them. Meanwhile, this classic sweet bread always brings a smile to the lips of those who taste it, and it will especially please any Parakeets who just like the thought of monkeys making bread. The truth remains, however, that we're all cavemen in faded aprons or something like that.

INGREDIENTS:

½ c water (105° to 115° F)
2¼ t active dry yeast
1 c milk (105° to 115° F)
¼ c granulated sugar

¼ T salt
1 egg, beaten
¼ c shortening, melted
4 c flour
½ c butter, melted
Sugar & cinnamon, to taste

PREPARATION:

Proof the yeast by combining the ½ c of warm water and sugar in a large mixing bowl. Stir the yeast into the water until it has dissolved. Allow this to stand until bubbles appear in the surface foam.

In a small saucepan, warm the milk over medium heat.

When the yeast has proofed, add the warm milk to the mixing bowl, then stir in the salt and the shortening.

In a small bowl, beat the egg well, then add to the mixing bowl.

Gradually stir in half the flour with a spoon.

Add more flour until the dough becomes too stiff to mix with the spoon.

Turn the dough out onto a well-floured surface and knead until dough is smooth and elastic, about 10 minutes. Add more flour as needed.

Lightly oil a large mixing bowl.

Form the dough into a ball and place in the bowl. Turn the dough to cover the surface with oil, then cover with a damp cloth. Allow the dough to rise until double in volume.

When the dough has doubled, punch it down to its original size and let it again rise until doubled.

When the dough has again doubled, break off small pieces of dough and roll each into small balls about the size of a walnut. This recipe should yield between 40 to 45 such balls.

In a small saucepan, melt the ½ c of butter.

Mix together the sugar and cinnamon in a shallow dish.

Pour the melted butter into a shallow dish.

Grease a 9-inch bundt pan or a tube cake pan.

Roll each ball of dough in melted butter, then roll each in the sugar-cinnamon mixture until coated. Arrange them loosely in the baking pan, then allow the dough balls to rise until double in bulk.

Preheat your over to 375° F.

Place the pan on the center rack of your oven and bake until the top is browned, about 30 to 35 minutes.

With an oven mitt, remove the pan from the oven and allow it to cool on a rack for 15 minutes.

Using an oven mitt, invert the pan onto a large plate, then remove the pan.

Serve warm.

Cuban Bread

Yields 2 loaves

Indeed, there is a *very* fine line between FRENCH BREAD and CUBAN BREAD, and the difference is not so much in their flours or even their shape, but most importantly in their process. Unlike the familiar long, thin French loaves, the round Cuban loaves must begin their baking in a cold oven.

INGREDIENTS:

½ c plus 2 c water (100° F to 110° F)
2 T active dry yeast
1 T granulated sugar
1 T salt
7 c all-purpose or hard-wheat flour
3 T yellow cornmeal
1 T egg white
1 T water

PREPARATION:

Proof the yeast by combining the ½ c of warm water and the sugar in a large mixing bowl. Stir the yeast into the water until it has dissolved.

Allow this to stand until bubbles appear in the surface foam.

Meanwhile, combine the 1 T of salt with the flour.

Add to the yeast mixture the 2 other c of water, then add 1 c of flour and stir with a wooden spoon into a smooth batter.

Gradually add more flour, 1 c at a time, to your bowl and stir until it becomes very difficult to work the mixture.

Turn your stiff dough onto a clean, floured surface.

Knead the dough, adding enough of the remaining flour as you work until the dough has almost no stickiness, about 10 minutes.

Lightly oil a large mixing bowl.

Form the dough into a ball. Place the ball of dough into the bowl, then turn the dough until its entire surface is oiled.

Place a damp towel over the bowl and place the bowl in a warm place for 1½ to 2 hours.

When the dough has doubled in bulk, punch it down, then turn it out onto a clean, floured surface.

Divide the dough into two equal pieces, then form each into a round loaf.

Dust your bread peal with cornmeal, or place a sheet of parchment atop a baking sheet and dust the paper with cornmeal.

Place the loaves on the bread peel or baking sheet and allow them to rise for 5 minutes.

Do NOT preheat your oven.

In a small mixing bowl, combine the egg white and the T of water to make a egg wash.

Use a sharp knife or a razor blade to slash the top of the loaves diagonally in 2 or 3 places, then brush the tops lightly with the egg wash.

Place the loaves on the center shelf of a COLD oven, then set the oven temperature to 400° F.

On the bottom rack of your oven, you might want to place a pan of boiling water to enhance the crust.

The loaves need to bake until the crust is well browned, about 40 minutes.

When the bread appears done, use an oven mitt to remove the loaves from oven. Turn them over and gently tap the bottoms. If they do not sound somewhat hollow, they should be baked a bit longer.

Cool on a wire rack.

DESSERTS & GOODIES

Sponge Cake ☺ Apple Pie
Chocolate Pie ☺ Peach Cobbler
Blackberry Cobbler
Sweet Potato Pecan Pie ☺ Coconut Tart
Key Lime Pie ☺ Crème Brûlée
Citrus Crème Brûlée ☺ Blonde Stranger
New Orleans Bread Pudding
Banana Split ☺ No Plain Ol' Sundae
Desdemona's Brownies
Desdemona's Passion
Isabella's Coconut Wedding Cake
Fruitcake City Half-baked Fruitcake
Jamaican Holiday Rum Cake
Last Mango Fruitcake
Strawberry Shortcake
Tourte aux Cerises

Sponge Cake

— FROM "Margaritaville"
on CHANGES IN LATITUDES, CHANGES IN ATTITUDES

Yields one 12- by 17-inch sheet cake

Whether you're one of those folks who likes icing, or just one who likes cake, you still ought to know the subtle differences in the latter. After all, some people think that a SPONGE CAKE is the same as an angel cake, or that a SPONGE CAKE is the same as a pound cake, or that a SPONGE CAKE is the same as a Twinkie® (fer cryin' out loud!). In truth, though, a SPONGE CAKE is not like any of the above and has long remained a classic among French chefs. (Yes, they *do* have a word for it.)

INGREDIENTS:

½ c milk
1 T plus 2 t butter
8 large eggs
2 c plus 2 T sugar
1 c bleached flour
1 t baking powder
½ t salt
1 t pure vanilla extract

PREPARATION:

In a small saucepan, heat the milk and 1 T of butter over medium heat until it is 110° F.

Into a large mixing bowl, sift together the flour, baking powder, and salt.

In another large mixing bowl, whisk together the eggs, vanilla, and 2 c of sugar until the mixture is pale yellow, thick, and has tripled in volume.

Slowly whisk in the warm milk mixture.

Fold the bowl of dry ingredients into the bowl of liquids and mix until the batter is smooth.

Preheat your oven to 350° F.

Grease your sheet pan with the remaining butter, then sprinkle with the remaining 2 T of sugar.

Pour the batter evenly into the pan, then place it in the center rack of your oven and bake until the cake spring back when it is touched, about 15 minutes.

With an oven mitt, remove the cake from the oven and allow it to cool for about 2 minutes.

Sprinkle a piece of parchment paper with powdered sugar, then use a thin spatula or knife to loosen the edges of the cake and flip it over onto the sugared paper.

Allow the cake to cool completely.

KEY LIME CREAM CHEESE ICING

Okay, you've come this far with your SPONGE CAKE, so here's an alternative or two. One is to make this simple icing and frost the top of your cake; another is to make your iced SPONGE CAKE into a cake roll.

INGREDIENTS:

> *8 oz cream cheese, softened*
> *1½ c confectioners' sugar*

> *½ t vanilla*
> *1 t key lime zest*
> *2 t fresh key lime juice*
> *½ c secret ingredient*
> *1 T crystalized ginger, grated*

PREPARATION:

Of the frosting:
In a medium mixing bowl, cream together the softened cream cheese and the 2 T butter.

Add the confectioners' sugar and the vanilla, then beat the mixture until it is fluffy and smooth.

Beat in the zest and the lime juice.

Of the cake roll:
While your sponge cake is baking, prepare yourself to roll the cake. For this, you will need a clean kitchen towel sprinkled with powdered sugar. This towel will replace the sugared parchment paper in the final steps of the plain SPONGE CAKE recipe.

Use a thin spatula or knife to loosen the edges of the cake, then flip it over onto the sugared towel. (This is a neat place to brush ½ c of a good dark rum across the entire top, but don't tell anyone.)

Lift the towel along a short edge of the cake and fold it so that the cake rolls onto itself. Continue to lift the towel from the back and carefully roll the entire sponge cake. Allow to cool on a rack.

When the sponge cake has cooled, carefully unroll the cake and spread the KEY LIME CREAM CHEESE ICING across the top. Sprinkle with grated crystalized ginger.

Repeat the rolling process, then place seam side down on a clean plate.

Dust with confectioners' sugar.

Apple Pie

— FROM "Captain America"
on DOWN TO EARTH

Yields one 10-inch pie

What's good for America is also good for Margaritaville!

INGREDIENTS:

For the crust:

> *2 c all-purpose flour*
> *1 t salt*
> *¾ c shortening*
> *5 to 7 T ice water*

For the filling:

> *6 to 8 tart apples, peeled, cored & sliced*
> *1 cup sugar*
> *2 T all-purpose flour*
> *½ to 1 t fresh cinnamon, grated*
> *2 T butter*

PREPARATION:

Of the crust:

In a large bowl, mix with your fingertips the salt, shortening, and flour until they have the crumbly consistency of a corn meal.

Add 5 T of the ice water and mix well. Add more water if the dough is too dry.

Divide the dough into two equal balls, then pat one flat on a lightly-floured surface. With a rolling pin, work the flattened ball into a 12-inch circle, then place in the bottom of a 10-inch pie plate.

Repeat this procedure with the second ball of dough; however, leave it on your floured surface.

Of the apple filling:
Slice the apples into a large mixing bowl.

Combine the sugar, flour, and cinnamon in a small bowl, then add to your apple slices and toss

with your hands until the slices are coated evenly.

Of the pie:
Preheat your oven to 400° F.

Pour the seasoned apples into the bottom crust in your pie plate and dot with pieces of the butter, then place your second crust on top and crimp the edges tightly. Use the point of a sharp knife to vent the top crust with slits for the steam to escape.

Place your pie on the center rack of the oven and bake until the crust is golden, about 50 minutes.

With an oven mitt, remove the pie and allow it to cool.

Chocolate Pie

Yields one 10-inch pie

— FROM "The 10 Best Cheeseburgers"
in THE PARROT HEAD HANDBOOK / P. 27

While Jimmy truly savors the CHEESEBURGERS at the Camelia Grill in New Orleans, he says that their CHOCOLATE PIE is unbelievable. Note, please, that he is *not* speaking of chocolate cream pie that is lathered with a topping of whipped cream. Nor is he speaking of some filling that falls out of a box. In fact, the name itself keeps secret the other two flavors of coconut and pecans. But what makes this chocolate confection so decadent is a recipe that can only be made from scratch.

So, pinch yourself to prove it's real, then be absolutely certain that you make the filling with baking cocoa and *not* that stuff you make the kids' drinks with. When you're all done baking, you'll be a true believer.

INGREDIENTS:
For the crust:
 1 c all-purpose flour
 ½ t salt
 ½ c shortening
 3 to 4 T ice water

For the filling:

1½ c sugar

3½ T baking cocoa

6½ oz evaporated milk

2 eggs, beaten

¼ c butter

1 t vanilla extract

1 c fresh coconut, flaked

½ c pecans, shelled & chopped

PREPARATION:

In a large bowl, mix together with your fingertips the shortening, salt, and flour. Work these ingredients until they have the crumbly consistency of a corn meal.

Add 3 T of the ice water and mix well. Add more water if the dough is too dry.

Form the pastry dough into a ball, then pat this flat on a lightly floured surface.

With a rolling pin, work the flattened ball into a 12-inch circle of crust.

Place the crust in a 10-inch pie plate.

Of the filling:

In a small saucepan, melt the butter and set aside.

In a large mixing bowl, combine the sugar and the baking cocoa.

Stir in the evaporated milk, eggs, melted butter, and vanilla, then mix well.

Add the coconut and pecans, then stir well.

Of the finished pie:

Preheat your oven to 350° F.

Pour the filling into the unbaked pie shell.

Place the pie on the center rack of your over and bake until the filling has set around the edges, about 40 minutes.

Use an oven mitt to remove the pie from the oven, then allow the pie to cool on a wire rack.

Peach Cobbler

Yields 8 servings

Perhaps you recall that point in *Where is Joe Merchant?* when Desdemona has anchored the *Cosmic Muffin* just off Dog Island and she whips up a PEACH COBBLER with canned fruit and Bisquick®! As they say, "Any port in a storm."

In this case, though, I think we should rely more upon the home-cooked flavors that Frank Bama always can find at Bobalou's on Big Coppitt Key. That's where he can always find a real PEACH COBBLER. If you wish to serve this *a la mode*, you might want to select an ICE CREAM recipe.

INGREDIENTS:
For the filling:

> 8 c fresh peaches (about 10 medium),
> pitted & sliced
>
> 2 c sugar
>
> 2 T cornstarch
>
> ½ t nutmeg, grated fresh
>
> 1 t vanilla extract
>
> ¼ c butter

For the crust:

> *2 c all-purpose flour*
> *1 t salt*
> *¾ c shortening*
> *5 to 7 T ice water*

PREPARATION:

In a Dutch oven, combine the peaches, sugar, cornstarch, and nutmeg, then set them aside until a syrup forms from the juices.

Meanwhile, prepare your pastry dough.

In a large bowl, mix together with your fingertips the shortening, salt, and flour until they have the crumbly consistency of a corn meal.

Add 5 T of the ice water and mix well. Add more water if the dough is too dry.

Divide the pastry into 2 equal balls of dough.

Pat one pastry ball flat on a lightly floured surface.

With a rolling pin, work the flattened ball into a 10-inch square of crust.

Repeat this procedure with the second half of the pastry dough.

Place the Dutch oven on the stove and bring the peach mixture to the boil.

Reduce the heat to low, then simmer until the peaches are tender, about 10 minutes.

Lightly butter an 8-inch square pan, and preheat your oven to 475° F.

Remove the Dutch oven from the burner, then stir in the vanilla and butter.

Spoon half of the cooked peaches into the buttered pan, then top with 1 square of crust and trim the edges to fit pan.

Place the pan on the center rack of your oven and bake until the crust is lightly browned, about 12 minutes.

With an oven mitt, remove the pan from the oven. Spoon the remaining peach mixture over the baked pastry square.

Cut the remaining pastry square into strips 1-inch wide, then arrange them in a lattice design over the peaches.

Bake the cobbler an additional 15 to 18 minutes until browned.

With an oven mitt, remove the peach cobbler from the oven and allow to cool for 15 minutes.

Spoon the cobbler into serving bowls and top each with a scoop of ice cream.

BLACKBERRY COBBLER

Yields 8 servings

If you can't visit the Cupboard Diner in Memphis, where Tully Mars ate this dish, then maybe your cousin Baxter could pick enough blackberries.

Simply substitute this filling for the peach mixture in the previous recipe.

INGREDIENTS:

For the filling:

> *3 c fresh blackberries*
> *1 c sugar*
> *¼ c flour*
> *1½ c water*
> *1 t lemon juice*

PREPARATION:

Same as PEACH COBBLER, except you use fresh blackberries. Pretty clever, huh?

Sweet Potato Pecan Pie

Yields one 10-inch pie

— FROM "I Wish Lunch Could Last Forever"
in TALES FROM MARGARITAVILLE / P. 155

This item on the menu at Chéz Bar-B-Q Hill, says Jimmy, is straight from Isabella's days on Snake Bite Key, and it's a southern beauty that brings together the best of two great tastes. Loosen-up that belt a notch, because you'll probably be sneaking around for at least an extra slice. And you might want to go with that urge to drop a dollop of whipped cream on top just for good measure.

INGREDIENTS:

For the crust:

> *1 c all-purpose flour*
> *½ t salt*
> *½ c shortening*
> *3 to 4 T ice water*

For the filling:

> *1 lb sweet potatoes, boiled & peeled*
> *¼ c butter*
> *1 14-oz can sweetened condensed milk*
> *1 t orange zest, grated*
> *1 t vanilla extract*

1 t fresh cinnamon, grated

1 t fresh nutmeg, grated

¼ t salt

2 eggs

For the pecan topping:

1 egg

3 T dark corn syrup

1 t maple syrup

3 T light brown sugar, packed firm

1 T butter, melted

1 cup pecans, shelled & chopped

PREPARATION:

Of the crust:

In a large bowl, mix together with your fingertips the shortening, salt, and flour. Work these ingredients until they have the crumbly consistency of a corn meal.

Add 3 T of the ice water and mix well. Add more water if the dough is too dry.

Form the pastry dough into a ball, then pat this flat on a lightly-floured surface.

With a rolling pin, work the flattened ball into a 12-inch circle of crust.

Place this crust in the bottom of a 10-inch pie plate.

Of the filling:

Preheat your oven to 350° F.

In a large mixing bowl, mash the sweet potatoes with the butter, then beat until smooth.

Add to the bowl the sweetened condensed milk, orange zest, vanilla extract, cinnamon, nutmeg, salt and eggs, then mix them together well.

Pour the filling into the pastry shell and place on the center rack of your oven.

Bake for 30 minutes.

Of the pecan topping:

In a small mixing bowl, mix together the egg, corn syrup, maple syrup, brown sugar, and melted butter.

Stir in the chopped pecans.

Of the finished pie:

When the filling has baked for 30 minutes, use an oven mitt to remove the pie from the oven.

Spoon the pecan topping evenly over the top of the filling.

Use an oven mitt to place the pie back into the oven on the center rack.

Bake until the topping is golden brown, about 20 to 25 minutes.

Use an oven mitt to remove the pie from the oven and allow the pie to cool.

This can be served either warm or chilled.

Coconut Tart

Yields one 10-inch tart

— FROM "I Wish Lunch Could Last Forever"
on OFF TO SEE THE LIZARD

Get thee to a gourmet shop and buy yourself a tart pan with a removable bottom, as well as a pastry bag, otherwise you'll be missing out on this classic dessert. Before there was the book called *Tales from Margaritaville*, there was the album called *Off to See the Lizard*, and "I Wish Lunch Could Last Forever" was the name of a song before it was ever the name of a short story. Nonetheless, both the song and the story have revealed a great deal about Jimmy's cravings for fine food.

Though this tart isn't in the story, it certainly takes top billing in the song. In fact, Jimmy suggests that you start your lunch with this dessert, as well as with a CAFE AU LAIT. To save you a bit of time in your endless lunch, not only is the coffee added right to this tart, but also the recipe can be made a day ahead, as long as it is covered and refrigerated.

INGREDIENTS:
For the crust:

    ¾ c all-purpose flour
    ½ c sweet coconut, shredded & toasted

7 T chilled unsalted butter, in ½-inch pieces
½ c powdered sugar
1 t instant coffee crystals
¼ t salt

For the filling:
¼ c sugar
6¼ t instant coffee crystals
2 T cornstarch
½ c plus 2 T whipping cream
6 T cream of coconut
4 large egg yolks, beaten
½ t vanilla extract

For the topping:
¾ c whipping cream, chilled
¼ c cream of coconut
2 T powdered sugar
Sweetened coconut, shredded & toasted

PREPARATION:
Of the crust:
In a food processor, combine the flour, shredded coconut, butter, powdered sugar, instant coffee crystals, and salt. Process these ingredients until they form into moist clumps, about 1 minute.

Transfer the mixture to a 9-inch tart pan with a removable bottom, then press the dough onto the bottom and along the sides of the pan.

Place the pan in the freezer until the crust becomes firm, about 10 minutes.

Preheat your oven to 350° F.

Remove the tart pan from the freezer and place it on a baking sheet. With a toothpick, pierce the crust all over.

Place the baking sheet on the center rack of your oven and bake the crust until it is golden brown, about 25 minutes.

With an oven mitt, remove the baking sheet from the oven and allow the crust to cool.

Of the filling:
Before measuring your cream of coconut, blend it at high speed for 30 seconds.

In a medium saucepan, whisk together the sugar, coffee crystals and cornstarch until there are no lumps of cornstarch. Do not panic if all of the coffee crystals do not dissolve.

Gradually whisk in the cream, then whisk in the blendered cream of coconut.

Mix in the eggs yolks, then whisk the mixture over medium heat until it thickens and comes to the boil, about 8 minutes.

Remove the pan from the heat and occasionally whisk the mixture as you allow it to cool.

Whisk in the vanilla, then spread the filling into your crust.

Place the tart in the refrigerator to chill until cold, about 2 hours.

Of the topping:
Again, blend your cream of coconut before measuring any into the recipe.

In a medium mixing bowl, beat together the whipping cream, cream of coconut, and powdered sugar until firm peaks form.

Affix a medium star tip to your pastry bag, then fill the bag with the topping. Pipe the topping over the filling, then sprinkle with the shredded coconut.*

Place the tart in the refrigerator to chill for at least 1 hour before serving.

* If you're like me, you'll probably hold the topping and coconut garnish until you've served a slice of the tart. Then, you'll just dollop on the topping and sprinkle the coconut. Tastes just as good to me!

Key Lime Pie

— FROM "Are You Ready for Freddy?"
in TALES FROM MARGARITAVILLE / P. 181

Yields one 10-inch pie

Fishstick is just his stage name; Purvis is his real moniker. Some knew him simply as Freddy, lead singer of a group that opened for Joe Merchant; one knew him as her husband. That one, of course, was our fair Desdemona. Her band was Cats in Heat, but her talent was baking. And though Freddy might not have had the good sense to stick with our gal, at least he knew a classic dessert when he ate one. And this is the one that he and Jimmy had at the Big Pine Inn on their way to Cayo Hueso.

Chemically speaking, KEY LIME PIE is a ceviche, not unlike CONCH SALAD. In this case, though, the acid in the lime juice is "cooking" the protein in the eggs. Most people don't trust the limes, however, so they stick the pie in the oven to cook the eggs with some heat. That's okay, too.

The big question, however, is should the pie be made with a meringue top, as in lemon meringue pie? The big answer is NO! A lot of people do that simply because they don't have any other use for the egg whites. But because key limes and lemons both produce yellow pies, I think you ought to leave off the meringue from the lime pie just to set things straight. And because restaurants tend to overcharge customers for a sliver of this rather simple dessert, I always like to double this recipe and serve up jumbo slices. That only means that you'll have to drink a little more something to slosh down the extra serving of tartness.

Finally, some bakers like to tinker with this classic recipe by using a chocolate cookie crust. As for me, I like to use a crust of GINGER SNAPS, now and then.

INGREDIENTS:

For the crust:

> 18 graham cracker squares, crushed into crumbs
> ¼ lb butter
> ½ c sugar
> ¼ t fresh cinnamon, grated

For the filling:

> 1 14-oz can of sweetened condensed milk
> 3 egg yolks, beaten
> ½ c key lime juice

PREPARATION:

Of the crust:

Preheat your oven to 375° F.

In a large mixing bowl, combine the graham cracker crumbs, butter, sugar, and cinnamon.

Mix the ingredients together thoroughly with your fingertips, then pack them tightly into a 10-inch pie pan.

Place the pan in the center rack of your oven and bake for 10 minutes.

With an oven mitt, remove the pie crust from the oven.

If you plan to bake your pie, then reduce your oven heat to 350° F.

Of the filling:

In a large mixing bowl, mix together the condensed milk and egg yolks. This might take a little work at first until these two ingredients begin to blend together.

Gradually add in the key lime juice and continue mixing until the filling is rather thick and smooth.

Pour your filling mixture into the graham cracker crust.

Again, you may wish to allow your pie to "cook" overnight in the refrigerator as the citric acid and protein do their chemical interaction.

Otherwise, place the pie on the center rack of your oven and bake for 10 minutes.

With an oven mitt, remove your pie from the oven and allow to cool.

This pie *cannot* be served warm or else it will simply run all over your serving dishes and your pie plate.

You might wish to top with whipped cream.

Crème Brûlée

— FROM "Walkabout"
in TALES FROM MARGARITAVILLE / P. 6

Yields 8 5-oz servings

Ramekins is a three-syllable word that has nothing to do with either baby mountain goats or very little computer memory. In the kitchen, a *ramekin* is a small porcelain casserole used for baking individual servings, such as in this recipe. As for the CRÈME BRÛLÉE, itself, this is a French cousin to the CUSTARD and the FLAN, popular throughout Mexico and the Caribbean. While both the CUSTARD and the FLAN are generally cooked in a larger baking dish, the CRÈME BRÛLÉE also boasts a trademark finish of having the brown sugar on top caramelized with an open flame (or a boring broiler).

INGREDIENTS:

> 1¾ c heavy cream
> 1¾ c milk
> ½ vanilla bean, split
> 7 egg yolks
> 2 whole eggs
> ½ c sugar
> Brown sugar

PREPARATION:

In a large saucepan, combine the heavy cream, milk, and vanilla bean, then bring to the boil over a low heat.

Remove the saucepan from the heat and allow the vanilla bean to steep for 10 minutes.

With a spoon, scrape the seeds of the vanilla bean into the cream and milk.

In a large mixing bowl, combine the eggs and the ½ c of sugar with a mixer.

In a steady stream, pour the cream and milk mixture from the saucepan into the bowl and continue mixing.

Strain the custard mix into another large mixing bowl, then skim off any foam.

Preheat your oven to 325° F.

Set your 8 ramekins into a large baking dish and divide the custard mix equally among them. Being careful not to spill any hot water into the custard, add enough water so that it comes about halfway up the sides of the ramekins.

Carefully place the baking dish on the center rack of the oven and bake until the custard just sets, about 25 to 30 minutes.

With an oven mitt, *carefully* remove the baking dish from the oven and turn on the broiler.

Top each custard with brown sugar, then place under the broiler until the brown sugar has caramelized.

CITRUS CRÈME BRÛLÉE

Yields 8 5-oz servings

INGREDIENTS:

> Juice of 1 lime
> Juice of 1 lemon
> Juice of 2 oranges
> 2½ c heavy cream
> ½ c plus 1 T sugar
> 6 egg yolks

PREPARATION:

Preheat your oven to 300° F.

In a saucepan combine the juices, then cook over medium heat until they have been reduced to a very tart syrup of about ¼ cup.

Add to the saucepan the heavy cream and sugar, then stir and cook them until the sugar has completely dissolved. Set aside.

In a large mixing bowl, beat the egg yolks slightly. Gradually, mix in the citrus and cream mixture.

Use a fine sieve to strain the egg mixture into another bowl.

Set your 8 ramekins into a large baking dish and divide the custard mix equally among them. Being careful not to spill any hot water into the custard, add enough water so that it comes about halfway up the sides of the ramekins. Carefully place the baking dish on the center rack of the oven and bake until the custard just sets, about 1½ hours.

With an oven mitt, *carefully* remove the baking dish from the oven and allow the custard to cool in the water bath for 15 minutes.

Carefully remove the ramekins from the baking dish and allow the custard to cool completely.

Refrigerate at least 4 hours before serving.

Top each custard with brown sugar, then place under the broiler until the brown sugar has caramelized.

Blonde Stranger

— FROM "Who's the Blonde Stranger?"
on RIDDLES IN THE SAND

Among the jillions of things that New Orleans is known for, BREAD PUDDING ranks right up there at the top. Though Jimmy never has mentioned this in any of his songs or stories, Executive Chef Joe Tusa at The Margaritaville Cafe in New Orleans attributes the origin of this regional dish to the city's love of French bread. And because the loaves don't stay particularly fresh beyond a day, there is a lot of stale bread to be consumed in the Crescent City.

BLONDE STRANGER is the Cafe's interpretation of this local classic, adding ripe bananas to the pudding. To finish this off, each serving at Margaritaville is topped with medallions of banana, VANILLA ICE CREAM and their signature CARAMEL RUM SAUCE.

INGREDIENTS:
For the pudding:

> 4 c milk
> 2 eggs
> 2 t vanilla
> 1½ c sugar

8 oz stale French bread

1 t fresh cinnamon, grated

1 t fresh nutmeg, grated

1 c ripened banana, sliced

½ c golden raisins

For the caramel rum sauce:

4 c sugar

1 c water

1½ T fresh lemon juice

¼ T cream of tartar

1½ c heavy cream

¼ c dark rum

PREPARATION:

Of the bread pudding:
Tear the French bread into medium-sized chunks and place in a large mixing bowl.

Add the sliced banana, raisins, sugar, cinnamon, and nutmeg, then toss them together well.

In a separate mixing bowl, beat together the eggs, vanilla, and milk.

Pour the beaten egg-milk mixture into the bowl of dry ingredients and allow the bread to soak for 30 minutes.

Preheat your oven to 350° F.

Lightly grease a 9- by 13-inch baking dish.

Spread the mixture evenly in the baking dish, then grate some more fresh cinnamon on top.

Bake for 45 minutes.

With an oven mitt, remove the pudding from the oven and allow to cool.

Of the caramel rum sauce:
In a small saucepan, combine the sugar, cream of tartar, lime juice, and water, then cook over low heat until the sugar has melted.

Bring this sugar mixture to the full boil over high heat and cook until it has reached the caramel stage of golden to medium brown.

Remove the saucepan from the heat and gradually stir in the heavy cream until it has all been incorporated into the caramel.

Prepare a pan of ice into which you will be able to place the saucepan *after* the next step.

Return the saucepan to the heat and bring the caramel cream mixture to the boil for 2 minutes.

Remove the saucepan from the stove and place it in the pan of ice to cool the caramel cream.

Stir in the dark rum. If the sauce and rum separate during the cooling process, continue to stir them together.

Top each serving of pudding with the sauce.

TRADITIONAL NEW ORLEANS BREAD PUDDING

Yields 12 servings

INGREDIENTS:

10 oz stale French bread

1 c coconut, shredded

1 c pecans, chopped

1 c raisins

1 T fresh cinnamon, grated

1 T fresh nutmeg, grated

3 eggs

4 c milk

2 T vanilla

1¼ c sugar

PREPARATION:

Tear the French bread into medium-sized chunks and toss in a large mixing bowl, along with the coconut, pecans, raisins, cinnamon, and nutmeg.

In a separate mixing bowl, lightly beat the eggs with the milk and vanilla.

Add the sugar and stir until dissolved.

Pour the egg and milk mixture into the bowl with the dry ingredients and mix lightly with your fingertips so that the mixture is moist, but not soupy. Allow this to soak for 30 minutes.

Butter a 9- by 12-inch baking dish.

Pour the pudding mixture into the buttered baking dish, then place on the center rack of your *unheated* oven.

Set your oven to 350° F and bake until the top of the pudding is golden brown, about 1¼ hours.

With an oven mitt, remove the pudding from the oven and allow it to cool 30 minutes before serving.

Banana Split

Yields 4 servings

— FROM "I Will Play for Gumbo"
on BEACH HOUSE ON THE MOON

— FROM "They Don't Dance Like Carmen No More"
on A WHITE SPORT COAT AND A PINK CRUSTACEAN

— FROM "No Plane on Sunday"
on FLORIDAYS

Though Jimmy does sing about BANANA SPLITS in "I Will Play for Gumbo," I just couldn't muster the courage to tell you to slice a banana lengthwise, drop 3 scoops of ice cream in the cradle of fruit, pour on 3 different toppings, then top with whipped cream and nuts. (Oh, I guess I *did* get up the courage after all. Now, if I only had a brain . . .)

And knowing Jimmy's love of puns, it was only a matter of time that I tried to force upon you CARAMEL MIRANDA, which includes much of the fruit that the Brazilian bombshell wore "piled high to the sky," along with a rich, tropical ice cream, all adrift on a sea of creamy caramel sauce. At the Avalon® in Lahaina on the Hawaiian island of Maui, Chef Mark Ellman has created a signature dish he also calls CARAMEL MIRANDA. So, Chef Chas. Burger and I improvised a bit to finesse many of the same ingredients into NO PLAIN OL' SUNDAE. This can be served with any flavor ice cream you choose, but Chef Chas. prefers the COCONUT ICE CREAM.

In buying a fresh pineapple, look for one with the "gold" label that indicates it has ripened *be-*

fore being harvested. Depending upon the ripeness of your fruits, you might wish to sweeten the mix with a bit of sugar, or else tarten it with some lime juice.

No Plain Ol' Sundae

INGREDIENTS:
For the fruit:

> 2 c ripe pineapple, peeled & diced
> 1 c mango, peeled, seeded & diced
> 1 c ripe papaya, peeled, seeded & diced
> 1 vanilla bean
> ¼ cup dark rum
> Fresh mint, chopped
> Sugar or lime juice, to taste

For the topping:

> 4 c sugar
> 1 c water
> 1½ T fresh lemon juice
> ¼ T cream of tartar
> 1½ c heavy cream
> ¼ c dark rum
>
> 4 scoops ice cream

PREPARATION:
Of the fruit:
In a large mixing bowl, combine the pineapple, mango, and papaya.

With a sharp paring knife, slice the vanilla bean lengthwise, then scrape the seeds of the pod into the mixing bowl with the fruit.

Add the dark rum and chopped mint.

Toss the fruit mix lightly with your fingertips.

Cover the bowl with plastic wrap and allow the flavors to marry at room temperature for 1 hour.

Of the topping:
In a small saucepan, combine the sugar, cream of tartar, lime juice, and water, then cook over low heat until the sugar has melted.

Bring this sugar mixture to the full boil over high heat and cook until it has reached the caramel stage of golden to medium brown.

Remove the saucepan from the heat and gradually stir in the heavy cream until it has all been incorporated into the caramel.

Prepare a pan of ice into which you will be able to place the saucepan *after* the next step.

Return the saucepan to the heat and bring the caramel cream mixture to the boil for 2 minutes.

Remove the saucepan from the stove and place in the pan of ice to cool the caramel cream.

Stir in the dark rum. If the sauce and rum separate during the cooling process, continue to stir them together.

Of the presentation:
Spoon a layer of fruit into each ice cream dish.

Place 3 scoops of ICE CREAM atop the fruit.

Spoon the topping over the ICE CREAM.

Garnish each serving with a spring of mint.

Desdemona's Brownies

— FROM "Fruitcakes in the Galley,
Fruitcakes on the Street"
in WHERE IS JOE MERCHANT? / P. 72

Legendary folk singer Phil Ochs wrote a song called "Miranda," about a girl who not only was a Rudolf Valentino fan, but also baked brownies for the boys in the band. Definitely a 60s thing. And something which Desdemona (both women's names are Shakespearean) also did in the 60s. Presented here for your approval, then, is the absolutely best recipe for brownies which anyone could bake without any herbal additives (*wink, wink*). Maybe it's that missing ingredient which makes them so gooey that they must be made a day before they can be cut into squares. In any event, they are so dark, so sweet, and so crispy on top that you won't need the herbs to ride into orbit.

INGREDIENTS:

8 oz unsweetened chocolate
½ c unsalted butter
5 large eggs
2 T vanilla extract
¼ t salt
1 t almond extract

*1 T plus 1 t powdered (not granular)
espresso
3¾ c sugar
1¾ c all-purpose flour, sifted
2 c walnuts, chopped in large pieces*

PREPARATION:

Place an oven rack in the lower third of your oven and preheat the oven to 400° F.

Line a 9- by 13- by 2-inch pan with aluminum foil, then brush the foil well with melted butter and set it aside.

In the top of a large double boiler, melt together the chocolate and butter over medium heat. Stir until the chocolate and butter are mixed well, then remove from the heat and set aside.

In a large mixing bowl, combine the eggs, vanilla extract, salt, almond extract, dry espresso powder, and sugar, then beat at high speed for a full 10 minutes. (Yes, 10 minutes.)

Reduce the speed of the mixer to low, then add the melted butter and chocolate to the bowl. Beat until the batter is mixed well.

Add the sifted flour, then beat until it is just mixed with the other ingredients.

Remove the bowl from the mixer and stir the walnuts into the batter.

Transfer the batter to the buttered (aluminum foil in the) baking pan and smooth out the top.

Place the baking pan in the lower third of your oven and bake for 15 minutes. Watch during this period for even baking and turn the pan if necessary.

Bake for another 10 minutes, then insert a clean toothpick. Though the top of the brownies will be crisp, the toothpick should come out covered with wet chocolate. Have no fear! Your brownies are done.

With an oven mitt, remove the baking pan from the oven and allow it to cool to room temperature.

When the brownies are cool, place a wire rack on top of the baking pan, then invert the brownies onto the rack. Remove the baking pan and the buttered foil from the brownies, then cover the bottom of the brownies with a cookie sheet and invert them once again. If all is done correctly, the brownies should now be crispy side up.

Allow the brownies to stand for at least 8 hours, but preferably overnight.

Use a serrated knife to cut these gooey delights and wipe the knife clean with a damp cloth between each cutting.

Store the brownies in an airtight container with wax paper between the layers. Because you went through all the trouble to get these gooey, do *not* allow them to dry out!

Desdemona's Passion

— FROM "No Bird Flies by My Window"
in WHERE IS JOE MERCHANT? / P. 222

— FROM "Further Adventures
in Restless Behavior"
in WHERE IS JOE MERCHANT? / P. 380

— FROM "Desdemona's Building
A Rocket Ship"
on BANANA WIND

This woman's passion, sings Jimmy, is definitely cookies, and I think these recipes might show you why.

But I must add this galley note: To avoid burning the bottoms of these cookies, you might want to use either cushioned cookie sheets (or else doubled cookie sheets), then line them with parchment paper. You'll find that works much better than any other method.

CHOCOLATE CHIP

Yields 2½ dozen cookies

This is one of those recipes for chewy cookies which you *must* follow precisely without deviation. You'll be glad that you did.

INGREDIENTS:

3 c all-purpose flour

1 t salt

1 t baking soda

¼ t baking powder

¾ c unsalted butter, softened

1 c dark brown sugar, packed
½ c white sugar
1 T vanilla extract
1 T coffee liqueur
2 large eggs
2 T dark corn syrup
1 T milk
2 c semisweet chocolate chips
1½ c pecans, toasted & chopped coarse

PREPARATION:

Position your rack in the lower third of oven, then preheat your oven to 350° F.

In a medium mixing bowl, whisk together the flour, salt, baking soda and baking powder, then set them aside.

In a large mixing bowl, use an electric mixer at medium speed to cream together the butter and the sugars, along with the vanilla until the ingredients are light and creamy.

Add each egg and beat well after each one.

Add the corn syrup and milk to the bowl and mix well.

Reduce your mixer to low speed.

In 3 separate batches, add the dry ingredients to the larger bowl. Scrape down the bowl each time you add dry ingredients and make certain that you mix the ingredients well each time.

Stir in the chocolate morsels and nuts to make a very sticky dough.

Wet your hands under running water and shake 10 times before handling the dough. Plan to do this between the making of every third cookie.

Using a 1 T measuring spoon, scoop 2 level measures of dough into one hand, then roll with your wet hands into a ball

Place each ball of dough at least 2 inches apart on your cookie sheets, then slightly flatten each with your fingers.

Place your cookie sheet in the lower third of your oven and bake until the cookies are lightly golden around the edges, but still a bit puffy in the centers, about 14 minutes. (If you underbake these cookies, they will be too gooey.)

With an oven mitt, remove the cookie sheets from the oven and allow to cool 5 minutes on top of your stove.

Use a thin metal spatula to transfer each cookie to wire racks.

Discard any used parchment paper before making any more cookies.

Store the cooled cookies in an airtight container at room temperature.

BANANA SPICE

Yields 2½ dozen cookies

INGREDIENTS:

½ c butter
2¼ c all-purpose flour
1 c white sugar
2 eggs
1 t vanilla extract
½ t fresh cinnamon, grated
¼ t baking soda
¼ t cloves, ground
3 bananas, mashed
1 t baking powder
½ c pecans, toasted & chopped

PREPARATION:

Preheat your oven to 375° F.

In a large mixing bowl, use an electric mixer on high speed to beat the butter for 30 seconds.

Add 1 c of the flour, as well as the sugar, eggs, baking powder, vanilla, cinnamon, baking soda, and cloves, then beat them together well.

Stir in the rest of the flour.

Add the mashed bananas and nuts to the bowl, stir, then beat them well.

Wet your hands under running water and shake 10 times before handling the dough. Plan to do this between the making of every third cookie.

Using a 1 T measuring spoon, scoop 2 level measures of dough into one hand, then roll with your wet hands into a ball

Place each ball of dough at least 2 inches apart on your cookie sheets, then slightly flatten each with your fingers.

Place your cookie sheet in the lower third of your oven and bake until the cookies are lightly golden around the edge, but still a bit puffy in the center, about 14 minutes.

With an oven mitt, remove the cookie sheets from the oven and allow to cool 5 minutes on top of your stove.

Use a thin metal spatula to transfer each cookie to wire racks.

Discard any used parchment paper before making any more cookies.

Store the cooled cookies in an airtight container at room temperature.

BEER COOKIES

Yields 2½ dozen cookies

Though there is no beer in Heaven, Paradise just might not be Paradise without it.

INGREDIENTS:

> ½ c butter
> 2 c all-purpose flour
> ½ c brown sugar
> ½ t baking soda
> 1 t fresh cinnamon, grated
> 1¼ c warm beer
> ½ c walnuts

PREPARATION:

Preheat your oven to 350° F.

In a large mixing bowl, use an electric mixer on high speed to beat the butter for 30 seconds.

Add 1 c of the flour, as well as the sugar, baking soda, and cinnamon, then beat together well.

Stir in the rest of the flour.

Gradually, mix in the warm beer until you've formed a soft dough.

Wet your hands under running water and shake 10 times before handling the dough. Plan to do this between the making of every third cookie.

Using a 1 T measuring spoon, scoop 2 level measures of dough into one hand, then roll with your wet hands into a ball

Place each ball of dough at least 2 inches apart on your cookie sheets, then slightly flatten each with your fingers.

Sprinkle chopped walnuts on top of each cookie and press them in slightly with your fingertips.

Place your cookie sheet in the lower third of your

oven and bake until the cookies are lightly golden around the edges, but still a bit puffy in the centers, about 12 to 15 minutes.

With an oven mitt, remove the cookie sheets from the oven and allow to cool 5 minutes on top of your stove.

Use a thin metal spatula to transfer each cookie to wire racks.

Discard any used parchment paper before making any more cookies.

BRAZILIAN COFFEE

Yields 2½ dozen cookies

The texture of these little morsels is much the same as that of a GINGERSNAP, but the flavor is truly of Brazilian coffee. Each one is as good as a fun ticket.

INGREDIENTS:

> *2 c all-purpose flour*
> *½ t salt*
> *2 T powdered instant coffee*
> *¼ t baking soda*
> *¼ t baking powder*
> *½ c solid vegetable shortening*
> *½ c brown sugar*
> *½ c white sugar*
> *1½ t vanilla extract*
> *1 T milk*
> *1 egg*

PREPARATION:

Position your rack in the lower third of oven, then preheat your oven to 400° F.

In a medium mixing bowl, whisk together the flour, salt, powdered instant coffee, baking soda and baking powder, then set aside.

In a large mixing bowl, use an electric mixer at medium speed to cream together the solid shortening and the sugars, along with the vanilla and milk until the ingredients are light and creamy.

Add the egg and beat well.

Reduce your mixer to low speed.

In 3 separate batches, add the dry ingredients to the larger bowl. Scrape down the bowl each time you add dry ingredients and make certain that you mix the ingredients well each time.

Wet your hands under running water and shake 10 times before handling the dough. Plan to do this between the making of every third cookie.

Using a 1 T measuring spoon, scoop 2 level measures of dough into one hand, then roll with your wet hands into a ball

Place each ball of dough at least 2 inches apart on your cookie sheets.

Dip the bottom of a milk glass in sugar, then flatten each ball of dough to a cookie that is less than ¼-inch thick.

Place your cookie sheet in the lower third of your oven and bake until the cookies are lightly browned, about 8 to 10 minutes.

With an oven mitt, remove the cookie sheets from the oven and allow to cool 5 minutes on top of your stove.

Use a thin metal spatula to transfer each cookie to wire racks.

Discard any used parchment paper before making any more cookies.

Store the cooled cookies in an airtight container at room temperature.

Coconut Macaroons

Yields 2 dozen cookies

Ingredients:

2 egg whites
1 T corn starch
½ c white sugar
1 t vanilla extract
1 c coconut, flaked

Preparation:

Position your rack in the lower third of oven, then preheat your oven to 400° F.

In a medium mixing bowl, beat the egg whites until they are stiff, but not too dry.

Fold in the cornstarch.

Transfer the egg whites to the top portion of a double boiler, then set over low heat.

Stir the sugar into the egg whites and cook until the mixture begins to pull away from the edges of the double boiler, about 3 to 4 minutes.

Remove the top half of the double boiler from the heat, then stir in the vanilla.

Add the flaked coconut to the mixture and stir.

Use a teaspoon to drop the dough onto the parchment paper covering your cookie sheets and space each spoonful 1½ inches apart.

Place the cookie sheet in the lower third of your oven and bake until the macaroons are both golden brown and firm to the touch, about 20 to 25 minutes.

With an oven mitt, remove the cookie sheets from the oven and allow them to cool on your stove top for 5 minutes.

With a thin metal spatula, transfer the macaroons to a wire rack to cool completely.

Store in an airtight container in your refrigerator or freezer.

These are best served cold.

Chocolate Macaroons

Yields 2½ dozen cookies

These cookies can also be served partially frozen.

Ingredients:

1½ c semisweet chocolate chips
3 egg whites
1 pinch salt
¾ c white sugar
1 t vanilla extract
2 ¼ c shredded coconut
½ c toasted pecans, chopped fine

Preparation:

Position your rack in the lower third of oven, then preheat your oven to 325° F.

In a small saucepan, melt the semisweet chocolate over low heat. Set aside to cool.

In a medium mixing bowl, beat the egg whites until they are foamy.

Slowly add the salt and sugar until the egg whites stand in peaks.

Stir in the vanilla.

Fold the cooled chocolate, flaked coconut, and pecans into the mixture and stir only until blended.

Use a teaspoon to drop the dough onto the parchment paper covering your cookie sheets and space each spoonful 1½ inches apart.

Place the cookie sheet in the lower third of your oven and bake until the macaroons are firm to the touch, but still soft in the center, about 10 to 12 minutes.

With an oven mitt, remove the cookie sheets from the oven and allow them to cool on your stove top for 5 minutes.

With a thin metal spatula, transfer the cookies to a wire rack to cool completely.

Store in an airtight container in your refrigerator or freezer.

These are best served cold.

KEY LIME COOKIES

Yields 2 dozen cookies

Maybe it's ironic that these cookies with a Florida taste come from a rather traditional icebox dough, which can be made in larger batches, then frozen. If you wish, you could substitute either orange or lemon for the citrus flavor in these cookies.

INGREDIENTS:

- ½ c butter, unsalted
- ¾ c white sugar
- ½ c all-purpose flour
- ¼ t salt
- 1 T key lime juice
- 2 t lime zest, grated
- 1½ c all-purpose flour

PREPARATION:

In a large mixing bowl, use an electric mixer at medium speed to cream together the butter and the sugar until they are light and creamy.

Add the salt, lime zest, and lime juice, then beat well.

Reduce your mixer to low speed.

In 3 separate batches, add the flour to the mixture. Scrape down the bowl each time you add the flour and make certain that you mix the ingredients well each time.

Turn the dough out onto a lightly-floured surface, then use your hands to shape the dough into a log about 2½ inches in diameter.

Wrap tightly with plastic wrap and chill at least 4 hours. (You could also freeze the dough at this stage.)

Position your rack in the lower third of oven, then preheat your oven to 350° F.

Remove the wrap from the dough, then use a sharp knife to slice the dough into 24 cookies.

Place each slice of dough at least 2 inches apart on your cookie sheets.

Place your cookie sheet in the lower third of your oven and bake until the cookies are lightly browned, about 8 minutes.

With an oven mitt, remove the cookie sheets from the oven and allow to cool 5 minutes on top of your stove.

Use a thin metal spatula to transfer each cookie to wire racks.

Discard any used parchment paper before making any more cookies.

Store the cooled cookies in an airtight container at room temperature.

GINGER SNAP COOKIES

Yields 2 dozen cookies

INGREDIENTS:

- 2¼ c unbleached flour
- 2 t fresh ginger, grated

½ t salt
2 t baking soda
¾ c butter, unsalted
½ c brown sugar
¼ c molasses
1 egg
2 T fresh ginger, grated
½ c candied ginger, chopped fine

PREPARATION:
Position your rack in the lower third of oven, then preheat your oven to 350° F.

In a medium mixing bowl, whisk together the unbleached flour, ground ginger, salt, and baking soda, then set aside.

In a large mixing bowl, use an electric mixer at medium speed to cream together the solid butter and sugar until they are light and creamy.

Add the egg and molasses, then beat well.

Reduce your mixer to low speed.

In 3 separate batches, add the dry ingredients to the larger bowl. Scrape down the bowl each time you add dry ingredients and make certain that you mix the ingredients well each time.

Blend in the fresh ginger and the chopped candied ginger.

Wet your hands under running water and shake 10 times before handling the dough. Plan to do this between the making of every third cookie.

Using a 1 T measuring spoon, scoop 2 level measures of dough into one hand, then roll with your wet hands into a ball

Place each ball of dough at least 2 inches apart on your cookie sheets.

Dip the bottom of a milk glass in sugar, then flatten each ball of dough to a cookie that is less than ¼-inch thick.

Place your cookie sheet in the lower third of your oven and bake until the cookies are lightly browned, about 10 minutes.

With an oven mitt, remove the cookie sheets from the oven and allow to cool 5 minutes on top of your stove.

Use a thin metal spatula to transfer each cookie to wire racks.

Discard any used parchment paper before making any more cookies.

Store the cooled cookies in an airtight container at room temperature.

Coconut Cake

Yields 10 servings

— FROM "I Wish Lunch Could Last Forever"
in TALES FROM MARGARITAVILLE / P. 155

"Wedding" is the one word that's missing from the name on this recipe. COCONUT WEDDING CAKE is what Isabella called it, but I left out the "wedding" part for two simple reasons. For one thing, the word just didn't fit on the page well; for another, just reading that word gives some folks the heebie-jeebies. Besides, this cake shouldn't need any occasion to be baked and enjoyed, and it's too good for any bride to shove into her groom's face.

INGREDIENTS:

For the cake:

> 2 c sugar
> 1½ c solid vegetable shortening, softened
> ¼ c butter, softened
> 5 large eggs, separated
> 2 c all-purpose flour
> 1 t baking soda
> Pinch of salt
> 1 c buttermilk
> 2 c sweetened coconut, shredded
> 1 t vanilla extract

For the frosting:

> 16 oz cream cheese, softened
> 2 sticks butter, softened
> 2 t vanilla extract
> 2 lbs confectioner's sugar
> ¼ c sweetened coconut, shredded &
> toasted

PREPARATION:

Of the cake:

Lightly butter and flour 3 8-inch round cake pans.

Preheat your oven to 350° F.

In a large mixing bowl, cream together the sugar, shortening, and butter with an electric mixer until they are light and fluffy.

Separate the eggs, then add 1 yolk at a time to the mixing bowl. Beat well after each egg.

In a smaller mixing bowl, sift together the flour, baking soda, and salt.

In small batches, alternate adding the sifted dry ingredients and the buttermilk to the larger bowl. Mix between the adding of each ingredient.

Add both the shredded coconut and the vanilla to the batter, then stir.

In another mixing bowl, beat the egg whites until they form soft peaks.

Fold the beaten egg whites into the cake batter.

Divide the batter evenly among the 3 cake pans.

Place the cake pans on the center rack of your oven and bake until an inserted toothpick can be cleanly removed, about 20 to 25 minutes.

With an oven mitt, remove the cake pans from the oven and allow to cool.

Of the frosting:

In a large mixing bowl, beat together the cream cheese, butter, vanilla, and sugar until smooth and creamy.

Transfer one layer of the cake from the baking pan to a serving dish, then spread a generous layer of frosting across the top.

Transfer a second layer of cake from the baking pan to the frosted top of the first layer, then spread a generous layer of frosting across its top.

Transfer the third layer of cake from the baking pan to the frosted top of the second layer, but spread its layer of frosting only to within a half inch of the outer edge.

Generously frost the sides of all three layers, then complete the frosting of the top layer.

Sprinkle the toasted coconut across the top of the cake.

Fruitcakes

— FROM "Fruitcakes"
on FRUITCAKES

What on earth would *ever* compel me to give you a recipe for something which rightfully has been maligned and ridiculed for generations? I won't even bother telling you anything about traditional fruitcakes, other than that the alleged fruit used in such things is not anything which mankind has ever found in a natural state. Did Darwin ever discover candied citron anywhere in his voyage of the *Beagle*? And why would anyone boast about baking something that apparently lasts forever because no one wants to eat such garbage? After all, what might be an admirable quality in roofing material is not necessarily a tribute to great taste. (Just put it right over there next to the mincemeat pie, please.)

Instead, then, I offer here some true cakes with real fruits, which not only are edible, but also shall be eaten!

FRUITCAKE CITY

Yields 12 adult servings (ID required)

In place of all those yucky candied fruits in a traditional fruitcake, this recipe includes the familiar dried fruits found in most supermarkets. Try to find a store that gives you the opportunity to be a little picky about what you're buying, then get as much dried banana, coconut, papaya, mango, and other tropical fruits as you can. Combined with the orange juice and spices (not to mention the rum!), these give this recipe a feeling for the little latitudes and not some dark and dank coal mine in Wales. A variation on this would be to use Grand Marnier instead of the rum.

INGREDIENTS:

4 c mixed dried fruit, chopped

2¼ c raisins

1 large green apple, peeled, cored & chopped

½ c pecans, chopped

¼ c orange juice

2 t orange zest, grated

½ c plus 2½ T dark rum

1¾ c cake flour

½ c almonds, ground

¾ t fresh cinnamon, grated

½ t fresh nutmeg, grated

¼ t salt

¾ c sugar

¼ c unsalted butter, softened

3 large eggs, room temperature

½ c light corn syrup

PREPARATION:

In a large mixing bowl, combine the dried fruits, raisins, apple, pecans, orange juice, and zest.

Stir the ½ c of rum into the mixture, then allow it to stand at room temperature until the liquids have been absorbed, about 30 minutes. Stir occasionally.

Generously butter a 10-c bundt pan, then lightly dust it with flour. Set aside.

Preheat your oven to 325° F.

In a small mixing bowl, combine the flour, almonds, cinnamon, nutmeg, and salt.

In another large mixing bowl, cream together the butter and sugar.

Add 1 egg at a time to the creamed butter and sugar, then beat well after each egg.

Transfer the bowl of fruit mixture to the bowl with the butter, sugar, and eggs, then blend together.

Add the bowl of dry ingredients to this larger bowl and mix well.

Pour the batter into the bundt pan, then place the pan in the center rack of your oven.

Bake until a knife inserted near the center of the cake can be removed clean, about 1¼ hours.

With an oven mitt, remove the cake from the oven and allow it to cool in the pan for 10 minutes.

Turn the cake out onto a wire rack and allow it to cool to room temperature.

In a small saucepan, combine the remaining 2½ T of rum with the corn syrup over low heat. Do not allow this to become anything other than warm, or else you will burn off the alcohol in the rum!

With a pastry brush, spread the warm glaze over the whole cake, including the bottom. When you've finished doing that once, give it another coat . . . even if it means making another batch of corn syrup and rum!!! (Hint.)

Seal the cake well in a good layer of heavy duty aluminum foil and allow the cake to mellow at room temperature for 1 day.

Store the cake in the refrigerator. In theory, this could last a good two weeks, but why should all that rum be sitting idle in your refrigerator?

HALF-BAKED FRUITCAKE

Yields to no one

INGREDIENTS:

1 c water
1 c sugar
4 large brown eggs
2 c dried fruit, chopped
1 t salt
1 c brown sugar
2 T lime juice
½ c pecans
1 qt premium rum

PREPARATION:

First of all, to make certain that your rum is of the highest quality, you should sample just a bit before assembling the rest of the ingredients.

Find a large mixing bowl, then check the quality of the rum once more, just to be certain. Pour a good level c of rum and swallow it down. Better do that again.

With your electric mixer, beat one c of butter in a large fluffy bowl.

Add 1 t of sugar and beat again.

Just to make sure the rum is still okay, better cry another tup.

Turn off the mixer.

Beat two leggs, add to the bowl, then chuck in the c of dried fruit.

Mix on the tuner. If the fried druit gets stuck in the beaterers, pry it loose with a drewscriver.

Check the rum for tonsisticity.

Sniff 2 c of salt. No, sift 2 c of salt. No, sift 2 c of something. Who gives a dried fig?

Better check the rum instead.

Chop the lemon juice and strain your nuts.

Add 1 Table. Spoon. Of sugar or something. Whatever you want, pal.

Grease the oven well. Turn the cake pan to 350° F.

Don't forget to mix off the turner.

Throw the bowl out the window, the check the rum one more time.

Better stumble off to your hammock before you hurt yourself.

SUMMER FRUITCAKE

Yields 8 servings

INGREDIENTS:

½ c brown sugar
½ c white sugar
2 c unbleached flour
2 t baking powder
½ t baking soda
½ t salt
½ c butter
1¼ c buttermilk
2 eggs
1 t vanilla
1½ c green apples, peeled & chopped
1 c fresh peaches, peeled & chopped
1 c bing cherries, pitted & chopped
½ brown sugar, packed
¼ c all-purpose flour
2 T butter
½ c almonds, chopped
1 t fresh cinnamon, grated

PREPARATION:

In a large mixing bowl, combine the brown and white sugars, the unbleached flour, the baking powder, the baking soda, and the salt.

Add the butter, then use your fingertips to mix the ingredients to the texture of cornmeal.

In a small mixing bowl, combine the eggs, buttermilk, and vanilla, then beat them together.

Add the beaten egg mixture to the larger bowl of dry ingredients, then stir just enough to mix them together.

Preheat your oven to 350° F.

Grease an 8- by 12-inch cake pan.

Transfer the batter to the cake pan, then spread the chopped fruit evenly across the top of the batter. Use a spatula to lightly press the fruit into the batter, but be careful not to sink it.

In another small mixing bowl, combine the ½ c of brown sugar, the ¼ c of all-purpose flour, the 2 T of butter, the chopped almonds, and the cinnamon. Crumble this topping evenly over the layer of fruit.

Place the cake on the center rack of your oven and bake for 1 hour.

With an oven mitt, remove the cake from the oven and allow to cool before cutting.

JAMAICAN HOLIDAY CAKE

Yields 12 adult servings (ID required)

Jamaicans call it RUM CAKE, but I call it *you-know-what* . . . except this recipe has a down island touch. As with all genus of this species, the longer you let it ripen, the better it somehow tastes. You know how it is: the drunker I sit here, the longer I get.

INGREDIENTS:

1 lb butter
4 c flour, sifted 4 times
4 t baking powder
1 t baking soda
½ t salt
1 c brown sugar
3 T browning
1½ c granulated sugar
½ c Jamaican white rum
2 c Jamaican dark rum
8 eggs
1 T vanilla extract
½ t fresh nutmeg, grated
½ c cherries, pitted & diced
¼ t cloves, ground
1 t rose water
½ c raisins
1 t almond paste
2 oz dried papaya, chopped
½ c dates, chopped

PREPARATION:

At least a day before baking, combine in a large saucepan the cherries, raisins, papaya, and dates, along with the 2 c of dark rum. Allow this mixture to cook over low heat just long enough for the raisins to puff slightly, but not long enough for the rum to have its alcohol evaporated.

Remove the saucepan from the heat and allow the ingredients to cool to room temperature. Cover the saucepan and refrigerate for at least 1 day.

On baking day, generously butter a 10-c bundt pan, then lightly dust with flour. Set aside.

Preheat your oven to 350° F.

In a large mixing bowl, cream together the butter with the dark and granulated sugars.

Add to the mixture the eggs, nutmeg, vanilla, and cloves, then beat until mixed.

In a small mixing bowl, combine the flour, salt, baking powder, and baking soda, then gradually add these dry ingredients to the larger mixing bowl.

Into a measuring cup, drain the dark rum from the fruits. Add enough white rum to make ½ c (in addition to the ½ c of rum in the ingredients).

Add to the large bowl the browning, the ½ c of Jamaican white rum, and the ½ c of rum drained from the fruits, as well as the almond paste and rose water. Mix well.

Fold into the mixture the drained fruits.

Pour the batter into the bundt pan, then place the pan in the center rack of your oven.

Bake until a knife inserted near the center of the cake can be removed clean, about 1¼ hours.

With an oven mitt, remove the cake from the oven and allow it to cool in the pan for 10 minutes.

Turn the cake out onto a wire rack and allow it to cool to room temperature.

Cut a piece of cheesecloth large enough to wrap well around the cake. Soak the cheesecloth in a small bowl of rum while the cake is cooling.

Wrap the cake well in a the rum-soaked cheesecloth, then seal the cake in a layer of heavy aluminum foil.

Store the rum cake in the refrigerator and allow it to ripen for several days.

Serve this with proper ID.

LAST MANGO FRUITCAKE

Yields 8 servings

This is one small cake for a man; one giant slice for mangokind.

INGREDIENTS:

½ c self-rising flour
½ c butter, softened
½ unrefined sugar
1¼ t baking powder
4 eggs
1 large ripened banana, mashed
1 large papaya, peeled, seeded & chopped
1 small mango, peeled, seeded & chopped
1 T fresh cinnamon, grated
1 T confectioner's sugar

PREPARATION:

In a large mixing bowl, combine the flour, butter, sugar, and baking powder, then stir with a spoon.

Add 1 egg at a time, then stir well after adding each egg.

Add the chopped fruit and stir just until mixed.

Preheat your oven to 350° F.

Butter an 8-inch round cake pan, then dust lightly with flour.

Place the cake pan on the center rack of your oven and bake until the cake is golden brown and an inserted tester can be removed clean, about 20 minutes.

With an oven mitt, remove the cake and allow it to cool for 10 minutes.

Turn the cake out onto a wire rack to cool.

When cool, dust with a combination of cinnamon and confectioner's sugar.

Strawberry Shortcake

Yields 8 servings

— FROM "I Wish Lunch Could Last Forever"
in TALES FROM MARGARITAVILLE / P. 153

Here's one of those traditional recipes that could explode into a jillion different dimensions simply by adding a flavor, here or there, to either the shortcake, the strawberries, or the whipped cream. You might already have a favorite, but Jimmy's way is to state the dessert as STRAWBERRY SHORTCAKE WITH FRAISES & CRÈME CHANTILLY. But don't let that frighten you. CRÈME CHANTILLY is nothing more than WHIPPED CREAM. FRAISES is a liqueur made from strawberries and has a high content of sugar; FRAISES DES BOIS, on the other hand, is made from wild strawberry, a plant which bears small berries with a distinctive and delicate flavor. If you can find them, they would add a singular new dimension in themselves.

INGREDIENTS:

For the berries:

> *4 c fraises des bois (or cultured strawber-*
> *ries), hulled & sliced*
> *½ c granulated sugar*
> *1 T fraises des bois*

For the shortcakes:

>½ c butter, softened & divided
>
>2 c all-purpose flour
>
>1 ½ T baking powder
>
>¼ t salt
>
>¼ c granulated sugar
>
>1 t lemon zest, grated
>
>½ c milk
>
>2 eggs, separated
>
>¼ c granulated sugar, for the wash

For the crème chantilly:

>1 c heavy cream
>
>½ c confectioner's sugar, sifted
>
>1 T fraises

PREPARATION:

Of the berries:

Set aside 8 whole berries for a garnish.

Rinse the berries well, then remove the hulls and slice into a large mixing bowl.

Into the bowl, add the ½ c of granulated sugar and the fraises des bois.

Stir gently, then chill for at least 1 hour.

Of the shortcake:

Preheat your oven to 425° F.

In a large mixing bowl, combine the flour, baking powder, salt, the ¼ c of granulated sugar, and the lemon zest.

Add the butter and use your fingers to blend the ingredients into a coarse meal.

Separate the egg yolks and whites.

In a small mixing bowl, beat the milk and yolks.

Pour the milk and yolk into the dry ingredients, then stir with a fork until a soft dough forms.

Divide the dough into 8 somewhat equal portions and drop them as 8 mounds on an ungreased cookie sheet.

In a small mixing bowl, beat the egg whites until they are stiff, but not dry.

Brush the surface of each mound of dough with a wash of beaten egg whites, then sprinkle each with the remaining ¼ c of granulated sugar.

Place the cookie sheet on the center rack of your oven and bake until the shortcakes are golden brown, about 11 to 12 minutes.

With an oven mitt, remove the cookie sheet from your oven and allow the shortcakes to cool for 5 minutes before serving or moving to a wire rack to further cool.

Of the crème chantilly:

In a small mixing bowl, beat the heavy cream and fraises until foamy.

Gradually add the confectioner's sugar and beat the cream until soft peaks form.

Of the presentation:

Split a shortcake in half so that you have a top and a bottom portion. If you're serving them warm, you might want to butter each half.

Place the bottom half on your serving plate, then cover generously with the chilled strawberries and their juices, as well as crème chantilly.

Place the second half, then top with another dollop of crème chantilly.

Garnish each shortcake with a whole strawberry.

Tourte aux Cerises

Yields 8 servings

— FROM "At Arm's Length"
in WHERE IS JOE MERCHANT? / P. 307

Anyone who began reading this book from the very beginning ought to have some inkling that this TOURTE AUX CERISES WITH CRÈME FRAÎCHE of which Jimmy writes is not the sort of French cuisine found in any tin can wrapped with a Franco American label. Oh that life were so simple!

INGREDIENTS:

For the tourte:

> *3 c cake flour*
> *2 c brown sugar*
> *½ t salt*
> *1 c butter, sliced*
> *1 egg, slightly beaten*
> *1 c buttermilk*
> *1 t baking soda*
> *½ c pecans, chopped*
> *1 c cerrise liqueur*

For the crème fraîche:

> *1½ c heavy cream*
> *½ c granulated sugar*

¼ c yogurt

2 T fresh lemon juice

For the cherries:

5 c fresh cherries, pitted & chopped

1 c whole, fresh cherries, pitted for garnish

ॐ

PREPARATION:

Of the tourte:

Preheat your oven to 375° F.

Lightly grease two 9-inch round pans and line the bottoms with 9-inch circles of waxed paper.

In a large mixing bowl, combine the cake flour, brown sugar, salt, and butter. With your fingers, mix these together to form a coarse meal.

Reserve ½ c of this mixture.

In a small mixing bowl, beat together the egg, buttermilk, and baking soda.

Add the wet ingredients to the bowl of dry ingredients, then blend well.

Divide the batter between the 2 cake pans, then sprinkle the reserved ½ c of unmixed dough across the top of one of the layers, which you will later use as your top layer.

Sprinkle the chopped nuts equally upon the top of both layers.

Place the cake pans on the center rack of your oven and bake until each layer is done, about 25 to 30 minutes.

With an oven mitt, remove the cake pans from your oven and allow them to cool.

Of the crème fraîche:

In a small mixing bowl, stir together the heavy cream with the sugar, yogurt, and lemon juice until the sugar is dissolved and the ingredients are blended.

Place a piece of cheesecloth loosely over the top of the bowl and allow this to stand at room temperature until thickened, about 24 hours.

Line a strainer with a double layer of cheese cloth, then place the strainer over a large bowl.

Transfer the thickened mixture from the original mixing bowl into the sieve, then place this into the refrigerator until the liquid drains from the sieve and a thickened crème fraîche remains, about 2 hours.

Transfer this crème fraîche to a clean bowl and refrigerate until you're ready to use it.

Of the cherries:

In a medium mixing bowl, combine the sliced cherries with 2 T of the cerrise, then slightly mash them together. Add any sugar, to taste.

Remove the bottom layer from its pan, then peel the waxed paper from the bottom. Place the bottom layer, nut side up, on a serving plate.

Brush the top of the bottom layer generously with the cherry liqueur, then spread half of the chopped cherries. Top the cherries with a layer of crème fraîche.

Remove the top layer from its pan, then peel the waxed paper from the bottom. Place this layer atop the layer of crème fraîche.

Brush the remaining liqueur across the top layer, then spread the remaining chopped cherries.

Leaving a circle of chopped cherries exposed in the center of the top layer, spread the remaining crème fraîche.

Garnish by placing the reserved whole cherries around the bottom edge of the tourte.

FROZEN CONFECTIONS

Coconut Ice Cream ❦ Orange Dreamsicle
Georgia Peach Ice Cream
Cinnamon Ice Cream ❦ Ginger Ice Cream
Mango Ice Cream ❦ Papaya Ice Cream
Island Vanilla Ice Cream
Mexican Chocolate Ice Cream
Pink Grapefruit Ice Cream
Banana-Orange Freeze
Margarita Granita ❦ Mimosa Granita
Peach Frozen Yogurt
Daiquiri Sorbet ❦ Chocolate Sorbet
Honeydo Sorbet ❦ Coconut Sorbet

Coconut Ice Cream

Yields about ½ gallon

When it comes to ICE CREAM, there is absolutely no substitute for the *true* variety made with an old-fashioned ice cream maker, cranked in a tub of crushed ice and rock salt. These machines are not expensive, and the motorized ones are certainly not labor intensive. The drawbacks, though, are these: you need the ice and the rock salt; you need to enjoy a *gallon* of whatever you're making; you need the space to store that gallon (even if you divide it into smaller containers); and you need to let your ice cream "cure" for 24 hours to reach the true consistency. And even if you devour the "uncured" stuff as you would soft-serve ice cream, it's still the best in the world. You probably need to double these recipes for that type of ice cream maker.

That said, there are acceptable ice cream/frozen yogurt makers that have a bowl which must first be chilled in the freezer, but then yields a fairly good ICE CREAM or FROZEN YOGURT almost immediately after you've made it. These machines are a bit more pricey, but you're paying for that immediate gratification. This recipe can be used for those machines, but might need to be halved for some. Similarly, other recipes in this chapter are for the newer machines and might need to be doubled or even quadrupled for the old-fashioned ones.

In either instance, most recipes require that you first prepare a sweet cream base for a custard, then add the signature ingredients when the custard is placed in the ice cream maker.

Some of the other recipes that follow do not require any special machines at all, but they are still pretty good variations of these frozen confections.

INGREDIENTS:

> 4 c whole milk
> 2 c heavy cream
> 1 c Coco Lopez® cream of coconut
> 1 c sugar
> Pinch of black pepper
> 8 egg yolks, beaten
> 10 oz fresh coconut, grated

PREPARATION:

Begin by making a custard for your ice cream maker. In a large saucepan, combine the milk, cream, Coco Lopez®, sugar, and pepper.

Whisk these together over medium heat until the sugar is dissolved.

Bring the mixture up to the boil, then reduce to a simmer. This will scald the milk.

Temper the beaten eggs yolks by first scooping a cup of the scalded milk into a medium mixing bowl. As you whisk the milk, gradually add the beaten egg until it begins to thicken without becoming scrambled.

Add the bowl of tempered egg to the pan of scalded milk and continue to cook until the mixture returns to the boil.

When this mixture is thick enough to coat the back of a spoon, remove the pan from the heat and strain the custard into a glass bowl.

Fold in the fresh coconut.

Cover the top of the mixture with plastic wrap and allow to cool completely.

When the custard has reached room temperature, place it in the refrigerator and chill.

Pour the custard into your ice cream machine and follow the directions for making ice cream.

ORANGE DREAMSICLE

Yields 1 quart

INGREDIENTS:

> 2 eggs
> ¾ c sugar
> 2 c heavy cream
> 1 c milk
> ½ c orange juice concentrate, thawed
> 2 t vanilla

PREPARATION:

In a large mixing bowl, make your sweet cream base by whisking together the eggs until they are light and fluffy, about 2 minutes.

Gradually whisk in the sugar until it has been completely blended, about 1 more minute.

Add the cream and the milk to the bowl, then whisk until blended.

To the sweet cream base, add the orange juice concentrate and the vanilla.

Blend together well.

Transfer the mixture to an ice cream maker and freeze according to the manufacturer's instructions.

GEORGIA PEACH ICE CREAM

Yields 1 quart

Though using small peaches might require a little more work, they have a much better flavor, as well as much less water than do the larger ones.

INGREDIENTS:

> 2 c ripe peaches, chopped fine
> 1¼ c sugar
> Juice of ½ lemon
> 2 eggs
> 2 c heavy cream
> 1 c milk

PREPARATION:

In a large mixing bowl, combine the chopped peaches, ½ c of the sugar, and the lemon juice. Toss together lightly with your fingers, then cover tightly with plastic wrap and refrigerate for 2 hours.

During the refrigeration period, stir the peach mixture every half hour.

Remove the peach mixture from the refrigerator and drain any juices into a bowl. Set the juices aside, then return the peaches to the refrigerator.

In a large mixing bowl, make your sweet cream base by whisking together the eggs until they are light and fluffy, about 2 minutes.

Gradually whisk in the sugar until it has been completely blended, about 1 more minute.

Add the cream and the milk to the bowl, then whisk until blended.

Add the reserved peach juice to the sweet cream base and blend well.

Transfer the mixture to an ice cream maker and freeze following manufacturer's instructions.

When the base begins to stiffen in the ice cream maker (about 2 minutes before completion), add the chilled peaches from the refrigerator to the machine.

Continue following the manufacturer's instructions until the ice cream is ready.

CINNAMON ICE CREAM

Yields 1 quart

INGREDIENTS:

> 3 c half & half
> 1¼ c sugar
> ½ oz cinnamon stick, in small pieces
> 6 egg yolks
> 1 fresh vanilla bean, split lengthwise
> 1 c heavy cream

PREPARATION:

In a medium saucepan, combine the half & half, the cinnamon stick pieces, and the split vanilla bean. Scald the mixture over very low heat.

Remove the saucepan from the heat, cover, and allow to stand at room temperature at least 1 hour.

Meanwhile, in a large mixing bowl combine the sugar and the egg yolks, then beat together until a raised beater drips a slow ribbon of the mixture.

Return to low heat the saucepan of cooled half & half mixture.

When the half & half has reheated, temper the egg mixture by gradually beating ½ c of the half & half mixture into the mixing bowl.

Stir the tempered egg mixture into the pan of heated half & half mixture.

Over low heat, stir constantly until the custard coats the back of a spoon, about 180° F. Do not allow the custard to come to the boil.

Pour the custard into a large, heatproof bowl and allow it to cool at least 2 hours.

Strain the custard and discard the cinnamon pieces and vanilla bean.

Add the heavy cream to the bowl and whisk together well.

Transfer the mixture to an ice cream maker and freeze following manufacturer's instructions.

GINGER ICE CREAM

Yields 1 quart

INGREDIENTS:

> ½ c water
> ¼ c granulated sugar
> 2 T fresh ginger, peeled & grated
> 1¼ c milk
> 3 c heavy cream
> ½ c granulated sugar
> 3 egg yolks
> 1 T crystallized ginger, chopped fine

PREPARATION:

In a small saucepan, make a simple syrup by combining the water, ¼ c of sugar, and the fresh ginger. Simmer over low heat about 4 minutes, stirring occasionally.

Remove the simple syrup from the heat and allow to cool.

In a medium saucepan, combine the milk and whipping cream. Over low heat, allow the mixture to scald. Do not let it come to the boil.

Remove the saucepan of scalded milk and cream

from the heat, then stir in the cool simple syrup. Allow this to cool at least 15 minutes.

Strain the cooled mixture into a large bowl and discard any ginger solids.

Return the strained mixture to the top half of a double boiler, then whisk in the egg yolks and chopped crystallized ginger.

Heat this mixture gently and constantly stir until a thin custard forms which will coat the back of your spoon, about 180° F. Do not allow the custard to come to the boil.

Remove from the heat and allow to cool.

Transfer the mixture to an ice cream maker and freeze following manufacturer's instructions.

MANGO ICE CREAM

Yields 1 quart

INGREDIENTS:

> 1 mango, peeled & chopped
> 1 T lemon juice
> 2 t cornstarch
> ½ c sugar
> 1½ c half & half
> 1 egg yolk, beaten
> 2 T light corn syrup

PREPARATION:

In a food processor, combine the chopped mango and lemon juice, then purée.

In a medium saucepan, combine the cornstarch and sugar. Stir in the half & half, the beaten egg yolk, and the corn syrup.

Continue to stir the mixture and cook over medium heat until bubbles form on the surface.

Cook 1 more minute.

Remove the saucepan from the heat and allow the mixture to cool.

Stir the puréed mango into the cooled mixture.

Transfer the mixture to an ice cream maker and freeze following manufacturer's instructions.

PAPAYA ICE CREAM

Yields 1 quart

INGREDIENTS:

    1 ripe papaya, peeled, seeded & sliced
    1 T lemon juice
    ¾ c sugar
    2 egg yolks, beaten
    1 c milk
    1 c heavy cream

PREPARATION:

In a food processor, combine the sliced papaya and lemon juice, then purée.

In a medium saucepan, combine the beaten egg yolks, and the milk.

Continue to stir the mixture and cook over medium heat until the custard thickens and coats the back of your spoon, about 180° F. Do not allow the custard to come to the boil.

Remove the saucepan from the heat and allow the mixture to cool.

Add the puréed papaya and whipping cream to the cooled mixture, then stir.

Transfer the mixture to an ice cream maker and freeze following manufacturer's instructions.

ISLAND VANILLA

Yields 1 quart

INGREDIENTS:

    1 vanilla bean, split lengthwise in 4 pieces
    2 c milk
    2 c heavy cream
    6 egg yolks
    1 c sugar

PREPARATION:

In a medium saucepan, combine the vanilla bean and milk, then bring to the boil over low heat.

Remove the saucepan from the heat.

In the top half of a double boiler, combine the egg yolks and sugar, then whisk until they are foamy.

Strain the cooled milk into the egg mixture, then put the double boiler together.

With a wooden spoon, stir the mixture until the custard thickens and coats the back of the spoon.

Remove the top of the double boiler from the heat, then stir in the heavy cream.

Place the mixture in the refrigerator until it becomes cold.

Transfer the mixture to an ice cream maker and freeze following manufacturer's instructions.

MEXICAN CHOCOLATE

Yields 1 quart

INGREDIENTS:

    4 oz semisweet chocolate
    ½ c sugar
    3 egg yolks

2 c milk, warm
2 c heavy cream
1 vanilla bean, split lengthwise

PREPARATION:

In the top of a double boiler, melt the semisweet chocolate. Stir occasionally to make certain that the chocolate does not scorch.

In a medium mixing bowl, combine the sugar and egg yolks, then beat well until they are a smooth, creamy yellow. Set aside.

In a large saucepan, combine the milk, heavy cream, and vanilla bean. Bring to the boil over medium heat.

Remove the saucepan from the heat.

Temper the beaten egg mixture by stirring about ¼ of the hot milk to the bowl and whisking well.

Whisk the hot milk mixture as you add the bowl of tempered egg mixture into the saucepan.

Return the saucepan to the heat and cook together the milk and egg mixtures.

Continue to stir with a wooden spoon until the heated custard is thick enough to coat the back of the spoon, about 180° F. Do not allow the custard to come to the boil.

Remove the saucepan from the heat.

Add the melted chocolate to the custard and whip together well with a whisk.

Set a large heatproof bowl in a bath of ice, then strain the chocolate custard into the bowl. This will remove the vanilla bean and seeds, as well as chill the custard before it is refrigerated.

Place the bowl of chocolate custard in the refrigerator for at least 2 hours.

Transfer the mixture to an ice cream maker and freeze following manufacturer's instructions.

PINK GRAPEFRUIT

Yields 1 quart

Neither a sherbet, a sorbet, or a granita, this recipe is a genuine citrus ice cream that is much, much tastier than you might ever imagine. Though you might contemplate cheating on this recipe by using bottled grapefruit juice, *don't!* Use juice that you've squeezed fresh from pink grapefruit. If you're still not convinced, you can use any other type of citrus juice and still make a great ice cream.

Meanwhile, let me also point out that this recipe does not require any cooking.

INGREDIENTS:

1 c pink grapefruit juice, squeezed fresh
½ c whole milk
1 c heavy cream
1 c sugar

PREPARATION:

In a large mixing bowl, combine the grapefruit juice, milk, heavy cream, and sugar, then stir well until the sugar has dissolved.

Place the mixture in the refrigerator until it becomes cold.

Transfer the mixture to an ice cream maker and freeze following manufacturer's instructions.

Banana Orange Freeze

Yields 6 servings

Though this recipe doesn't require any special tools, it must be made in three small batches, then brought together as one.

INGREDIENTS:

12 very ripe bananas, sliced
1 c honey
Juice of 6 oranges
½ c macadamia nuts, chopped

PREPARATION:

Into a blender, slice 4 of the bananas, then add in ½ c of honey along with the juices of 2 oranges.

Blend the mixture on a medium speed until smooth.

Transfer this mixture to a large mixing bowl.

Repeat this process twice more until you have blended all of the bananas, honey, and juice, then combined them in the mixing bowl.

Stir in the chopped macadamia nuts.

Pour the mixture into a shallow freezer tray and place in the freezer.

After the first 2 hours of freezing, remove the tray briefly every hour or so, then stir up the mixture well. This will improve the texture.

Return the tray to the freezer.

Altogether, the mixture should freeze at least 12 hours.

Margarita Granita

Yields 4 servings

Short of a margaritacicle, this recipe is probably the ultimate FROZEN MARGARITA. In fact, it must be served in a margarita glass that has been rimmed with lime juice and sugar, then garnished with a slice of lime. Unlike a margarita, though, you don't get a hangover the next morning; you get an ice cream headache right away! (Only kidding.)

Granita is a Mexican ice, not unlike Italian ices in their recipes, but whose process involves the creating of shaved ice particles for a rougher, grainier texture.

INGREDIENTS:

3 c water
1 c sugar
Juice of 2 key limes
Juice of 1 lemon
6 T triple sec
6 T gold tequila
2 t lime zest, grated

Sugar, for garnish
Lime slices, for garnish

PREPARATION:

In a large saucepan, make a simple syrup by combining the water and sugar over medium heat until the sugar has dissolved.

Bring the mixture to the boil, then stir for 1 more minute.

Carefully pour your hot syrup into a heatproof bowl. Stir in the lime and lemon juices, triple sec, tequila, and lime zest.

Cover the bowl with plastic wrap and place the mixture in your freezer.

While you do want this to freeze, you also want to shave it every hour by scraping this into crystals to create a bowl of small, frozen margarita crystals,

Serve this as you would a margarita, except give your guests each a spoon.

Mimosa Granita

Yields 4 servings

Rather than shaving the frozen ingredients to create your dish of ice crystals, this method of making a granita with your food processor can also be applied to any others you have in mind. The true convenience here, though, is not necessarily in using the food processor, but in making the recipe up to a week ahead of time, then keeping it frozen until you're just about ready to serve.

INGREDIENTS:

> *2 c fresh juice from 3 oranges*
> *1 c sugar*
> *2½ c sparkling wine*
> *2 T lime juice*

PREPARATION:

In a large mixing bowl, combine the orange juice and sugar, then whisk them together until the sugar is dissolved.

Stir in the sparkling wine and lime juice.

Transfer the mimosa mixture to 2 ice cube trays, then freeze until firm.

Once the ingredients have frozen, you can seal the mimosa cubes in freezer bags for up to 1 week.

To finish the granita, fit your food processor with a steel blade.

Place just enough of the frozen mimosa cubes in the bowl of your food processor to create a single layer.

Pulse the cubes just enough so that there are no large chunks; about 10 or 12 times.

Spoon or scoop the mimosa crystals into fluted champagne glasses.

Repeat the process to make the remaining servings.

Serve immediately.

Peach Frozen Yogurt

Yields 1 quart

Every now and then, along comes a recipe that appears much too simple to be any good, and yet it turns out to be great. This is one of those.

INGREDIENTS:

3 c peaches, peeled & sliced
½ c superfine sugar
½ c plain non-fat yogurt
1 t fresh lemon juice

PREPARATION:

Combine the peaches and sugar in a food processor, then pulse until the peaches have been coarsely chopped.

In a small mixing bowl, stir together the yogurt and lemon juice.

Once again start the food processor with the peaches, then gradually add the yogurt mixture.

Once or twice, stop the processor to scrape down the sides of the bowl with a spatula. Otherwise, process the peaches and yogurt until the mixture is smooth and creamy.

Use an ice cream scoop to divide the peaches and yogurt mixture into freezer-proof serving dishes, then cover and freeze until the yogurt has firmed up slightly, about 30 minutes.

Daiquiri Sorbet

Yields 1 quart

That old saying that "It all depends on how you slice it" just about explains the difference between a SORBET and a GRANITA. The only difference is in how you freeze it. Rather than freeze these ingredients and shave them, you place them into your ice cream maker. That process, however, does *not* make this into a SHERBET. For that, you'd need to add some dairy product.

INGREDIENTS:

> *4 c fresh strawberries, rinsed & hulled*
> *1 c sugar*
> *2 T light rum*
> *1½ T fresh lime juice*

PREPARATION:

In your blender, purée the strawberries until quite smooth.

If you prefer, you can strain the puréed berries to remove the seeds.

In a medium mixing bowl, combine the strawberry purée, sugar, rum, and lime juice, then blend well with a whisk.

Cover tightly and refrigerate until cold, at least 2 hours, but no more than 3 *days*.

Remove the mixture from the refrigerator and whisk once again to blend all of the ingredients together well.

Transfer the mixture to an ice cream maker and freeze following manufacturer's instructions.

At this point your frozen sorbet will be edible, but somewhat soft. You may wish to transfer the sorbet from the ice cream maker into a freezer-safe container and freeze it for another 2 hours.

CHOCOLATE SORBET

Yields 1 quart

INGREDIENTS:

> 3 c water
> 1¼ c sugar
> 3 T light corn syrup
> ¾ c unsweetened cocoa powder
> 2 oz semisweet chocolate
> 1 T pure vanilla

PREPARATION:

In a large saucepan, combine the water, sugar, and corn syrup over low heat. Stir until the sugar has dissolved.

Over medium heat, bring the mixture to the boil and cook for 2 minutes.

Reduce the heat, whisk in the cocoa powder, then simmer for 2 more minutes.

Remove the saucepan from the heat.

Add the semisweet chocolate to the hot mixture.

Stir until the chocolate has melted completely and is smooth.

Allow the chocolate mixture to cool to room temperature.

Add the vanilla and stir well.

Cover the saucepan and refrigerate at least 1 hour.

Remove the saucepan from the refrigerator.

Transfer the mixture to an ice cream maker and freeze following manufacturer's instructions.

At this point the frozen sorbet will be edible, but somewhat soft. You may wish to transfer the sorbet from the ice cream maker to a freezer-safe container and freeze for another 2 hours.

HONEYDO SORBET

Yields 1 quart

INGREDIENTS:

> 1 c sugar
> 1¼ c water
> 1 honeydew melon
> 1 t fresh lime juice

PREPARATION:

In a medium saucepan, combine the sugar and water, then bring to the boil over high heat.

Stir until the sugar has dissolved into a simple syrup.

Remove the saucepan from the heat and allow this mixture to cool to room temperature.

Cut the melon in half, then spoon out and discard the seeds.

Scoop the flesh of the melon from the rind into a blender. Purée the melon pieces until smooth, about 2 minutes.

In a medium mixing bowl, combine the melon purée, the cooled simple syrup, and the lime juice.

Transfer the mixture to an ice cream maker and freeze following manufacturer's instructions.

At this point the frozen sorbet will be edible, but somewhat soft. You may wish to transfer the sorbet from the ice cream maker to a freezer-safe container and freeze for another 2 hours.

COCONUT SORBET

Yields 1 quart

INGREDIENTS:

> 1 c sweetened coconut milk
> 2 c water
> ¼ c coconut, toasted

PREPARATION:

In a medium mixing bowl, combine the sweetened coconut milk and the water.

Cover and refrigerate at least 6 hours.

Remove the mixture from the refrigerator.

Transfer the mixture to an ice cream maker and freeze following manufacturer's instructions.

At this point the frozen sorbet will be somewhat soft. Add the toasted coconut and blend well with a spoon.

You may serve the sorbet in this soft state or you might want to transfer the sorbet from the ice cream maker to a freezer-safe container and freeze for another 2 hours.

GALLEY NOTES:

CONDIMENTS, ETC...

Last Mango Salsas
Mango~Ginger ∞ Orange~Mango
Mango, Black Bean & Pepper Salsa
Watermelon~Honeydo Salsa
Papaya~Pepper ∞ Pineapple~Chipotle
Orange~Tomato ∞ Mayan Xnipec Salsa
Creole Tartar Sauce
Cajun Rémoulade ∞ Shrimp Rémoulade
Big Kosher Pickles

Last Mango Salsas

Yields 1½ cups

There are several variations of MANGO SALSA, most of which deal with the sort of onion and/or pepper that most suits your taste. So, I'll offer a few here for your tasting.

INGREDIENTS:

> 2 ripe mangos, peeled & in ¼-inch cubes
> 1 large serrano chile, minced
> 3 green onions, sliced fine
> ¼ red bell pepper, diced
> Juice of 2 key limes

PREPARATION:

In a large mixing bowl, combine all the ingredients and mix thoroughly with a fork.

Cover the bowl with plastic wrap and allow to stand at room temperature for 2 hours so that the flavors will marry.

If not using immediately after that, store sealed in your refrigerator.

Mango~Ginger Salsa

Yields 2½ cups

This salsa is close to being a chutney, which balances sweet and sour. This is especially good with grilled meats and fishes, or even as a side dish.

Ingredients:

2 ripe mangos, peeled & diced
1 cucumber, peeled, seeded & diced
1 jalapeño, seeded & minced
2 t fresh ginger, grated
¼ c fresh cilantro, chopped
1 T light brown sugar, packed
Juice of 2 key limes
Salt, to taste
Black pepper, cracked fresh, to taste

Preparation:

In a large mixing bowl, combine all the ingredients and toss gently with a fork.

Taste, then adjust seasonings and juice to taste.

Cover the bowl with plastic wrap and allow to stand at room temperature for 2 hours so that the flavors will marry.

If not using immediately after that, store sealed in your refrigerator.

Orange~Mango Salsa

Yields 1½ cups

Ingredients:

Juice of 3 oranges
2 ripened mangos, peeled & diced
¼ cup cilantro, chopped
Salt & pepper, to taste

Preparation:

In a small saucepan, warm the orange juice.

Add to the pan the chopped mangos and cilantro.

Taste, then adjust the seasonings with salt & pepper.

Being careful not to allow the salsa to come to the boil, cook for another 3 minutes.

Remove the saucepan from the heat.

This salsa can be served either hot or cold.

Mango~Black Bean & Roasted Red Pepper

Yields 4 cups

When in doubt, serve up this recipe, because it will go well with anything and everything.

Ingredients:

1 red bell pepper, seeded & roasted
1½ c mango, peeled & in chunks
1 15-oz can black beans, rinsed & drained
½ c red onion, diced fine
1 jalapeño pepper, seeded & minced
2 T fresh cilantro, chopped fine
2 T lime juice
Salt, to taste

Preparation:

Preheat your broiler.

Slice the red pepper lengthwise, then remove the core and seeds.

On a lightly oiled baking sheet, place the pepper cut-sides down and put under the broiler until the skin is charred, about 15 minutes.

With an oven mitt, remove the baking sheet and allow the pepper to cool.

When the pepper is cool enough to handle,

remove the charred skin under running water. Dry the pepper, then dice.

In a large mixing bowl, combine the diced roasted pepper with the mango chunks, black beans, onion, jalapeño, cilantro, and lime juice.

Stir well, taste, then adjust the seasonings.

Serve immediately or refrigerate in a covered container.

Watermelon~Honeydo Salsa

Yields 4 cups

This salsa is not only good with grilled chicken breasts, but also with tortilla chips. Its only drawback is that is does not store well and must be served immediately.

INGREDIENTS:

2 c watermelon, peeled, seeded & diced
2 c honeydew, peeled, seeded & diced
¼ c scallion, chopped fine
2 jalapeño peppers, chopped fine
2 T fresh cilantro, chopped
1 t sugar
Juice and pulp of 2 key limes
Salt, to taste, just before serving

PREPARATION:

In a large glass mixing bowl, combine all the ingredients and toss gently with your fingertips.

Cover the bowl with plastic wrap and refrigerate for no more than 1 hour.

Papaya~Pepper Salsa

Yields 1¼ cup

The flip side to the sweet WATERMELON-HONEYDO salsa is this one, which is great with grilled tuna or any white fish.

INGREDIENTS:

1 papaya, peeled, seeded & diced
¼ green bell pepper, seeded & diced
¼ red bell pepper, seeded & diced
1 serrano chile, seeded & diced
1 T cilantro, minced
Juice of ½ key lime
Juice of ½ orange
½ t red pepper flakes, crushed

PREPARATION:

In a medium mixing bowl, combine all the ingredients and mix thoroughly with a fork.

Cover the bowl with plastic wrap and refrigerate for at least 2 hours so that the flavors will marry.

This salsa will not keep for more than 24 hours.

Pineapple~Chipotle Salsa

Yields 3 cups

The Caribbean flavors in this recipe go well with JAMAICAN JERK CHICKEN.

INGREDIENTS:

1 ripened pineapple, peeled & diced
1 green bell pepper, seeded & diced
1 red bell pepper, seeded & diced
1 red onion, diced
3 chipotle peppers, seeded & minced
¼ c cilantro, chopped
2 limes, zested & juiced
½ c sugar
2 t chili powder
2 t coriander
2 t cumin
2 t salt

PREPARATION:

In a large mixing bowl, combine all the ingredients and mix thoroughly with a fork.

Cover the bowl with plastic wrap and allow to stand at room temperature for 2 hours so that the flavors will marry.

If not using immediately after that, store sealed in your refrigerator.

Orange~Tomato Salsa

Yields 2 cups

INGREDIENTS:

1 ripe tomato, seeded & diced
1 orange, peeled & diced
½ red onion, diced
1½ T fresh mint, chopped
1½ T fresh basil, chopped
1½ T fresh cilanto, chopped
½ jalapeño pepper, seeded & minced
Juice of 1 key lime
Juice of 1 orange

PREPARATION:

In a large mixing bowl, combine all the ingredients and mix thoroughly with a fork.

Cover the bowl with plastic wrap and allow to stand at room temperature for 2 hours so that the flavors will marry.

If not using immediately, store sealed in your refrigerator.

Mayan Xnipec Salsa

Yields 1 cup

Forget about your Mayan eyes; this salsa is about your Mayan dog's nose! In the Yucatan, they call this xnipec (SHNEE-pek), Mayan for dog (xni) nose (pec), because it makes your nose moist like a dog's.

INGREDIENTS:

> *1 tomato, diced*
> *½ onion, chopped*
> *3 habañero peppers, chopped*
> *¼ cup cilantro, chopped*
> *Juice of 1 lime*
> *Salt & pepper, to taste*

PREPARATION:

You might want to start by using only 1 habañero, then add more if you dare.

In a large mixing bowl, combine all the ingredients and mix thoroughly with a fork.

Cover the bowl with plastic wrap and refrigerate for 2 hours so that the flavors will marry.

Creole Tartar Sauce

Yields 1 cup

Mayonnaise is *not* an ingredient in this recipe, but the Creole mustard is essential. Made from mustard seeds marinated in vinegar, the Creole mustard can be substituted with a dijon mustard.

INGREDIENTS:

> ¼ c celery, chopped fine
> ¼ c parsley, chopped fine
> 3 T tomato paste
> ½ t paprika
> 2 T Creole mustard
> 2 T olive oil
> 1 T white wine vinegar
> ¾ t Crystal® sauce

PREPARATION:

In a small mixing bowl, combine the celery, parsley, tomato paste, paprika, mustard, and oil.

Stir in the vinegar and Crystal® sauce, taste, then adjust the seasonings with more/less Crystal®.

Cajun Rémoulade

Yields 2¾ cups

Though you won't find this mayonnaise sauce in any of Jimmy's writings, it's long been a staple of New Orleans cuisine, especially in the Margaritaville Cafe, where it can be served over fish, meat, or shrimp.

The name, itself, comes from a French dialect of the word *ramolas*, which means "horseradish," but the New Orleans version is even spicier than the French. Some variations include hard-boiled eggs, and others have chopped parsley. It's an easy thing to prepare and gives you another item to make your cooking a bit more distinctive.

INGREDIENTS:

> 2 c mayonnaise
> 2 T Creole mustard
> ½ t blackening seasoning
> ½ t chili powder
> 1 t kosher salt
> 1 roasted red bell pepper, peeled, seeded & diced fine
> 1 T scallion (green only), chopped fine

PREPARATION:

In a large mixing bowl, combine the mayonnaise, Creole mustard, blackening seasoning, chili powder, and salt.

Add the roasted red pepper and chopped scallion, then stir well.

Cover the bowl tightly with plastic wrap, then refrigerate for at least 12 hours before serving.

SHRIMP RÉMOULADE

Yields 4 servings

This is one variation which can serve as a lunch or appetizer, as well as a sauce. An important part of its taste comes from the fact that you are actually making a fresh mayonnaise within the process of the recipe.

INGREDIENTS:

2 eggs
¼ c Creole mustard
3 T brown mustard
½ c ketchup
1¾ T red wine vinegar
3 T horseradish
2 T Worcestershire
1 T paprika
1 celery rib, chopped coarse
4 garlic cloves, minced
¼ c parsley, chopped
2 bay leaves
1 t salt
2 T fresh lemon juice,
1 t Crystal® sauce
½ c olive oil
2 lbs cooked shrimp, peeled & deveined
Lettuce, washed & dried
Lemon, quartered for garnish

PREPARATION:

In the bowl of your food processor, combine the eggs, mustards, ketchup, red wine vinegar, horseradish, Worcestershire, paprika, celery, garlic, parsley, bay leaves, salt, fresh lemon juice, and Crystal® sauce.

Process the ingredients until they are smooth.

Slowly add the olive oil and continue to process until it is blended well with the rest of the ingredients.

Transfer the remoulade to a large mixing bowl, then cover tightly with plastic wrap and refrigerate for at least 1 hour.

Place a lettuce leaf on each plate, then spoon a base of sauce.

Arrange the shrimp on the sauce, then garnish with a lemon wedge.

Big Kosher Pickles

Yields 4 to 6 quarts

— FROM "Cheeseburger in Paradise"
on SON OF A SON OF A SAILOR

Hey, whoever thought you'd be making pickles? Well, this cookbook would be definitely inadequate if we didn't try these babies. Besides, you might be looking someday for a quick gift, and what could say more than a quart jar of homemade KOSHER PICKLES? (I know, a can of homemade beer with a pop top, but that's out of the question.) Quite frankly, though, I think a gift of homemade pickles would just about say it all. (Or maybe just enough?) So, that's why I've saved the best for last.

Before you get too excited, make certain you gather up a half dozen quart-size pickling jars and sterilize them according to their directions. (Yes, they *will* have directions.)

INGREDIENTS:

> 36 small, firm pickling cukes
> 6 T kosher salt (not *table salt*)
> 12 T white vinegar
> 12 garlic cloves
> 12 dill sprigs

2 t pickling spice
4 qts water, boiling

PREPARATION:

While you're sterilizing those jars, wash your cucumbers well in cold water, but don't use any soap! The point is simply to remove any dirt and other garden debris.

In a large pot, bring the water for the brine to the boil.

Once the jars have been sterilized, pack each jar with cukes in the upright position. Depending upon the size of your cucumbers, you'll have anywhere from 4 to 6 jars.

Put the jars in your sink before you continue any further.

Place 1 T of kosher salt into each jar, along with 2 T of white vinegar, 2 garlic cloves, and 2 dill sprigs.

Carefully ladle boiling water into each jar until it overflows.

Seal the jars and store in a cool, dark place for at least 10 days. [NOTE: *The brine will become a bit cloudy as the cucumbers become pickles.*]

Chill each jar before opening, then keep them refrigerated thereafter.

GALLEY NOTES:

GALLEY NOTES:

INDEX

pecan waffles 40
pepper vodka 21
petit punch 24
picadillo 143
pickles 278
PIE
  apple 216
  chocolate 217
  coconut tart 223
  key lime 225
  sweet potato pecan 221
pineapple-chipotle salsa 272
pizza 66
plantation muffins 54
po'boy sandwich 154
pommes de terre soufflées 62
pompano en papillote 161
popcorn 79
  brittle 80
popcorn rice 185
pork 141, 146
  Cuban roast pork 141
  jerk 146
Porter, Aurora 84
Porter, Boring Alice 84
POT COOKIN'
  bouillabaisse 105
  Cajun gumbo 112
  callaloo 100
  Chinese claypot duck 124
  conch chowder 114
  Creole gumbo 111
  jambalaya 109
  Nantucket chowders 116
  oyster stew 118
  pumpkin soup 121
  shrimp étouffée 122
  turtle soup 108
potato salad 94
Prudhomme, Chef Paul 21
pumpkin soup 121
Purvis, Freddy 225

~ Q ~
quahaug chowder 116
"Que Pasa?" 77, 153
quesadillas 76

~ R ~
raisin bread 206
Rancho Deluxe 69
Rancho La Gloria 13
rasta pasta 188
red beans & rice 183
red eye gravy 139
red snapper 15
"Reggae Accident" 188
remittance man 190
rémoulade 276
rhum vieux 150
rice 183, 184, 185
rice & beans 153
Riddles in the Sand 229
risotto 173, 189
Rivière, Isabella 23, 24, 34, 46, 62, 84, 150, 194, 242
roast chicken 95, 135
roast pork 95
"Rolling with the Punches" 32
root beer float 27
rouille 105, 131
Ruby's 130
rum 14
  cake 247
  sauce 229

~ S ~
Sailor Jack's popcorn 79
SALADS OF SORTS
  Cajun crawfish 88
  cheapskate's lobster 97
  conch 85
  crab & mango 87
  grilled lobster 98
  Jamaican crawfish 89
  lentil 93
  lobster 96
  lobster, southern-style 97
  lone palm 90
  muffalata 92
  potato 94
  salpicón 95
  shrimp ceviche 86
  West Indies crab 84
salmon 172
salpicón 95
SALSA
  mango 268
  mango, black bean & roasted red pepper 269
  mango-ginger 269
  Mayan xnipec 274
  orange-mango 269
  orange-tomato 273
  papaya-pepper 271
  pineapple-chipotle 272
  watermelon-honeydo 270
San Padre oyster stew 119
SANDWICH
  brisket 131
  Cuban mix 147
  flying fish 152
  meatloaf 142
  muffalata 92
  oyster loaf 155
  po'boy 154
  shark 153
Saturday Night (Live) 160
"Sauce Boss" 185
"Saxophones" 111
scallop stew 117
seviche 86. *See also* Ceviche
shark sandwich 153
"Shelter in the Storm" 142
sherbet 264
SHRIMP 169, 170, 176
  boil 159
  Caribbean 171
  ceviche 86
  coconut beer 170
  étouffée 122
  fried 169
  rémoulade 277
SIDE DISHES
  black beans 186
  French fried potatoes 180
  hushpuppies 181
  oyster dressing 191
  popcorn rice 185
  potato salad 94
  rasta pasta 188
  red beans & rice 183
  risotto & truffles 189
  Spanish onion rings 190
  yellow rice 184
  zucchini fettucine 187
simple syrup 25